Citizens' Report on
Governance and Development 2010

ADVISORY COMMITTEE MEMBERS

Advisory group

Amitabh Kundu
Gowridasan Nair
Jagadananda
Lalit Surjan
Maja Daruwala
P.V. Rajagopal
Pamela Philipose
Rajesh Tandon
Vinod Vyasulu

Contributors
Parliament

Girish Nikam

Inputs and involvement of A. Surya Prakash, Chakshu Roy, Rajesh Jha and Venkitesh Ramakrishnan is acknowledged and deeply appreciated.

Judiciary

Videh Upadhyay

Policies and practices

Amit Sengupta, Bhaskar Goswami, Kaushik Ganguly, Manish Sisodia, Pooja Parvati, Sanjay Vashisht, Subrat Das, Surajit Mazumdar

Local self-government

Abhijit Dutta, Debolina Kundu, Manoj Rai

Editors

Amitabh Behar
John Samuel
Yogesh Kumar

Research and report coordinating team

Himanshu Jha
Ashwini K. Swain

Administrative support

Shubhro Roy
Bhairav Dutt

We acknowledge the support of NOVIB for their generous support towards research and publication of this Report. We express our deep sense of gratitude and acknowledgement to CYSD for housing and facilitating Social Watch as one of our national ally in the National Social Watch Coalition.

Citizens' Report on
Governance and Development 2010

NATIONAL SOCIAL WATCH

$SAGE   www.sagepublications.com
Los Angeles • London • New Delhi • Singapore • Washington DC

First published in 2011 by

SAGE Publications India Pvt Ltd
B1/I-1 Mohan Cooperative Industrial Area
Mathura Road, New Delhi 110 044, India
www.sagepub.in

SAGE Publications Inc
2455 Teller Road
Thousand Oaks, California 91320, USA

SAGE Publications Ltd
1 Oliver's Yard, 55 City Road
London EC1Y 1SP, United Kingdom

SAGE Publications Asia-Pacific Pte Ltd
33 Pekin Street
#02-01 Far East Square
Singapore 048763

Published by Vivek Mehra for SAGE Publications India Pvt Ltd, typeset in 10/13 Minion by Star Compugraphics Private Limited, Delhi and printed at Artxel, New Delhi.

Library of Congress Cataloging-in-Publication Data Available

ISBN: 978-81-321-0627-2 (PB)

The SAGE Team: Rekha Natarajan, Arpita Dasgupta, Rajib Chatterjee and Umesh Kashyap

Contents

4. THE STATE OF DECENTRALISATION AND LOCAL GOVERNANCE IN INDIA: INTERROGATING INSTITUTIONS, PROGRAMMES AND SERVICE DELIVERY   111

List of Tables, Figures, Boxes and Annexures

Tables

Figures

Boxes

Annexures

Preface

Democracy in India has come of age. Both democracy and democratisation in the country has matured in the last 60 years to such an extent that it is regarded as a model of a vibrant and effective system in the world over. The process has widened and deepened to reach every nook and corner of the country, and has provided space to the citizens to expect and demand their rights, reflected not only in their active participation, but also in decision-making. Popular participation is an objective as well as the mechanism for achieving democracy and development. The widening of democracy is also perceptible in the nature and membership of the popularly elected representatives which reflects the representation of varied identities. This poses a daunting challenge to the institutions of governance to work out a viable and satisfactory agenda of governance, which satisfies both, the rising demands and the aspirations of the people, as also the changing nature of the representatives.

Democracy, development and governance, it seems, are at the crossroads, caught in the contradictions of our times, some of which are new and have emerged in the midst of the older. The ultimate test of effective governance is the fulfilment of its commitments to the citizens, ensuring delivery of public services right up to the excluded and marginalised sections of the society. The biggest challenge for governance then, is the sustainability and the wider reach of economic growth from the point of view of the desired level of social development.

In this light, it is important to reiterate the importance of institutions of governance and their functionaries, who are the vehicles to carry the governance agenda forward. They represent the connecting link between the state and the citizens in terms of the programmes of development. Institutions (of governance) are the mechanisms of actualising both democracy and development. It is important to monitor the performance of these institutions by civil society organisations like Social Watch, who have acted as 'watchdogs' and have created a heightened sense of citizens' rights through their forceful articulations.

This year as well, Social Watch remains committed to its endeavour to 'democratise knowledge' by putting this valuable information in the public domain. While we continue with our previous focus on the performance of the four nodal institutions of governance namely—the Parliament, the Judiciary, the Policy-making and the institutions of local self-governance—we have also critically examined some new issues and policies like price rise and climate change. Perhaps a first by any civil society network, we have attempted to evaluate the performance of the Members of Parliament in the House and also reflected on the issue of conflict of interest. We are sure that this year as well, the Report will reveal some interesting insights about the working of these institutions, generating considerable interest among the civil society groups, media, academia, policy-makers and legislators.

It is our pleasure to announce that apart from the annual Social Watch Reports, we have recently undertaken an initiative for publishing perspective papers and organising informed policy dialogues around it to bring forth the specific issues relating to the agencies of governance.

It is heartening to see that the lateral expansion of the process in 14 states (Madhya Pradesh, Orissa, Karnataka, Maharashtra, Andhra Pradesh, Tamil Nadu, Rajasthan, Uttar Pradesh, Bihar, Jharkhand, West Bengal, Chhattisgarh, Kerala and Gujarat) has brought together a number of civil society actors, academia and concerned citizens to enrich the process as a whole and analyse the issues that capture the variety and complexity of situations in different states, thus enriching the process further.

At this point, we would like to express our indebtedness to numerous contributors of the Report representing varied viewpoints and constituencies, which not only broadened the base of the process, but also made this Report wholesome and rich in terms of its content and coverage. The names of these contributors are mentioned on the first page of this Report. We express our thanks and gratitude to the Advisory Members of National Social Watch who have constantly provided their guidance and support to steer the process forward and provide their valuable feedback. Thanks are also due to Pradip Kumar Jha and Shazia Wahid for providing research support during the preparation of this Report. Above all, the Social Watch Coalition partners deserve our deep appreciation for their support and encouragement without which this process would not have been successful.

Amitabh Behar
National Social Watch

Introduction

Governance is a development issue and good governance is a key requirement for effective and inclusive development. Governance is about the way decisions are made in villages, towns, cities, provinces and countries. For those in government, it is the *exercise of authority* to manage the affairs of a constituency. While the government normally has the final say when it comes to public policies, programmes, laws and regulations, it is not the only player. Citizens, civil society organisations and the private sector also have a role to play. Governance is about how the government, civil society and the private sector work together. Governance tells us *how* the government functions, *who* is involved in the policy process and *where* the effects, both positive and negative, of political activity, are distributed in a society.

Development is 'the process of enlarging peoples' choices to live long and healthy lives, to have access to knowledge, and to have access to income and assets: to enjoy a decent standard of living.'[1] Reflecting on the elements of governance in a country can tell us a great deal about the people's options, their access to knowledge and opportunities. Each of the elements, and good governance itself, can be understood to be both a means and a goal of development. Assessing governance and its elements will lend insight into how development efforts are succeeding (or not succeeding) in securing choices for the people the government represents. *Citizens' Report on Governance and Development* is an effort to understand the process and institutions of governance in India and its implications for development.

After more than six decades of independence and state formation, India is faced with serious development challenges. These challenges are aggravated by the recent global financial crisis and climate change. India's recent growth performance has been impressive and the country remains one of the fastest growing economies in the world.[2] However, there is an alarming inter- and intra-state disparity that challenges the development in India. Two major developmental challenges of India are maintaining rapid growth while spreading the benefits of growth more widely and improving the delivery of core public services. These are the two areas where India has been frequently failing, even after continuous efforts. The current government, in its second term, aims to achieve a rapid expansion in economic growth while also giving every citizen a sense of partnership in economic processes, welfare programmes and developmental activities. It places special emphasis on ensuring equality of opportunity for individual advancement and social upliftment of all sections of Indian society.[3] In this report, we aim to examine how far these objectives have been met by interrogating the four key institutions of governance.

While the deadline for achieving Millennium Development Goals (MDGs) is approaching, India is far from achieving the goals. One-third of the Indian population is still living in poverty. Almost two decades of basic education programmes have expanded access to schools in India,[4] but the quality of education remains poor resulting in low literacy level (66 per cent). Most of those deprived of primary education are from marginalised social groups. The challenge is reach to 8 million children and to ensure that they remain in schools till they complete elementary education, and at the same time improve the quality of education. Even though serious efforts like Women's Reservation Act are being made, ensuring gender equity, women empowerment is still a major concern for India. Health services in India are also considerably pitiable. The government sector is understaffed and underfinanced, poor services at state-run hospitals force many people to visit private medical practitioners. National policy lacks specific measures to achieve broad stated goals. Particular problems include the failure to integrate health services with wider economic and social development, the lack of nutritional support and sanitation, and the poor participatory involvement at the local level. In this context, it is essential for India to improve the delivery of core public services such as health care, education, power and water supply to all citizens. This means empowering the citizens to demand better services through reforms that create more effective systems of public sector accountability. *Citizens' Report on Governance and Development* is an effort in that direction. The report aims to assess the governance and development process in India and inform the citizens so that a debate can be generated and public sector accountability can be ensured. With this objective, the report attempts to evaluate the four key institutions of governance, namely the Parliament, the Judiciary, the Executive and Local Self-Government. We look at the health of these institutions, their constitutional responsibilities, how far these responsibilities are met, what are the implications for inclusive development and why these institutions fail.

PARLIAMENT WATCH

The title of the Parliament section[5] encapsulates the issues which face the Indian Parliament in terms of three challenges of 'Representativeness', 'Responsiveness' and 'Responsibility'. In this light, the present section is divided into five sub-sections looking at various aspects of the functioning and performance of the Parliament for the year 2009.

Functioning of the Parliament: Conducting Business

The first section indicates the existing health of the Indian Parliament by examining and establishing some worrying trends in the way in which the Parliament functions and conducts its business. The section notes that disruptions leading to unscheduled adjournments have become the biggest bane of Indian Parliament. In contrast to the 14th Lok Sabha, the initial session of the 15th Lok Sabha was quite peaceful. In fact, in the short session of over seven days, there was neither a single adjournment nor disruption, the opposition benches stayed calm and allowed smooth functioning of the House. However, it was business as usual in the monsoon session which followed, where issues like rise of petroleum prices, the Indo–Pak Prime Ministers' meet at Sharm-el-Sheikh raised the temperatures on both sides, forcing adjournments. As a result, 23 hours and 45 minutes in the Lok Sabha and 9 hours and 30 minutes in the Rajya Sabha were lost. The winter session was worse hit, witnessing a lost over 30 per cent of its scheduled time in Parliament, while the Rajya Sabha lost nearly 13 per cent of its scheduled time. For the first time in recent years, on 30 November 2009, Lok Sabha witnessed the shocking collapse of the question hour when 28 members in whose names the starred questions were listed, played truant. Despite the Lok Sabha sitting for 64 days in the year and Rajya Sabha for 63 days, the number of bills passed saw a decline from 47 in 2008 to 41 in 2009. The time devoted to legislative business has been showing a continuous declining trend and the 15th Lok Sabha is no exception to this. Both the Houses of the Parliament have spent less than one-fifth of their total time on legislative business. In 2009, 27 per cent of the Bills passed in the Lok Sabha were done in less than five minutes. Only 17 per cent of the Bills took over three hours of discussion. It is also interesting to note that the number of MPs participating in the discussions on legislations have come down from 11.5 per Bill in 2008 to just 8.8 in 2009.

Inside the Parliament: The 15th Lok Sabha So Far

The second section gives a bird's eye view of what happened inside the Parliament in 2009. Starting with the re-election of the United Progressive Alliance(UPA) government, the section notes that for the first time since 1971, a government returned to power under the same Prime Minister (PM) and after completing its full term in office. The other significant feature of the newly formed 15th Lok Sabha was that for the first time after 1991, the leading party in the government had more than 200 seats in the Lok Sabha with the Congress winning 207 seats. Last the Congress had won more than 200 seats was in 1991. Another major landmark, which Dr Manmohan Singh rightly dubbed as a 'historic moment', was the election of a woman as the Speaker (Meira Kumar) of the Lok Sabha.

The Opposition benches also acquired some new gloss as some of its leading lights which had been out of the Lok Sabha returned to add glamour as well as punch. BJP leaders like Sushma Swaraj, Jaswant Singh, Yeshwant Sinha to name a few, and Janata Dal(U)'s Sharad Yadav, occupying the opposition benches in the Lok Sabha, meant that much more challenging days ahead for the government.

It was evident right from the beginning of the new House that issues like price rise would be a hot topic and virtually in every one of the three sessions during the year, it found echo in both Houses, in the form of discussions, calling attentions and also during zero and question hours. The Monsoon session however proved to be the most productive one. With both the Railway and General Budget being presented for the year, the session acquired new meaning. The session also witnessed very important legislations being passed including the momentous Right to Education Bill. If the Right to Education Bill was a major achievement of the UPA-II then the Judges (Declaration of Assets and Liabilities) Bill, 2009, known as the 'Judges Bill' turned out to be a major embarrassment. The Law Minister Veerappa Moily introduced it in the Rajya Sabha, hoping to get it passed without a hitch, but had to face ignominy when he was forced to withdraw it.

Even as the early part of the session was dominated by the budget and its fall outs, the visit of Prime Minister to Sharm-el-Sheikh in Egypt, midway during the session, his controversial meeting with the Pakistan Prime Minister, Yusuf Raza Gilani, and the subsequent statements, created a furore in the Parliament. While the foreign policy, especially related to Pakistan had occupied the Parliament's time considerably, the looming drought and expected failure of monsoon also caught the attention of the two Houses, quite a bit. By the time the Winter session began, some new issues and some old ones surfaced, resulting in some stormy days when both Houses remained paralysed and emotions ran high. Starting with the concern showed to the farmers on the sugarcane pricing issue, which resulted in both Houses of Parliament being stalled on the first day itself, the stormy scenes continued throughout the 21-day session.

The leak of the Liberhan report in the media right at the beginning of the session, resulted in turbulent disruptions. The Rajya Sabha witnessed some of the ugliest scenes ever witnessed when the BJP and Samajwadi Party members almost came to blows on the floor of the House.

Amid all this high drama witnessed during the session, the government however managed to push through over a dozen Bills, most of them without a discussion, and while the Houses were witnessing unruly scenes. Unfortunately this has now become a tradition for all governments, which has resulted in the Parliament itself coming under question.

Performance of the Members: Who is the Best Performing MP?

This year, the report decided to look into the actual performance of the MPs in as objective terms as possible. After much thought and discussion, a methodology was evolved—which is pathbreaking on its own—to assess the performance of the MPs within the House. For the first time in the Indian Parliamentary history we have been able to evolve this method, which has assisted in rating the MPs purely based on their performance in the House. This should encourage the MPs in future to perform better. In this pioneering exercise, we decided to assess the performance of the MPs in the 14th Lok Sabha, which came to an end in mid-2009. Parameters, which are based on Social Watch's perception of vital role of the Parliament in governance and development, were evolved to evaluate as objectively as possible, the performance of all the 545 MPs and see where they stand. Social Watch India (SWI) holds that the Parliament is supposed to formulate effective policies, as well as keep a tab on the working of the government, as the union government is major spender of the national funds. Being the highest deliberative institution, we believe that policy-making role of an MP should be pronounced as state and sub-state level legislative bodies can take care of implementation and accountability dimensions. The allocation of points to different parameters has been done keeping in mind these guiding concerns of the SWI.

The study decided to look at these four parameters, and short listed the top 25 members under the four categories—attendance, participation in debates, number of questions asked and number of Private Members' Bills (PMBs) proposed. For arriving at the final result of who were the best 10 performing MPs in all these four departments, we decided on weightage to each of the five parameters on a total scale of 10. The MPs were ranked on this scale of 10, in which questions amounted to 1.25, supplementary questions to 1.75, debates to 3, attendance to 2 and PMBs to 2.

The final outcome was quite revealing. It went on to prove the fact that the performance of the members inside the Parliament has almost no bearing on their popularity or otherwise among their electorate. Among the top 10 performers in the 14th Lok Sabha, only four have managed to return to the 15th Lok Sabha, and most of the 10 have hardly ever been on national news networks. It is also interesting to note that among the top 10, all major political parties are represented. The pointers from this analysis raise serious questions about both the parliamentary performance of the members, as well as the centrality of such performance in the broader political process, especially the electoral process.

Conflict of Interest

This section looks at the issue of conflict of interest by establishing some patterns and by providing some clues to solve this predicament that the Indian Parliament is facing for quite some time, especially in the recent years when the industrialists and businesspersons have been increasingly getting into both houses of Parliament. Their presence in the various standing and other committees and their

potential to influence decision-making has also been a matter of concern.

In the last 10 years or so, one has witnessed an exponential growth in industrialists, businessmen or others from allied communities getting elected to the Lok Sabha, as well as occupying the hallowed precincts of the Rajya Sabha. This growth is also reflected in the astonishing growth of *crorepati*s in both Houses of Parliament.

Since we had 15th Lok Sabha elections in the middle of 2009, the section looks at the composition of the members profession-wise (those who have declared themselves to be 'industrialists', 'businesspersons', 'traders' and 'builders'). The findings were startling: 128 out of the 543 members in the Lok Sabha, it emerged, belonged to one or more of these four above mentioned categories. This means about 25 per cent of the strength of the Lok Sabha belong to the industrialist/trader/businessperson/builder category. A similar list was compiled for Rajya Sabha, where the number of members belonging to the four above-mentioned categories number 25 out of the total strength of 245, including 12 nominated members. A more modest 10 per cent, compared to the 25 per cent in the Lok Sabha. Though there is no intention to jump to any conclusions on this basis about any conflict of interest, the potential can never be undermined. Some specific cases of conflict of interest have been cited from both the Houses.

The viewpoint of the MPs on the issue is highlighted in the section, as an alternate opinion from inside the Parliament.

The Working of the Parliamentary Committees

This section while acknowledging the growing importance of the committees and their role in legislation, also looks at some systemic problems in terms of the committee's functioning and performance. It is noted that the government's response to the reports generated by Standing Committees is at best lukewarm—only 53 per cent recommendations were accepted in 2005–06, while in 2006–07 this was 53.56 per cent. From 10th Lok Sabha onwards, there has been a steady increase, from 1.4 per cent in the 7th Lok Sabha to 25.3 per cent in the 12th Lok Sabha and finally 68.84 per cent in the 14th Lok Sabha. The process is becoming more consultative as various stake holders including the state governments are presenting their case *suo moto* or on the behest of a committee.

The figures are not very encouraging if we look at the average attendance of the 16 Standing Committees in the Lok Sabha. In 2005–06, the average attendance was 42 per cent (13 out of 31) which increased marginally to 45 per cent (14 out of 31) in 2006–07. In most of the committees, the average attendance was ranging from 14–16 members. Out of 18 committees, only six committees, i.e., one-third of them could register the attendance of 50 per cent and more. On an average each committees spends 182 minutes to approve a draft, in many cases it is less than 120 minutes.

The section also describes the emerging trends in the committee system in the 15th Lok Sabha and gives out some concrete recommendations, such as the need for strict rationalisation of the committee system especially in terms of their tenure, reduction in the number of members in the Standing Committees and the Financial Committees to 20, using Business Advisory Committee (BAC) as a platform for coordination in more effective way, opening of deliberations and examination of witnesses to the public and dedicated research staff for each committee. The section also points out that the Standing Committees, while scrutinising the Bills, should be like the Select Committee/ Joint Select Committee in terms of procedure and reporting.

POLICY WATCH

A systematic and thorough review of policy initiatives of the government provides us a useful window to view the state's will as well as its capacity, both political and administrative, to design and formulate viable and effective public policies. Examining such contours of public policy also provides a unique lens to evaluate the administrative capacity of the state to effectively carry the policy initiatives in terms

of its reach and delivery. In this light, a bottom-up perception of the policies provides a view from the other end of the spectrum, i.e., at the very end of the delivery chain.

While the current crises in the implementation of the key policies continue to plague the administrative apparatus, some new challenges have emerged at both the national and global level, such as the financial crisis, price rise and climate change. The policy section examines the health of the executive by evaluating public policy response in the key sectors of health, education and agriculture. The policy response of the government in tackling emerging challenges in terms of price rise and climate change is also discussed. Accountability, transparency and effectiveness remain the fulcrum of our analysis and understanding of the entire public policy apparatus.

To what extent have the existing and emerging patterns in public policy in the country been able to address the issues of growth and equity? Are these policies specifically directed towards the millions who are still in the periphery? How inclusive is our public policy in its design and implementation? These are some of the searching questions we have attempted to answer in the current section.

With the objective of providing an informed input in the public domain especially to the civil society, policy-makers and citizens, this review of policy is divided in four sections. The first section provides an overview of fiscal issues and maps out the patterns in public expenditure especially on the social sector. The second section evaluates the current policies around the sectors of health, education, agriculture and rural development. The third presents a comprehensive picture of the emerging issues of climate change and price rise by critically examining the policy response to smoothen out these emerging challenges. Finally, the last section looks at the implementation of the Right to Information (RTI) Act within the whole gamut of accountability and transparency, a pre-requisite to effective administration.

The realities of emerging patterns in the current public policy paradigm belie the objective of 'inclusive growth' and fail to address the issues of growth and equity. While the public expenditure in key social sectors are still largely insufficient, the flagship programmes themselves have not been able to fine-tune themselves to myriad problems of implementation at the grassroots. A prudent fiscal policy and an effective administrative apparatus would facilitate in turning these flagship programmes into reality. Paradoxically, the crisis in agriculture deepened with the plight of the farmers while the rise in the prices of essential commodities has continued unabated. Climate change has added to the challenge, which is not only a standalone problem, but has a multi-dimensional effect on other sectors as well. In this light, there is an urgent need to mainstream the climate issues in the public policy priorities. RTI heralded as the most powerful and potent tool to ensure administrative accountability has no doubt empowered the citizens and this can be seen in the growing number of RTI applications. However, in addition to some inherent systemic problems, there have been attempts to dilute the spirit and content of the Act.

There is an urgent need to make the policy process more participatory starting from the formulation right up to the implementation. The recent People's Mid-Term Appraisal of the 11th Five-Year Plan by civil society organisations is a case in point. The state has to reorient its policy direction in order to fulfil the global commitments made in form of the MDGs and its own commitments in the 11th Five-Year Plan.

JUDICIARY WATCH

This section is divided in two parts and deals with specific cases, issues and proposals on judicial accountability and reforms. A critical overview of the judiciary is undertaken by looking in depth at the key issues such as, transparency and judicial corruption, proposals of the Law Commission of India on restructuring of courts, law reforms for the 'have-nots' and on mending practices of lawyers. It also includes new proposals of the Ministry of Law and Justice on judicial reforms, and regulation of the instrument of public interest litigation by the Supreme Court.

The issues in judicial corruption and transparency discussed in the first part bring to light instances in 2009 for which the judiciary was in the news almost every day, and on many occasions for wrong reasons. A range of verdicts and decisions discussed at length in the first part above, takes us through some of these controversies. Justice Saumitra Sen, Justice Dinakaran, and 'cash at the door of judge' scam made repeated appearances in the newspapers. The conduct of the Supreme Court itself on the judges' assets declaration and the Justice Dinakaran controversy was questionable. One may also add here that it is also dangerous to see the entire issue as a limited controversy around a one judge. The Supreme Court had observed in ringing words in 1991 that a judicial scandal around a single dishonest judge (unlike a scandal involving a legislator or an administrator) can potentially endanger the foundation of the state. Corruption at the level of lawyers also emerged as an issue during a sting operation by NDTV where when two Senior Counsels at the Delhi High Court were shown, as part of a 'Sting Operation', being involved in influencing and winning over a witness for one of the parties to the litigation. On this issue, the Supreme Court took up the opportunity to observe on media reporting and commenting in a matter sub judice before court. It held that media cannot be left free to deal with a sub judice matter as they please. However in the present matter, the telecast was held to be in the larger public interest, which served as an important public cause. It, in no way interfered with or obstructed due course of any judicial proceedings, rather it was intended to prevent an attempt to interfere with or obstruct the due course of law. The Court also noted at some length the general erosion of professional values among lawyers at all levels and impressed upon the immediate need to arrest and reverse the trend, lest it would have very deleterious consequences for administration of justice in the country.

The role of some of the judges of the Delhi High Court along with the bodies like the Central Information Commission (CIC) needs acknowledgement and appreciation by the civil society. On 6 January 2009, the CIC upheld the request of a public individual for the supply of information concerning the declaration of personal assets by the judges of the Supreme Court. In an appeal before the Delhi High Court, the Central Public Information Officer, Supreme Court of India was quick to question the correctness and legality of the said order. However, in a landmark verdict delivered on 6 September 2009, Justice S. Ravindra Bhat of the Delhi High Court ruled that the CIC was correct in its order dated 6 January 2009. In the subsequent appeal, a three-judge bench headed by Justice A.P. Shah of the Delhi High Court, in a verdict delivered on 12 January 2010, held that the judgement delivered by Justice Bhat in September 2009 was correct, thus confirming and amplifying his findings. Meanwhile, in a separate case before it, the CIC held on 24 November 2009, that the appointment of judges was a 'public activity' which the Supreme Court could not withhold from disclosure. In this light, each of the verdicts are discussed in detail in view of their far reaching importance.

The second part of the section maps out a range of positive pronouncements by the High Courts and the Supreme Court in the last one year, on areas of civil liberties, social and economic rights, environment and development, and on issues regarding rural and urban self-governance. A review of some of the key cases of the year gone by show that there has been a range of positive pronouncements by the Supreme Court and the High Courts in areas of civil liberties, social and economic rights, environment and development, and on issues in rural and urban self-governance. Together they tell a story that the judiciary continues to play its vital role as a guardian of rights and of order in society. Indeed some of the judges, and in particular, Justice A.P. Shah from the High Court of Delhi, wrote some landmark judgements throughout the last year, but what the story of the cases discussed above hide is that some of these cases are occasioned primarily due to judicial pronouncements of the past remaining unimplemented. This trend had motivated the chairperson of the Law Commission of India to write to the Union Law minister while forwarding the 223rd Report of the Commission to the Ministry in April 2009. He said:

Various laws have been enacted to eradicate poverty: some of them directly deal with them and some of them indirectly. Nevertheless, their tardy implementation makes us lag behind in effectively dealing with the problem… We are of the view that the Union and the State Governments should accord top priority to implementation of the judgments rendered by our Supreme Court in their letter and spirit in order that the lot of the have-nots is ameliorated.

A mapping of key verdicts of the Supreme Court and the High Court show that the courts have been accessible to a range of public issues. However, this also is not the whole truth. It has been pointed out in first part of the review that research has established that in 2008, the Supreme Court received 24,666 letters, postcards, or petitions asking for its intervention in cases that might be considered Public Interest Litigation (PIL). Of these, only 226 were placed before judges on admission days, and only a small fraction of these were heard as regular hearing matters. The rest were rejected. Numbers may not reveal all but they do suggest that the jury is out on the accessibility of the Supreme Court on public interest issues today. The trends also point to the imperative of understanding the instrument of PIL better. There is a need to understand the various distinct traditions within the PIL jurisprudence resulting from the different categories of public interest issues brought in the higher courts. Such an understanding is central to evolving more nuanced and effective approaches on the issues and concerns around PIL in future.

The section also highlights the positive role of Committee on Judicial Accountability and some senior and respected lawyers, which should also not be lost sight of. They infused hope and optimism. Some of the new proposals of the Ministry of Law and Justice are also potentially far reaching, though a touch ambitious. Articulation of a National Litigation Policy and proposal to create of a National Arrears Grid deserve a close follow up especially in the light of pendency cases in all the high courts. The trends show that some of the 'bigger' High Courts have huge problems of pendency, for example, the High Court of Allahabad. Out of the total pendency of over

40 lakh cases in all the 21 high courts, almost one-fourth is from one single court, i.e., the High Court of Allahabad. It is interesting to note that the same High Court that has the largest pendency also has the largest vacancy of judges as on 15 February 2009. The total pendency in all the high courts on 31 December 2009 was more than 40 lakh cases (4,076,837 to be exact).

LOCAL GOVERNMENT WATCH

Decentralised local governance is frequently promoted as a solution to the failure of centralised development and as an alternative mode of local development, not only in India, but globally. It is assumed that decentralised local governance would facilitate effective people's participation, an enhanced degree of transparency and ensure greater accountability, which in turn will lead to effective and competitive delivery of services at the local level. The underlying argument is that centralised planning has been relatively unsuccessful in the delivery of developmental goals as it failed to consider local issues and contexts. Grassroots institutions and local people have a better understanding of local issues and context, so they can manage local development better and make development inclusive.

In recent years, however, decentralised local governance has become a fluid and flexible discourse that can be utilised by different ideological interests. Interpretation of the concept is wide enough to include informal community-based participatory initiatives, micro-privatisation, public–private initiatives and formal grassroots institutions of governance. The local governance section of this report focuses on the formal aspect of the concept, i.e., the local government. The previous five editions of the *Citizens' Report on Governance and Development* had focused on different aspects of formal local governments in India. The reports analysed the institutional structure, performance, accountability, level of decentralisation and governance process.

This report focuses on three key institutions—the State Election Commission, the State Finance Commission and the District Planning Committee (the 3Cs)—responsible for ensuring effectively functioning local governments and three Centrally Sponsored Schemes—the Mahatma Gandhi Rural Employment Guarantee Act (MGREGA), the National Rural Health Mission (NRHM), and the Jawaharlal Nehru National Urban Renewal Mission (JNNURM)—implemented at the local level by local government institutions. The report also interrogates the quality of delivery of basic services at grassroots levels. The objective is to assess the effectiveness of local governments in India, make some policy recommendations for improvement of the same, and improvement in quality of service delivery at grassroots level.

The report finds that level of decentralisation and its effectiveness varies across states due the difference in the efforts of state governments towards strengthening local governance. Since decentralisation is defined by the Constitution as a state subject, states have pursued varying strategies to empower local governments. The institutions for ensuring effective local governance are established in all states, but their strength, capability and thus effectiveness could be challenged. Though the Centrally Sponsored Schemes (CSS) have made various provisions to empower the institutions of local governance and given them a key role, it has hardly empowered the local government institutions due to weak devolution at the state level. On the other hand, the outcome decentralisation in public service delivery has a pitiable result and again varies across states. Though decentralised public service delivery has been effective in improving the access to services, the quality of services is still to be improved. In an ideal world, the institutions of local governance could assume their constitutionally mandated role of 'planning for economic development and social justice' and function as institutions of self-government without outside help or support. However, in the real world, a lot more has to be accomplished on the road of devolution, capacity building and animation of local governance processes for realising the Constitutional ideals. The journey until now has been modest; it must continue with vigour.

The chapter on local governance concludes that the state of decentralisation and (formal) local governance is far from effective. There is a long way to go before decentralised local governance can produce real gains for the marginalised sections of the society. In its current form, decentralisation in India seems to be a tool for reinforcing central control in local governance. The belated action to activate local government in India after more than half a century of the country's independence through the 73rd and 74th Constitutional Amendments, has had a limited success mainly due to opposition from the states as also because of the limited scope, bureaucratic drafting and faulty method of functional and fiscal devolution. The main shortcoming of these amendments was the political strategy to empower local governments from outside the 7th Schedule. This has not worked and any future attempt to energise local government must, of necessity, start from restructuring the 7th Schedule to conform to the ethos of a multilevel governance system through an open system of reform.

There is a dire need to bring in clarity in decentralisation, i.e., clarity in responsibilities delegated and need to be delegated to the local government institutions, matching devolution of finances and administrative autonomy to meet with the responsibilities. Empowerment of not only local government institutions but also the other institutions responsible for making local governance effective is required to gain the real benefits of decentralisation for the poor. In its current form, decentralisation and local governance serves to the interest of a small group of well-off as it promotes rent-seeking. The problem is not only in the implementation, but also in design of local governance in India. The institutions of local governance, like many other public institutions in India, are designed in a way that they serve perverse interests and endorse rent-seeking. Thus, improving local governance in India would require breaking down the nexus of perverse interests, bringing in radical changes, and probably, institutional shifts.

LOOKING AHEAD

Review of the four key institutions of governance—the Parliament, the executive, the judiciary and the local government—indicates some progress forward but there are numerous problems in the working of these institutions, especially with regard to ensuring that the benefits of development reaches all sections of population and all regions of the country. While there are pockets of achievements, a large section of the poor and the marginalised remain neglected. These sections of population will be able to see some value in democracy and governance when they impact their lives.

The continued evaluation of these institutions and processes will go a long way in putting these burning issues and complexities in context.

NOTES

1 As defined by UNDP in Human Development Report, 1990.
2 In 2009, India's nominal GDP stood at USD 1.243 trillion, which makes it the 11th largest economy in the world. If PPP is taken into account, India's economy is the fourth largest in the world at USD 3.561 trillion, corresponding to a per capita income of USD 3,100. The country ranks 139th in nominal GDP per capita and 128th in GDP per capita at PPP. With an average annual GDP growth rate of 5.8 per cent for the past two decades, India is one of the fastest growing economies in the world.
3 The Prime Minister, in a foreword to *UPA Government Report to the People 2009–10*.
4 The number of out-of-school children decreased from 25 million in 2003 to an estimated 8.1 million in 2009.
5 Parliament: Challenges of Three Rs—Representativeness, Responsiveness and Responsibility.

Parliament: Challenges of Three Rs—Representativeness, Responsiveness and Responsibility[1]

chapter 1

INTRODUCTION

As an institution, the Parliament, holds primacy in any democracy, and in a country like India, which has nurtured its democracy rather painstakingly for the last 63 years, it holds a special place. It is therefore imperative, that this institution to be scrutinised and encouraged to continue to play the crucial role it is expected to in a functioning democracy.

National Social Watch has looked at the health of these institutions annually, and it will continue to do so in the coming years too. In continuation of this endeavour, the present report has looked into the functioning and performance of the Parliament for the year 2009.

While the report deals with various details about the functioning of the Parliament, which it has done all these years, it has also added some new features. Since 2009 happened to be an election year and the 15th Lok Sabha came into being, we have included a section on its composition which includes the criminal records of the newly elected MPs, among other details.

The flavours of this year's report however, are two new sections, which are quite pathbreaking and herald a new phase in the scrutiny of the Parliament.

For years, one of the biggest grouses of the MPs themselves has been that their real work in the Parliament does not get reflected either in the media or in public sphere. The advent of 24-hour news channels according to them, while bringing limelight on them, has however, also resulted in the trivialisation of their work, with mainly the unsavoury things which happen in the Parliament getting blown out of proportion and their actual work getting sidelined.

This year therefore, we decided to look into the actual performance of the MPs in as objective terms as possible. After much thought and discussion, a methodology was evolved, which is pathbreaking on its own, to assess the performance of the MPs within the House.

For the first time in Indian Parliamentary history, we have been able to evolve this method, which has assisted in rating the MPs based purely on their performance in the House. This should encourage the MPs to perform better in future. In this pioneering exercise, we decided to assess the performance of the MPs in the 14th Lok Sabha, which came to an end in mid-2009.

This process helped us to have a broader perspective on the entire five-year period. The results of this exercise gave us a lot of satisfaction, as those MPs, who are normally unheralded but are known to be hardworking members, have found the pride of place.

While this is one pioneering work that this report has come out with, the other equally, if not more important, has been to look into the issue of *conflict of interest*.

It is widely agreed that if there is anything which can derail democracy and replace it with crony capitalism, it is the misuse of power for personal aggrandisement rather than for public good. There has not been enough debate in this country on the issue of conflict of interest among parliamentarians, though there have been occasional bursts of interest in the media. In fact, some time back even the Prime Minister's Office took note of this potential danger, and issued a circular warning about it.

The potential for misuse is enormous if one considers what was brought out in the study conducted for this issue. It was quite surprising to find that nearly 25 per cent of the MPs were in the category of businessmen/industrialists/traders/builders. The study has also come out with some interesting findings on their assets and liabilities.

The committee system of the Parliament is another area which has been studied in this report. This system, introduced in the 1990s, was brought in to make up for the limited amount of time that the Parliament spends in scrutiny of the budgets, as well as other issues including legislations. However, the extent of its success is an issue which has been discussed here.

The report, apart from giving a bird's eye view of the issues facing the Parliament and taken up, it also gives a critical insight into its functioning.

FUNCTIONING OF THE PARLIAMENT: CONDUCTING BUSINESS

Disruptions leading to unscheduled adjournments have become the biggest bane of the Indian Parliament, and there just does not seem to be a solution to this. It has come to a stage when smooth functioning of the either House, especially in the morning hours, raises many an eyebrow nowadays. For those who follow the proceedings of the Parliament meticulously, the major question in the morning, before the two Houses assemble is, 'What is the issue which is going to disrupt the parliament today!'

All political parties, without a single exception, are responsible for this sorry state of affairs. No amount of pledges to ensure smooth functioning have been helpful in ensuring it, as these pledges, made on and off the floor of the two Houses, are broken with alarming regularity.

One of the biggest casualties of these disruptions is the question hour, which is considered the individual MPs' single most important tool to keep the government on its toes, and ensure accountability to the Parliament and through it, to the people of the country.

There is loss of precious time during the question hour, and on several days, the entire question hour itself gets short-changed. This loss of time also has direct impact on the quality of debates for other issues including legislations (see Table 1.1).

The trend however seemed to have had reversed when the first session of the newly formed 15th Lok Sabha met. In contrast to what one had witnessed in 2004, when the new UPA government came to the House in 2009, the proceedings were largely peaceful. In fact, in the short first session of seven days, there was neither a single adjournment nor disruption, and unlike in 2004, the opposition benches stayed calm and allowed smooth functioning of the House.

However, it turned out to be a classic instance of 'flatter to deceive'. Come the monsoon, and the substantial second session of the new Lok Sabha, all the old afflictions which had dogged the Parliament in the last couple of decades returned to haunt the two Houses.

Table 1.1 Time Lost in Both the Houses

Session	Total time of sitting (hours:minutes)	Time lost on adjournment (hours:minutes)	Percentage of time lost
		Lok Sabha	
14 (14th LS) (Part I & Part II)	96:15	21:32	22.37
15 (14th LS)	59:47	1:55	3.2
1 (15th LS)	28:03	–	–
2 (15th LS)	162:11	23:45	14.64
3 (15th LS)	105:12	31:49	30.24
		Rajya Sabha	
214	70:37	10:00 (+)	14.16
215	55:01	00:30 (about)	0.9
216	16:57	–	–
217	147:27	09:30 (+)	6.44
218	102:02	13:00 (+)	12.74

Source: PRS Legislative Research, New Delhi, 2009.
Notes: Resume of works, Rajya Sabha does not provide the precise amount of time lost due to adjournments. For example, the amount of time lost during Session 214 is more than 10 hours. In the table, we have taken 10 hours as the figure for interpretation, though we put a '+' mark to convey it. LS in the table denotes Lok Sabha.

Issues like rise of petroleum prices, the Indo–Pak Prime Ministers' meet at Sharm-el-Sheikh raised the temperatures on both sides, forcing adjournments. In the bargain, 23 hours 45 minutes in Lok Sabha and 9 hours and 30 minutes in Rajya Sabha were lost.

However, the winter session was the worst hit. The leakage of the Liberhan report on the demolition of Babri Masjid and its subsequent release had a major impact on the functioning of the two Houses. For days, the two Houses witnessed repeated disruptions and adjournments, and some of the ugliest scenes ever were witnessed in the Rajya Sabha. The decision to send a central team to West Bengal also had a volcanic impact on the Houses, with more disruptions and adjournments.

The Winter session saw the Lok Sabha lose over 30 per cent of its scheduled time, while the Rajya Sabha lost nearly 13 per cent of its scheduled time.

In 2009 however, despite the curtailment of the first session because of the impending Parliament elections, the two Houses managed to sit for more number of days than in the previous year. Yet, despite the Lok Sabha sitting for 64 days in the year and Rajya Sabha for 63 days, the number of Bills passed saw a decline from 47 in 2008 to 41 in 2009 (see Table 1.2).

However, one redeeming feature in 2009 was that despite the many disruptions and adjournments, the Lok Sabha spent over 95 hours discussing the budget, far better than in the previous year, when it had taken only 73 hours. However, 2008 and 2009 were far better than 2006 and 2007, when budget discussions were curtailed to only 58 and 57 hours respectively (see Table 1.3).

Table 1.2 Number of Days in Each Session

Year	Lok Sabha	Rajya Sabha
2004	48	46
2005	85	85
2006	77	77
2007	66	65
2008	46	46
2009	64	63

Source: PRS Legislative Research, New Delhi, 2009.

Table 1.3 Time Spent on Budget Discussions in Lok Sabha

Year	Time (hour:minute)
2000	57:97
2001	16:27
2002	46:53
2003	59:68
2004	45:57
2005	64:20
2006	58:42
2007	57:52
2008	73:22
2009	95:88

Source: PRS Legislative Research, New Delhi, 2009.

Box 1.1 Collapse of the Question Hour: Something Good Comes Out of It

The importance of the question hour in the Parliamentary scheme of things can never be over-emphasised. Every Parliamentarian knows the importance of it, and how it is the most significant tool in the hands of the individual members to scrutinise the functioning of the political executive and hold it accountable.

Despite this, on 30 November 2009, the Lok Sabha witnessed a shocking scene, when 28 members in whose names starred questions were listed, played truant. After three members posed their questions and the respective ministers replied to them, the Speaker Meira Kumar was horrified to find, as she called out the names of the 33 members in whose names the questions were listed, that all of them were absent. For the first time in many years, the Lok Sabha witnessed the collapse of the question hour, leading to the adjournment of the House.

The truant MPs cut across party lines. They included 10 from the Congress, 7 from the BJP, 4 from the JD(U), 2 each from the CPI(M) and the CPI, 3 from the Shiv Sena, and one each from the MIM, the BJD, the Kerala Congress (M), and 2 independents. The 33 who failed to turn up that day, leading to the one of the most embarrassing moments in the history of the House were, Pradeep Majhi, Madhu Gowd Yaskhi, Botcha Jhansi Lakshmi, Anto Antony, B.B. Patil, Eknath M. Gaikwad, Shruti Chowdhry, Ahir Vikram Bhai Arjanbhai Madaam, P.T. Thomas and Kodikkunil Suresh (from the Congress), G.S. Basavaraj, Sanjay Dhotre, Varun Gandhi, Dr Sanjat Jaiswal, G.M. Siddeswara, Anurag Singh Thakur and Radha Mohan Singh (from the BJP), Dr Monazir Hasan, Jagdish Sharma, Meena Singh and Rajiv Ranjan (Lalan) Singh, Anandrao Rao Adsul, Adhalrao Patil Shivaji and Bhausaheb Rajaram Wakchaure (from the Shiv Sena), Dr Pulin Bihari Baske and Mahendra Kumar Roy (from the CPI-M), Prabodh Panda and P. Lingam (from the CPI), Baijayant Panda (from the BJD), JoseK. Mani (from Kerala Congress-M), Assaduddin Owaisi (from the MIM) and Jaya Prada and Kirori Lal Meena (as Independent candidates).

While this was an extraordinary occurrence that embarrassed every party and hastened them to find solutions to avert such a disaster in future, it was rather ironical because the question hour normally fails to provide sufficient time for all the starred questions from being answered.

For instance, in 2009, out of the 1,100 questions listed under the starred category, only 209 questions were answered due to lack of time. In 2008, only 152 of the 919 listed were answered. It meant that only 19 per cent of the questions were taken up on the floor of the House in 2009, while in 2008 this was only 17 per cent. When the listed questions do not get asked, it virtually lets off the ministers from being subjected to scrutiny. No wonder that many of the ministers who get let off in such a manner heave a huge sigh of relief.

However, the collapse of the question hour in the Lok Sabha, followed by a mini-collapse in the Rajya Sabha, both in the same winter session, lead the presiding officers of both Houses to find ways to avert such an eventuality in the future.

The Chairperson of the Rajya Sabha, Dr Hamid Ansari took the lead in February 2010 by changing the rules and making it mandatory for the starred questions listed for the day to be taken up for reply by the ministers, regardless of the presence of the members asking them.

As mentioned earlier, repeated disruptions and adjournments have an impact on the time spent on passing legislations. With the government always anxious to get the Bills passed, it is

Table 1.4 Number of Bills Passed

Year	Number of bills passed
2004	18
2005	56
2006	65
2007	46
2008	47
2009	41

Source: PRS Legislative Research, New Delhi, 2009.

Box 1.2 Parliament as a 'Talking Shop': An Analysis of Parliamentary Debates

The role of the Parliament as a 'talking shop' is often derided by those who do not understand the importance of debates and healthy ones at that, in a functioning democracy. The picture of the Indian Parliament in the minds of the ordinary citizen, boosted to a large extent by the images portrayed by the media, is that of a chaotic, cacophonous and disorganised institution, which does nothing but waste the precious money of the tax payers.

Fortunately, this impression is far from truth. If the media images can be left aside, and one looks at the actual functioning which is largely ignored by the media, there is a lot that gets done. The primary focus in all these debates is without a doubt, the concerns of the common people, national integrity and policies which touch every citizen of the country.

A detailed look at what the Lok Sabha (to a large extent the same issues were also discussed in the Rajya Sabha) discussed during the year 2009 gives some solace that the MPs are after all not as heartless and selfish as they are made out to be.

The two substantial sessions in 2009, the monsoon and winter session, had eight discussions on issues of urgent national importance under Rule 193. This is a rule which is often employed by members to raise issues affecting larger common interest. It is significant that the members spent over 40 hours discussing it.

The issues which were discussed varied from spread of swine flu to the Prime Minister's visit to foreign countries, specifically in the context of the talks between the Indian and Pakistani Prime Minister on issues related to terrorism, and India–US nuclear deal with United States of America.

One issue which affects every common man, the price rise, was taken up for discussion in both sessions. Drought and floods, which affected different parts of the country, natural calamities and impact of climate change on the country, were also discussed with all seriousness that these issues demand.

Anyone wanting to understand the nitty-gritties of these issues and how it pans out across the country would do well to go through these debates. It would surprise many how some of the members participating in these debates bring into it, perspectives and concerns that normally do not get reflected in the media.

The debate on climate change for instance, held in the Lok Sabha on 3 December 2009, witnessed an extremely interesting mix of opinions and concerns expressed by a mix of 25, both old and young members. It was heartening to see younger members like Sandeep Dikshit, M.B. Rajesh, Supriya Sule, Naveen Jindal and Jyoti Mirdha, participating passionately and with well prepared interventions, which brought in a fresh perspective on the issue. The Minister for Environment and Forests, Jairam Ramesh's mastery over the subject matched the high quality of debate witnessed on that day.

In 2009, it was after some time that one witnessed interesting and peaceful discussions on the demands for grants of five key ministries. While the discussion on the Home Ministry witnessed 45 members participating in the debate, Women and Child Welfare had 27 participating members, while 46 members spoke on the Power Ministry, and 30 on the HRD ministry. However, agriculture, consumer affairs, and food and public distribution found the most voices, with 54 members participating in the debate.

The debate which had the maximum number of interested members continued to be the Railways Ministry. The discussion on the Railway budget had 198 members participating in it, while the General Budget discussions witnessed 90 members speaking on it.

Unlike the popular perception, many of these debates are highly informative and bring a national perspective on issues which cannot otherwise be found under one roof.

However one lacuna which still dogs Indian parliamentary debates is the specialisation of members on various topics. It is often witnessed that glamorous and powerful members of various political parties dominate these debates, with many of these members, insisting on participating on all or most issues, which does not bring in the necessary expertise and sharpness to the debates. The Indian political parties are yet to adopt some of the leading western democracy models where certain members are encouraged to specialise in certain subjects, which goes on to make parliamentary debates, so much more interesting. This also would help governments in formulating policies apart from keeping it on its toes.

---

common to see that several Bills get passed in the melee, with no scope for any discussions. It happened both during the Monsoon and Winter session, when nine Bills were hustled through without discussion in the Lok Sabha, even as the House continued to be in disarray (see Table 1.4).

We are living in rapidly changing and complicated times where law-making requires very meticulous treatment, but the way our Parliament is treating this job seems to very sketchy. The time devoted to legislative business has been showing a continuous declining trend and the 15th Lok Sabha is no exception. Both the Houses of the Parliament have spent less than one-fifth of their total time on legislative business (see Figures 1.1 and 1.2).

For instance, the Information Technology (Amendment) Bill, which has large scale repercussions on individual privacy and also on the crucial sector itself, was passed in just 21 minutes in the Lok Sabha on 22 December 2008. Similarly, the Payment of Gratuity (Amendment) Bill, which affects lakhs of workers, was passed in just two minutes in the Lok Sabha on 16 December 2009, though fortunately the Rajya Sabha deliberated over it for an hour and 29 minutes. Similarly, the Legal Metrology Bill 2008, another important piece of legislation with wide repercussions, was passed in just three minutes in the Lok Sabha on the same day as the earlier Bill mentioned, though again the Rajya Sabha scrutinised it for two hours.

Two days later, on 18 December, the members of the Lok Sabha passed the all important (for themselves) Salaries and Allowances of Ministers (Amendment) Bill in just one minute, and the Rajya Sabha repeated the feat by passing it in just two minutes on 22 December 2009.

Figure 1.1 Broad Distribution of Official Time

(a) Distribution of Time Spent: Lok Sabha

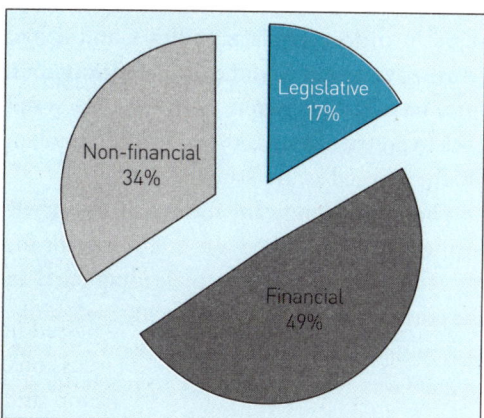

Source: *Annual Report 2009–10*, Ministry of Parliamentary Affairs, Government of India.

(b) Distribution of Time Spent: Rajya Sabha

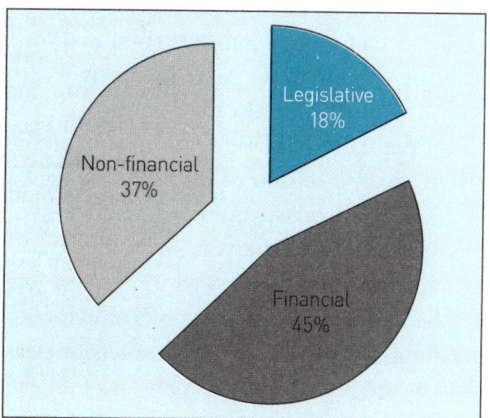

Source: *Annual Report 2009–10*, Ministry of Parliamentary Affairs, Government of India.

In these circumstances it comes as no surprise that in 2009, 27 per cent of the Bills passed in the Lok Sabha were dealt with for less than five minutes each (see Figure 1.2). Only 17 per cent of the Bills took over three hours of discussion. With such scant scrutiny of the Bills, no wonder demands for amendments or dissatisfaction over the quality of the legislations keep springing periodically, both inside the House and also among the civil society groups and concerned citizens.

It is also interesting to note that the number of MPs participating in the discussions on legislations has come down from 11.5 per Bill in 2008 to just 8.8 in 2009. These Bills however, do not include the Finance and Appropriation Bills.

On a positive note, what has been heartening to observe in the 15th Lok Sabha has been the active participation of the younger MPs. It has been happily noted that on most issues, these younger MPs have been taking an interest and have been able to put across their point of view, many a times adopting an apolitical stand. This development has indeed come as a breath of fresh air.

INSIDE THE PARLIAMENT: THE 15th LOK SABHA SO FAR

This section gives an overview of the 15th Lok Sabha, elaborating on the issues and trends which were important, both from the point

Box 1.3 Women's Reservation Bill

The saga of the Women's Reservation Bill continues to haunt the country. The Bill, which took shape for the first time in 1996, and seeks to reserve 33 per cent of the seats for women in State Legislative Assemblies and the Lok Sabha, lies in suspended animation. As soon as the new Lok Sabha was convened, one of the major issues which caught the attention of the members was this Bill.

During the President's address to the Joint Session, she pledged the government's resolve to get this bill passed within the first hundred days of its existence. The immediate and severe reaction from certain members including the JD(U) leader Sharad Yadav, RJD leader Lalu Yadav and Samajwadi Party Leader Mulayam Singh Yadav, on the first day of the first session, though on expected lines, only sought to underline the thorny path which needs to be crossed before achieving the goal of reservation for women.

In fact, in all the three sessions of the 15th Lok Sabha during the year 2009, the government kept pledging that it would bring the Bill for consideration, but eventually failed to do so. Its refrain that it was consulting with the parties to arrive at a consensus frustrated the supporters of the bill. It was common to see during every session, women MPs, cutting across all parties, queuing up before the Parliament with placards and all, demonstrating and demanding early passing of the legislation. The civil society groups including women's groups, also left no stone unturned.

The pledges of the various political parties in support of the Bill notwithstanding, the reason for the delay in getting the Bill through has been the underlying tensions and anonymous opposition within each of these parties.

However after the tortuous path that the Bill has taken in the last 14 years, it was finally introduced and passed during the first session of 2010, in the face of tremendous opposition in the Rajya Sabha. The fact that some opposition members had to be physically evicted from the House, before the Bill could even be discussed and passed, clearly indicated the hurdles which still lie in the path. No wonder the government has decided to put off bringing the Bill before the Lok Sabha.

However, despite the unsavoury tactics employed to push the Bill through the Rajya Sabha in the first session of 2010, the Bill has indeed made progress, though when and whether in the same form the Bill will be finally passed in the Lok Sabha remains to be seen.

Figure 1.2   Time Taken to Discuss a Bill: Lok Sabha, 2009

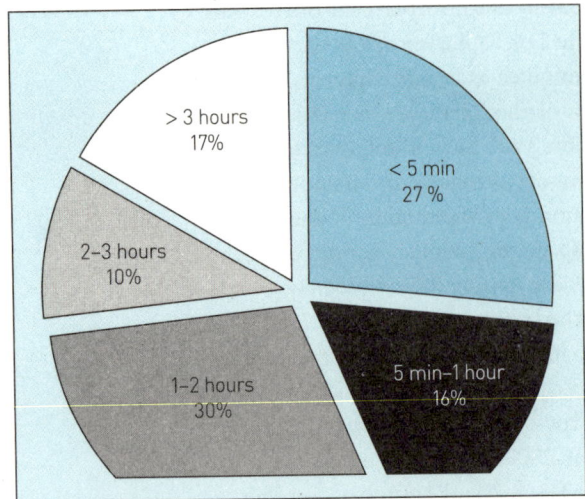

Source: PRS Legislative Research, New Delhi, 2009.
Note: This analysis does not include Finance and Appropriation Bills.

Figure 1.3   Average Number of MPs that Discuss a Bill in Lok Sabha

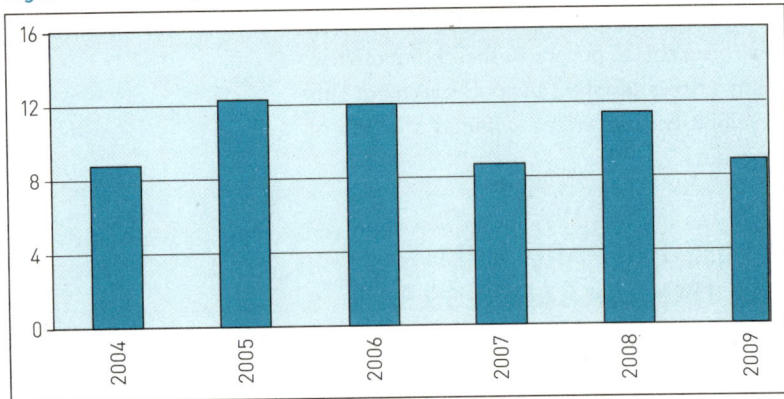

Source: PRS Legislative Research, New Delhi, 2009.

of view of the Parliament and the parliamentary democracy itself. The section also gives a synopsis of the debates which dominated the parliamentary proceedings during the year.

The 15th Lok Sabha: Post Elections Patterns

The year 2009 turned out to be a very significant one for the Indian Parliament. Apart from being an election year, when the transition from the 14th to the 15th Lok Sabha took place, it marked another significant landmark. For the first time since 1971, a government had returned to power under the same Prime Minister, after completing its full term in office.

For Dr Manmohan Singh and the UPA, it was an achievement which they could be justifiably proud of. It was way back in 1971, after four years in office that Mrs Indira Gandhi had returned to power. No other Prime Minister has since had the distinction, until the UPA swept back to power in May 2009, and Dr Manmohan Singh returned as the Prime Minister.

The other significant feature of the newly formed 15th Lok Sabha was that it was for the first time since 1991 that the leading party in the government had more than 200 seats in the Lok Sabha. The Congress, which won 207 seats in 2009 was also the last party to reach the 200 mark in 1991.

Yet another major landmark, which Dr Manmohan Singh rightly dubbed as a 'historic moment' was the election of a woman as the Speaker of the Lok Sabha. Meira Kumar, who achieved that distinction, surprised everyone by being chosen by her party, the Congress, to the Chair, as she had already been sworn in as a Minister. This dramatic development, on the eve of the first session of the 15th Lok Sabha in June 2009, raised quite a few eyebrows, though by the end of the year Meira Kumar had established herself pretty well in her new job, and had also earned much appreciation for her handling of the House. She also had made clear right at the beginning that there was no need for her to quit the party, after her election as Speaker, as some quarters had suggested.

The other interesting feature of the 15th Lok Sabha, was that unlike the 14th Lok Sabha, the new House took off in a more organised and peaceful manner. There was none of the disruptions and angry exchanges which one had witnessed when the first UPA government took the floor in 2004. The Opposition benches were orderly that resulted in the Prime Minister being able to perform his duties of introducing the members of his ministry to the House, without any of the ugly scenes we had witnessed in 2004.

The larger presence of the leading party, the Congress, in the UPA coalition, meant that it had to rely less on its allies than in its previous avatar. One of the most striking aspects of the new Lok Sabha was the marginalisation of the Left parties, who had during a large part of the 14th Lok Sabha held considerable power over the government.

The Opposition benches also acquired some new gloss as some of its leading lights who had been out of the Lok Sabha returned to add glamour as well as punch. With BJP leaders like Sushma Swaraj, Jaswant Singh, Yeshwant Sinha, and JD(U)'s Sharad Yadav occupying the opposition benches in the Lok Sabha, it was clear that far more challenging days lay ahead for the government. The leadership of the Opposition on which there was much debate at the beginning, was finally retained by L.K. Advani. By the end of the year however, the much debated generational shift within the BJP happened, Advani was elevated to the role of the Chairperson of the NDA and Sushma Swaraj took over as the Opposition leader.

Inside the Parliament: Issues Debated

In tune with the smooth take off witnessed of the 15th Lok Sabha, the transition from the UPA-I to UPA-II was equally smooth, with the *aam aadmi* election slogan again gaining precedence and this was evident in the President's address during the first session. Some of the key promises included the enactment of the National Food Security Act, the Women's Reservation Bill, a communal violence legislation, the provision of cheap rice to the poor and the financial sector reforms. Interestingly, BJP's campaign during the elections about bringing back black money from Swiss banks also figured in the President's address.

It was evident right from the very beginning of the new House that issues like price rise would be a hot topic and in virtually every one of the three sessions during the year, it found echo in both Houses in the form of discussions, calling attentions, and also during zero and question hours. Also, right at the beginning of the session, Pakistan was a matter of concern, which forced the Prime Minister Dr Manmohan Singh to speak about continuing to 'forge ties' with the neighbour, even as he made firm noises about countering terrorism. The Naxal problem also has been a recurring theme in all the sessions.

While the first session of the new Lok Sabha went off relatively quietly, the Monsoon session,

which was virtually the Budget Session, turned out to be much noisier though it was still was a marked improvement over the first budget session of the 14th Lok Sabha. The budget session in 2004 lost over 47 hours due to forced adjournments and interruptions and the 2009 Monsoon session fared much better with only over 23 hours being disrupted.

The Monsoon session however proved to be the most productive one. With both the Railway and General Budget being presented for the year, the session acquired a new meaning. Both the budgets came in for praise, as both laid the path for the new government's intentions in the coming five years. The session also witnessed the passing of some very important legislations including the momentous Right to Education Bill. This Bill, which had been in the works ever since 1996, was successfully piloted by the new HRD Minister, Kapil Sibal. However, even after a year it was passed, the implementation of this legislation is facing many hurdles.

If the Right to Education Bill was a major achievement of UPA-II, the Judges (Declaration of Assets and Liabilities) Bill, 2009, known as the Judges Bill, turned out to be a major embarrassment. The Law Minister, Veerappa Moily, introduced it in the Rajya Sabha with the hope of getting it passed without a hitch but instead had to face ignomity when he was forced to withdraw it. The hostile Opposition, which found many drawbacks in the Bill, was unwilling to accept it in its present form and hence forced the government to withdraw it. The Bill, which sought to make it mandatory for the judges of the higher courts to declare their assets and liabilities, however, weaved in a confidentiality clause. According to this clause, the declarations were not to be made public, thereby defeating the entire purpose of the legislation. The Bill continues to languish in cold storage with the government not being able to decide on its final form.

Even as the early part of the session was dominated by the budget and its fall outs, the visit of the Prime Minister to Sharm-el-Sheikh in Egypt, midway during the session, and his controversial meeting with the Pakistan Prime Minister, Yusuf Raza Gilani and the subsequent statements, created a furore in the

Parliament. For several days the issue gripped the Parliament, with the Opposition charging the government of compromising on the foreign policy. The statement that India was open to enquiry on its role in Baluchistan upped the ante of the opposition parties, which disrupted proceedings in the House. The Prime Minister also was brought under the scanner for 'delinking terrorism with composite dialogue' and despite statements by Prime Minister and Foreign Minister, S.M. Krishna denying any change, the Opposition was not satisfied and while the Prime Minister was charged with compromising India's foreign policy, Krishna came in for some fierce criticism and even his competence to head the ministry came into question.

The foreign policy, especially related to Pakistan occupied the Parliament's time considerably but the looming drought and expected failure of monsoon also managed to catch the attention of the two Houses, albeit not much. The Food and Agriculture Minister Sharad Pawar was repeatedly called to explain the situ-ation, and sometimes his frank assessment that the monsoon was indeed failing and that tough times lay ahead, brought gloom to the scenario.

By the time the Winter session began, some new issues and some old ones surfaced, resulting in some stormy days when both Houses remained paralysed, emotions ran high and the weather outside appeared to have no impact on the weather inside the two Houses. Starting with the concern showed to the farmers on the sugarcane pricing issue, which resulted in both Houses of Parliament being stalled on the first day itself, the stormy scenes continued throughout the 21-day session.

While the sugarcane issue, which brought the proceedings to halt in the beginning of the session, found some solution with the passing of a legislation in the latter half which promised to undo the earlier provision of state governments having to fill up for the difference in the remunerative and fair price, the Liberhan report disrupted the proceedings in both the Houses for a few days.

The leak of the Liberhan report in the media, just at the beginning of the session, resulted in turbulent disruptions. The Rajya Sabha witnessed some of the ugliest scenes ever when the BJP and Samajawadi Party members almost came to blows on the floor of the House. Amar Singh, the Samajwadi Party member who was later expelled from the party, was in fury when he walked across the well and held the collar of the BJP member, S.S. Ahluwalia. It was one of the most embarrassing incidents witnessed in the House of Elders for a long time. Finally, when the two Houses got down to discussing the report in a more peaceful atmosphere, other issues had already taken over in importance.

During the discussion too some unpleasant scenes were witnessed when a Congress member, Beni Prasad Verma made unparliamentary remarks against the former Prime Minister Atal Behari Vajpayee. After much disruption over the remark, the Prime Minister Manmohan Singh had to close the issue by making a personal apology in the House.

However, as the Liberhan report debate ended with BJP finding itself in the dock, the Telangana issue broke out after the Home Minister's statement about the process of the formation of a new state having begun. The issue rocked the two Houses repeatedly. The Lok Sabha witnessed dreadful scenes when the rival party members from Andhra Pradesh clashed over the issue. Both the Houses had to be adjourned numerous times as the divide within the Congress over the issue became clear. Finally, the Lok Sabha had to be adjourned sine die, following the two days of disruptions towards the end of the session.

The Lok Sabha meanwhile witnessed one of the most embarrassing moments when the question hour collapsed as not even one member whose question was listed for the day were present in the House (see Box 1.4). The virus seemed to have spread to the Rajya Sabha too, as on another day, six members whose questions were listed did the disappearing act.

The two Houses were exercised for several days over the Copenhagen summit on climate change. The Forests and Environment Minister Jairam Ramesh found himself under constant scrutiny in both Houses over India's stand at the Summit. The marathon debates in both Houses, while scrutinising the government's stand, also gave strength to the government in its negotiations in Copenhagen. The debate in both Houses was of a very high standard,

---

Box 1.4 Methodology for an MP's Composite Performance Index in the 14th Lok Sabha

The study decided to include four parameters, namely—attendance, participation in debates, number of questions asked and number of PMBs proposed. The parameters, which are based on our perception of the vital role of the Parliament in governance and development, were evolved to evaluate as objectively as possible, the performance of all the 545 MPs and to see where they stand. We hold that the Parliament is supposed to formulate effective policies as well as keep a tab on the working of the government as the union government is major spender of the national funds. Being the highest deliberative institution, we believe that policy-making role of an MP should be pronounced, as the state and sub-state level legislative bodies can take care of implementation and accountability dimensions. The allocation of points to different parameters has been done keeping in mind these guiding concerns.

An MP's (we have left the ministers out of the study) task in the House as a law maker and a scrutiniser of the government's performance revolves around four basic instruments that he/she has, the question hour, participation in debates concerning issues, passing of legislations and the PMBs, which is his individual instrument. It was also felt that attendance was also a key issue as regularity and punctuality lay down the foundation for effective performance in any field.

We further looked at those who have asked the most questions to check how many have actually asked supplementary questions, which would give us an idea of the presence of the members in the House and their preparation regarding the questions they had posed.

For arriving at the final result of who were the 10 best performing MPs in all these four departments, we decided on weightage to each of the five parameters on a total of 10. The MPs were ranked on a scale of 10, in which questions were given a weight of 1.25, supplementary questions with 1.75 points, debates with 3, attendance with 2 and PMBs with 2. The supplementary questions were given more weightage as compared to the questions asked because it was felt that concerned MPs might have done some home work on the matter and he/she must be more attentive. The member topping in a category was given the maximum weightage marks in that particular category, and those below them were marked accordingly in descending proportion. For instance, an MP with 100 per cent attendance gets 2 points. If next MP is with 95 per cent attendance then he/she gets $2*95/100 = 1.9$. The MP with highest number of questions $(N = x)$ gets 1.25 points. The MP next in the ranking asked y number of questions $(N = y)$ and gets $1.25*y/x$ point. Similar is the case in other categories. In the end, the points acquired by all the listed MPs in different categories were summed up, which gave us the composite performance ranking on the scale of 10.

Here we tried to apply a yardstick by which subjectivity could not creep in the evaluation. Second, here the focus has been on an MP's role in parliamentary proceedings as our main concern is evaluation of the Parliament as an institution in the process of governance and development.

---

with some members displaying impressive knowledge, redeeming the Parliament's prestige for a change.

The judiciary, which has been under the scrutiny of the Parliament in recent years was once again put on the dock when for the first time in years, the prospect of a senior judge facing impeachment proceedings loomed large. Seventy-six MPs of Rajya Sabha moved a petition seeking impeachment of the Chief Justice of Karnataka High Court, Justice P.D. Dinakaran. The petition was later admitted by the Rajya Sabha Chairman, Hamid Ansari, who subsequently has formed a three-member committee to go into the charges and give a report.

Amid all this high drama and unruly scenes in the two Houses, the government managed to push through over a dozen Bills, most of them without a discussion. Unfortunately, it has now become a tradition for all governments, which puts the Parliament itself under question.

TOP PERFORMERS OF THE 14th LOK SABHA

In the last several years, one of the biggest challenges faced by the Indian Parliament has been the gradual erosion in interest towards its functioning. The Parliamentarians them-

selves blame the media for trivialising issues and sensationalising events which do not deserve as much importance as they are given. Though there is truth in this charge against the media, the members themselves have to also take part of the blame because it is generally felt by many that the standard of debate and the general standard of behaviour in the leaves much to be desired.

Despite this blame game between the media and the parliamentarians, the fact remains that considerable work actually gets done in the Parliament, though a lot is left to be desired, be it the passage of bills, debates on various issues, and the crucial question hour. In short, it is imperative to scrutinise the functioning of the political and permanent executive and its role as a law-making institution.

The Parliamentarians, in fairness to them, are quick to admit that there are many lacunas in their functioning, and have continuously tried to correct them through periodical trysts to improve themselves. Resolutions have been passed, pledges have been made to improve the functioning and display better behaviour, only to be forgotten under the pressure of political one-upmanship.

Despite this, the fact remains that serious business indeed gets done when peace prevails in the Houses, and sometimes even amidst pandemonium. One of the biggest complaints of the members is that all this serious work gets ignored while trivia gets sensationalised. The result of this lopsided approach means the work of those MPs, who strive day in and day out to contribute to the functioning of the Parliament, goes almost unnoticed. That there is no recognition for good work done and only those who are glamorous or seen as powerful get noticed, is a constant refrain of the Parliamentarians themselves.

There is a lot of truth in this as one can see that the almost anonymous MPs keep the sessions going with their punctuality, diligent interventions and prepared approach. One can see this during the question hour, the debates, and even during the much-ignored PMBs.

Can there therefore, be some way of judging the performance of the MPs in their role as law makers which means their performance in the House? After much deliberation, this year's annual report of Social Watch decided to go ahead and evaluate the performance of the MPs in the Lok Sabha. Since the year which is being looked at for this report was 2009, it was decided to go ahead and look after the performance of the Lok Sabha members in the 14th Lok Sabha (2004–09) as a whole.

Parameters were evolved to evaluate as objectively as possible the performance of all the 545 MPs and see where they stand. An MP's (we have left the Ministers out of the study) task in the House as a law maker and scrutiniser of the government's performance revolves around four basic instruments that he has—question hour, participation in debates concerning issues, passing legislations and the PMBs which is his individual instrument. It was also felt that attendance was also a key issue.

So the study decided to look at these four parameters, and short list the top 25 members under the four categories—attendance, participation in debates, number of questions asked and number of PMBs proposed. We further looked at those who have asked the most questions to check how many have actually asked supplementary questions, which would give us an idea of the presence of the members in the House and their preparation regarding the questions they had posed.

Having shortlisted the top 25 in all the categories, we started looking at all the over 100 MPs and their performance under all the five parameters. It was interesting to note that those who finally emerged in the top 10 were members who are little known, but diligent all-rounders. This exercise of cross checking their performance in other categories brought out certain very interesting facets. For instance the only member in the 14th Lok Sabha, who had 100 per cent attendance record, Errabelli Dayakar Rao, a Telugu Desam Party (TDP) member from Warangal, Andhra Pradesh, had a very poor record in all other parameters. He had asked just 26 questions in the entire five years, did not participate in a single debate nor ask a single supplementary nor moved a single PMB.

For arriving at the final result of who were the best 10 (25) performing MPs, we decided on weightage to each of the five parameters on a total of 10. Accordingly, questions were given a weight of 1.25, supplementary questions with 1.75 points, debates with 3, attendance with 2 and private Bills with 2. The member topping in all these five categories were given the maximum weightage marks, and those below them were marked accordingly.

Each of the 100 odd MPs were then marked according to their performance in each of the five categories, and the total of all the five categories were reached to decide who are the top 10 (25) MPs. This methodology has ensured that there is no element of subjectivity in the evaluation.

The final outcome was quite revealing and went on to confirm the woes of the Indian MPs that their performance inside the Parliament has almost no bearing on their popularity or otherwise among their electorate. Of the top 10 performers in the 14th Lok Sabha, only four have managed to return to the 15th Lok Sabha. Also most of the 10 are hardly ever on national news networks.

It is also interesting to note that among the top 10, all major political parties are represented, with C.K. Chandrappan of CPI from Kerala topping the list. Incidentally Chandrappan, despite his stellar performance in the 14th Lok Sabha, failed to get the nod of his electorate in the elections to the 15th Lok Sabha. Similar was the fate of the other four in the top five, Ramdas Athawale of RPI(A), Mohan Singh of Samajwadi Party, Braja Kishore Tripathy of BJD and S.K. Kharventhan of Congress. Ramjilal Suman of Samajwadi Party who stood seventh in the rankings, also failed to get re-elected.

However, the remaining four in the top 10 got re-elected and included, the fifth ranked, Anand Rao Adsul of Shiv Sena, eighth ranked Shailendra Kumar of Samajwadi Party, ninth ranked Hansraj Gangaram Ahir of BJP and tenth ranked Basudeb Acharia of CPI(M).

It is hoped that this evaluation and ranking of the MPs in the Lok Sabha will act as a motivator for other MPs to participate actively and vie for the top honours in the coming years. Social Watch intends to make this an annual exercise, and extend it to the Rajya Sabha also.

Even though we have included the average of all the indicators to arrive upon the top 10 performing members of the 14th Lok Sabha, it is interesting to note the top five members in each category (see Table 1.5). However, it must

---

Box 1.5 Top 10 Members of 14th Lok Sabha

One of the prerequisites for a vibrant deliberative democracy is a healthy Parliament which carries forward the deliberative and legislative role of the democracy. What happens on the floor of the Parliament hence attains much importance. Keeping in mind these pertinent aspects of the functioning of Parliament, we decided to examine the participation of the MPs on the basis of attendance, questions (including supplementary questions), PMBs, and their participation in the debates. On the basis of these criteria, the following are the top 10 performers of Parliament in the 14th Lok Sabha:

1 **C.K. Chandrappan**
Points Received: 6.13
Party Affiliation: Communist Party of India
State: Kerala
Constituency: Trichur
Elected to 15th Lok Sabha: No

2 **Ramdas Athawale**
Points Received: 5.84
Party Affiliation: Republican Party of India(A) [(RPI(A)]
State: Maharashtra
Constituency: Pandharpur
Elected to 15th Lok Sabha: No

3 **Mohan Singh**
Points Received: 5.55
Party Affiliation: Samajwadi Party
State: Uttar Pradesh
Constituency: Deoria
Elected to 15th Lok Sabha: No

4 **Braja Kishore Tripathy**
Points Received: 5.41
Party Affiliation: Biju Janata Dal
State: Orissa
Constituency: Puri
Elected to 15th Lok Sabha: No

5 **Salarapatty Kuppusamy Kharventhan**
Points Received: 5.39
Party Affiliation: Indian National Congress
State: Tamil Nadu
Constituency: Palani
Elected to 15th Lok Sabha: No

6 **Anandrao Adsul**
Points Received: 5.07
Party Affiliation: Shiv Sena
State: Maharashtra
Constituency: Buldhana
Elected to 15th Lok Sabha: Yes

7 **Ramji Lal Suman**
Points Received: 5.04
Party Affiliation: Samajwadi Party
State: Uttar Pradesh
Constituency: Firozabad
Elected to 15th Lok Sabha: No

8 **Shailendra Kumar**
Points Received: 4.96
Party Affiliation: Samajwadi Party
State: Uttar Pradesh
Constituency: Chail
Elected to 15th Lok Sabha: Yes

9 **Hansraj Gangaram Ahir**
Points Received: 4.89
Party Affiliation: Bharatiya Janta Party
State: Maharashtra
Constituency: Chandrapur
Elected to 15th Lok Sabha: Yes

10 **Basudeb Acharia**
Points Received: 4.88
Party Affiliation: Communist Party of India (Marxist)
State: West Bengal
Constituency: Bankura
Elected to 15th Lok Sabha: Yes

Top 10 members have been chosen on the basis of their participation on following indicators: attendance, questions (including supplementary questions), PMBs and participation in the debates. All the members were evaluated on a 10 point scale which was distributed across the indicators as following:
Attendance carrying 2 points, Questions (Including Supplementary Questions) carrying 3 points (1.25, General Questions and 1.75 Supplementary questions), PMBs carrying 2 points and Debates with 3 points.

be pointed out that a member performing better in one category has no bearing on his/her performance on other indicators or on performance overall.

The pointers from Box 1.5 raise serious questions about both the parliamentary performance of the members, as well as the centrality of such performance in the broader political process, especially the electoral process.

We have seen that six of the 10 high performers were not able to get re-elected. Does it mean that the parliamentary performance is not of utmost importance for the politician in the political and electoral process? The fact that these high performing MPs are not very prominent or visible either in the media or within the political parties they represent, also points towards a similar insularity between the political process and the parliamentary performance. Does this mean that the formal role of the legislators within the Parliament is of little consequence in the constituency, as well as within the party?

The disconnect between the institutional and the political process emphasises the need to bring in the importance of the role of Parliamentarians within these institutions. The performance of the MPs in the popular domain is often seen in the light of their work at the level of their constituency, their political party, and so on. Their role as citizen's representative to participate actively in the formal parliamentary process will

Table 1.5 Top Five Members of Parliament on the Basis of Attendance, Debates, Questions and the PMBs in the 14th Lok Sabha

Attendance		Debates		Questions		Private members' bills (PMBs)	
Rank name	Percentage	Rank name	No. of debates	Rank name	No. of questions	Rank name	No. of PMBs
1. Errabelli Dayakar Rao Party: TDP Constituency: Warangal, Andhra Pradesh	100	1. Shailendra Kumar Party: SP Constituency: Chail, UP	340	1. Anandrao Vithoba Adsul Party: Shiv Sena Constituency: Buldhana, Maharashtra	1,255	1. C.K. Chandrappan Party: CPI Constituency: Trichur, Kerala	32
2. Thokchom Meinya Party: INC Constituency: Inner Manipur, Manipur Devendra Prasad Yadav Party: RJD Constituency: Jhanjarpur, Bihar	96	2. Ram Kripal Yadav Party: RJD Constituency: Patna, Bihar	230	2. Shivaji Adhalrao Patil Party: Shiv Sena Constituency: Khed, Maharashtra	1,251	2. Mohan Singh Party: SP Constituency: Deora, UP	28
3. Abu Ayes Mondal Party: CPI-M Constituency: Katwa, WB Sajjan Kumar Party: INC Constituency: Outer Delhi, Delhi Pawan Kumar Bansal Party: INC Constituency: Chandigarh Surendra Prakash Goyal Party: INC Constituency: Hapur, UP Francisco Sardinha Party: INC Constituency: Marmugao, Goa Abdul Rehman Antulay Party: INC Constituency: Kulaba, Maharashtra V. Kishore Chandra. S. Deo Party: INC Constituency: Parvathipuram, Andhra Pradesh	95	3. Bhartruhari Mahtab Party: BJD Constituency: Cuttack, Orissa	227	3. Salarapatty Kuppusamy Kharventhan Party: INC Constituency: Palani, Tamil Nadu	1,108	3. Bachi Singh Rawat Party: BJP Constituency: Almora, Uttarakhand	20

(Table 1.5 continued)

(*Table 1.5 continued*)

Attendance		Debates		Questions		Private members' bills (PMBs)	
Rank name	Percentage	Rank name	No. of debates	Rank name	No. of questions	Rank name	No. of PMBs
4. M. Ramadass Party: PMK Constituency: Puducherry	94	4. Ramji Lal Suman Party: SP Constituency: Firozabad, UP	204	4. Sugrib Singh Party: BJD Constituency: Phulbani, Orissa	1,083	4. Hansraj Gangaram Ahir Party: BJP Constituency: Chandrapur, Maharashtra	17
Dhani Ram Shandil Party: INC Constituency: Shimla, Himachal Pradesh							
Rajendra Kumar Badi Party: SP Constituency: Haridwar, Uttarakhand							
Ganesh Prasad Singh Party: RJD Constituency: Jahanabad, Bihar							
Chandra Dev Prasad Rajbhar Party: SP Constituency: Ghosi, Uttar Pradesh							
Krishna Tirath Party: INC Constituency: Karol Bagh, Delhi							
Chandra Sekhar Sahu Party: INC Constituency: Berhampur, Orrisa							
Bhanwar Singh Dangawas Party: BJP Constituency: Nagpur, Rajasthan							
Basudeb Barman Party: CPI-M Constituency: Mathurapur, WB							
5. Eknath Mahadeo Gaikwad Party: INC Constituency: Mumbai North Central, Maharashtra	93	5. Rasa Singh Rawat Party: BJP Constituency: Ajmer, Rajasthan	194	5. Ravi Prakash Verma Party: SP Constituency: Kheri, UP	1,050	5. Kavuru Samba Siva Rao Party: BJP Constituency: Chandrapur, Maharashtra	14
Virjibhai Thummar Party: INC Constituency: Amreli, Gujarat							
Rajnarayan Budholiya Party: SP Constituency: Hamirpur, UP							
Virendra Kumar Party: BJP Constituency: Sagar, Madhya Pradesh							
Shafiqur Rahman Barq Party: SP Constituency: Moradabad, Uttar Pradesh							
Virchandra Paswan Party: RJD Constituency: Nawada, Bihar							
Karan Singh Yadav Party: INC Constituency: Alwar, Rajasthan							
Lalmuni Chaubey Party: BJP Constituency: Buxar, Bihar							
Biren Singh Engti Party: INC Constituency: Autonomous District, Assam							

Source: PRS Legislative Research, collated from MP Track Records, New Delhi, 2009.

Box 1.6 Membership of the Committees: Increasing Potential of Conflict of Interest

The Standing Committee on Health

The Standing Committee on Health has at least three members who run medical education institutions—Prabhakar B. Kore, the BJP MP from Karnataka, who is the chairman of the Karnataka Lingayat Education Society which runs 18 medical science institutions; M.A.M. Ramaswamy of the Janata Dal (S), Rajya Sabha MP from Karnataka, who is the pro-chancellor of the Annamalai University, which also has medical institutions including a medical college; and Wardha's Congress MP Datta Raghobaji Meghe, who is the president of the Radhikabai Meghe Memorial Medical Trust that manages a deemed university, the Datta Meghe Institute of Medical Sciences.

The Standing Committee on Finance

The 31 member Standing Committee on Finance is virtually a who's who of industry. Venture capitalist Rajeev Chandrasekhar (Independent) from Karnataka; Chief Minister hopeful of Andhra Pradesh and business magnate Y.S. Jaganmohan Reddy (Congress); Maharashtra-based industrialist Vijay Jawaharlal Darda (Congress); Sambasiva Rayapati; and industrialist Magunta Srinivasulu Reddy (Congress) from Andhra Pradesh.

The Standing Committee on Industry

The 26 member Standing Committee on Industry has Uttar Pradesh businessman Akhilesh Das (BSP) as its chairperson, while perfume baron Badruddin Ajmal (AUDF) and Andhra Pradesh textile manufacturer Gireesh Kumar Sanghi (Congress) are its members. Over a third of the members of the committee on industry—9 out of 26—are from business and industry.

The Public Accounts Committee

The Public Accounts Committee boasts of members like industrialist Navin Jindal (Congress), Andhra Pradesh based contractor Kavuri Sambasiva Rao (Congress) and Tamil Nadu educationist M. Thambi Durai (AIADMK).

Source: Rahman Shaffi, 'Business of the Day', *India Today*, 12 November 2009.

---

have to be mainstreamed as one of the criteria of their performance. Social Watch, by initiating this exercise, aims to establish this particular interface in the popular domain. It is our intention to carry on with this exercise to enrich on the one hand, the criteria of performance to include other 'informal' institutional processes operating at the subterranean levels, and on the other to seek the parliamentarian's views on the centrality of the parliamentary performance in the political arena.

CONFLICT OF INTEREST

Conflict of interest among the elected political representatives and the bureaucrats is an issue which has existed in the world for many years. However, as nations got democratised and transparency became a key word, the issue gained importance and many democratic countries have since made a lot of efforts to bring about rules and laws to govern this. The aim is to clearly demarcate the public duties of the elected representatives and bureaucracy, and

their private aims, so that they do not come into conflict.

As far as the Indian Parliament is concerned, the issue remains unresolved. During the last 58 years of the functioning of the Indian Parliament, we have been a witness to this issue gripping the system periodically. Sadly, the response has been ad hoc from the Parliament itself.

In the recent past, the issue has gained prominence again, especially after the media reports about industrialists and businesspersons getting entry into both the Houses of the Parliament. Their presence in the various standing and other committees, and their potential to influence decision-making has also been a matter of concern. The committees on Finance and Industry have been witnessing dominant presence of businesspersons/traders/industrialists. One committee, the Committee on Public Undertakings (CoPU) was in the news some time back, when its Chairman issued a notice to a few of its members, raising the issue of potential conflict of interest (see Box 1.6). He had asked them also why they should not be asked to withdraw from certain meetings, as the issue on the agenda was directly related to their businesses.

The latest is the case of Union Minister of State for External Affairs, Shashi Tharoor and his links to the Kochi IPL Team.

Except for rare instances of attempts to self-correct, like in the case of the CoPU, the Parliament has woefully fallen behind in taking up the issue head on. The Rajya Sabha however, has fared better than the Lok Sabha on this score. It created what is called a 'Register of Members' Interest', which entails members to register their 'pecuniary interests' (see Annexure 1.3). However, this register has not been made available to the public. Organisations and individuals' attempts to access this register have so far proven to be futile. This is however, better than the Lok Sabha, which has not even created a 'Register of Interest'.

Many western democracies including USA, Australia and Great Britain among others have clearly spelt out rules and laws pertaining to the issue of potential conflict of interest of the members. In fact, the US Senate, as well as Australian Parliament have elaborate rules and procedures to deal with the issue, and it has also been implemented with rigour.

Tim Lankester of the University of Oxford, in a paper titled, 'Conflict of Interest—A Historical and Comparative Perspective', published in 2007, points out how in Great Britain, after a series of allegations, they set up a Committee on Standards in Public Life in 1994, headed by a judge, which resulted in new and 'strengthened mechanisms for regulating the conduct of MPs, Ministers, Political parties and Civil Servants'.

Referring to the United States, Lankester points out that conflict of interest is a much more serious problem there, due to the dominance of the business interests in political and cultural life. Unlike in Great Britain, politicians and senior officials very often come from the business sector and return to it, after a stint in the government, a trend which is slowly being witnessed in India as well, though it is still in the initial phase.

In United States however, efforts have been made by bringing in a number of 'ethics legislations' to govern and control the possible conflict of interest. However as Lankester noted:

Today, political patronage remains more widespread, and accepted, than in most western democracies. For example, ambassadors are routinely chosen on the basis of a connection with the President, a friendship or financial support for his election. And thousands of other senior officials in the federal government are appointed on the basis of their political affiliation. Furthermore, conflicts of interest are not adequately controlled, especially in the area of public procurement and public spending more generally.

In India too, the issue has become much more serious at present, as increasingly we are witnessing more and more members from the business and industry class getting into both houses of Parliament. (Cases of Nathwani and Rahul Bajaj, as shown in the Box 1.7, are indicating towards the complicated nature of this issue in Indian political context.) With 'money power' becoming a key element in elections at all levels, 'money bags' have found prominence in getting tickets, regardless of political parties, save for some honourable exceptions. In a way, despite our Parliamentary system being based on the Westminster model, we seem to be moving more towards the American model.

Increase in 'Wealthy' Members in Both the Houses

During the early years of the Indian Parliament, it was the 'advocates/lawyers' and 'agriculturists', who used to dominate the Lok Sabha, with a right mix of educationists, artists, intellectuals, industry leaders, sportsmen and social workers in the Rajya Sabha. It was rarely that one found industrialists, businessmen or others from allied communities in the Lok Sabha right until the 1990s.

However, in the last 10 years or so, one has witnessed an exponential growth in people belonging to this category getting elected to the Lok Sabha, as well as occupying the hallowed precincts of the Rajya Sabha.

This growth is also reflected in the astonishing growth of *crorepati*s in both Houses of Parliament. Though in the past no one had access to the assets and liabilities of MPs, it could have been safely assumed from the backgrounds of the MPs that there were far fewer *lakhpati*s and *crorepati*s. However, now with the help of Supreme Court interventions and the hard work done by civil society activists for more

---

Box 1.7 Rule 294, Clause 1 (Register of Interest) Questioned

Rule 294, Clause 1 under which a member can register their interest in advance was questioned by Ms Brinda Karat (CPM) when Mr Piramal Nathwani (Member, Rajya Sabha and Reliance Industries Limited (RIL) Group President) defended RIL on the issue of natural gas for power generation and on the issue of KG Basin assets contract being handed over to private contractors. He responded to the calling of the attention motion raised by the CPI(M) Mr Tapan Sen on the availability of natural gas for power generation and other national priorities at affordable price throughout the country (6 August 2009, Rajya Sabha).

Nathwani's open advocacy of RIL resulted in Brinda Karat seeking reconsideration of Rule 294, Clause 1 under which a member can declare conflict of interest right before he/she speaks. Just after the calling attention got over, Karat met Rajya Sabha Chairperson Hamid Ansari and gave him a representation seeking review of Rule 294, Clause 1. She said, speaking on the issue after declaring conflict of interest, 'It does not strengthen or uphold dignity of the House and the floor of the House should not be used.' Karat added, 'Given the reality that industrialists and/or their associates/employees are honorable members of the House, it has become a common occurrence and will therefore extend from conflict of interest to a conflict of dignity of the House.'*

Protest on Potential Conflict of Interest on the Question Raised by Rajya Sabha Member Rahul Bajaj

Similar scenes were witnessed in Rajya Sabha on 15 December 2008, when noted industrialist Mr Rahul Bajaj asked a question relating to automobile industry regarding the steps taken by the finance ministry to ameliorate the problems faced by the industry during the financial crisis. Ms Brinda Karat and Mr Amar Singh opposed Mr Bajaj asking a question related to the automobile industry, citing potential conflict of interest as Bajaj Company itself is a major player in the automobile industry.

* For details see: http://gujaratmoney.com/2009/08/08/parimal-nathwani-defends-ril-in-rajya-sabha-brinda-karat-objects/

Table 1.6 Dramatic Increase in Assets: Some Specific Examples from Lok Sabha

Name	Party	2004 assets (liabilities) (A)	2009 assets (liabilities) (B)	Percentage increase (B–A/A*100)
Rayapati Sambasiva Rao	Congress	4.81 cr. (98.89 lakh)	14.71 cr. (4.52 cr.)	+205.8 (+357.1)
L. Rajgopal	Congress	9.25 cr.	288.94 cr. (8.31 cr.)	+3023.7
Uday Singh	BJP	3.06 cr. (7.31 lakh)	43.86 cr. (14.10 lakh)	+1333.3 (+92.9)
Avtar Singh Bhadana	Congress	96.20 lakh	4.28 cr. (1.22 lakh)	+344.9
Naveen Jindal	Congress	12.12 cr.	131.09 cr. (4.26 cr.)	+981.6
H.D. Kumaraswamy	JD(S)	3.06 cr. (21.13 lakh) April 2004*	49.85 cr. (35.94 cr.)	+1529.1 (+16908.9)
Suresh Angadi	BJP	4.55 cr. (81.48 lakh)	22.54 cr. (4.34 cr.)	+395.4 (+432.6)
G.M. Siddeshwara	BJP	5.38 cr. (20 lakh)	14.28 cr. (5.03 lakh)	+165.4 (–74.9)
Prahalad Joshi	BJP	71.79 lakh (3.15 cr.)	75.38 lakh (27.96 lakh)	+5.0 (–91.1)
Praful Patel	NCP	NA (1.31 cr.)	94.88 cr. (21.07 cr.)	NA (+1508.4)
Milind Deora	Congress	4.98 cr.	25.86 cr.	+419.3
Dushyant Singh	BJP	70.82 lakh	6.41 cr. (27.75 lakh)	+805.1
D. Napolean	DMK	1.4 cr. May 2006*	19.08 cr. (1.1 cr.)	+1262.9
T.R. Baalu	DMK	2.69 cr.	7.84 cr.	+191.4
Maneka Gandhi	BJP	6.32 cr.	17.60 cr.	+178.5
Ambica Banerjee	AITC	23.18 lakh (2000) May 2006*	6.29 cr.	+2613.5

Source: Collated from affidavits submitted to the Election Commission of India, Report on Lok Sabha Ministry-wise Analysis, National Election Watch and Association for Democratic Reforms, 2009 and Parliament of India. Available online at: http://loksabha.nic.in/

Notes: In percentage column, + indicates increasing asset/liabilities, whereas–indicate declining trend as compared to figures in Column (A).

* These MPs did not contest in 2004 Lok Sabha elections. However, they have contested in respective state assembly elections around 2004. We taken details of their assets and liabilities in 2004 (or the closest year) from the affidavits submitted for state assembly elections.

A more detailed table containing details of 128 members of Lok Sabha is provided in the Annexure 1.1 along with another table on assets of members of Rajya Sabha.

transparency, those contesting elections are duty-bound to declare their assets and liabilities.

However, Rajya Sabha members continued to escape this scrutiny as their assets and liabilities were not available in the public domain. After every effort to get access to them had been stonewalled, the Association of Democratic Reforms (ADR) and National Election Watch (NEW) managed to get access through the RTI Act.

The Changing Nature of Membership: Potential Conflict of Interest?

During the process of evaluating the performance of the Parliament for this report, it was therefore felt to have a look at the Members of both Lok Sabha and Rajya Sabha in the context of potential conflict of interest. The recent media reports, as well as concerns expressed both in public and private by several MPs themselves, apart from social activists and concerned citizens, was a motivating factor behind this exercise. What started as an innocent exercise, however as we went along, turned out to be quite a revealing one, to say the least.

Since we had 15th Lok Sabha elected in the middle of 2009, it was decided to take a look at the composition of the members profession-wise. However, only those who had declared themselves to be 'industrialists', 'businesspersons', 'traders' and 'builders' were listed. Some well known MPs who were known to be industrialists/businesspersons, but who had not listed themselves as one in their resume, were also included. However, this number is very quite low.

The recent reports in the media about such people had apparently touched only the tip of the iceberg, as this exercise revealed. While majority of the media reports had focussed on the big-wig industrialists in the Rajya Sabha, what emerged from the Lok Sabha was astonishing. One hundred and twenty-eight out of the 543 members in the Lok Sabha, it emerged, belonged to one or more of the aforementioned categories. This means that about 25 per cent of the strength of the Lok Sabha belong to the industrialist/trader/businessperson/builder category, a far cry from the early days of the Indian Parliament.

The membership of these members, in various committees of the Parliament, has also been listed (see Annexure 1.1). Though there is no intention to jump to any conclusions on this basis, about any conflict of interest, the potential can never be undermined.

Meanwhile what however is more revealing are the assets and liabilities of these members over the last five years. The table is self-explanatory. Though many members in this list are first timers in the Lok Sabha, many of them have been MLAs in their respective states, because of which it was possible to access their assets and liabilities statements when they contested elections for the state assemblies. Although no connection is sought to be made in a hurry, between the bourgeoning wealth of some of these MPs and their access to corridors of power as MPs, a closer scrutiny of it in the coming days is certainly becoming inevitable.

We have also compiled a similar list of members in the Rajya Sabha. The number of members belonging to the four above mentioned categories, number 25 out of the total strength of 245, including 12 nominated members—a more modest 10 per cent, compared to the 25 per cent in the Lok Sabha.

During the exercise, it was also found that it was virtually impossible to understand the specific business interests of the members, as their resume only states in broad terms, their profession as one of the four mentioned categories, without any details as to what areas they operate in. It makes it that much more difficult to come to any conclusion on their potential conflict of interest, if we consider the various committees that they are members of.

As stated earlier, there is no attempt to jump to conclusions on the basis of what has been revealed from this exercise, however, these revelations undoubtedly makes out a strong case for a serious debate and action on the issue of conflict of interest. The Parliament and its members, in their own interest, will have to think of a more resilient and trustworthy rules and laws to curb the potential conflict of interest, and to regulate any attempts to misuse their positions as members to serve personal rather than public interest.

THE WORKING OF THE PARLIAMENTARY COMMITTEES

Committees, of one form or another, have become central to modern governance… Parliamentary committees have become 'mini legislatures' helping Parliament in scrutinizing executive and legislative action. They are a link between Parliament and people on one hand and administration and Parliament on the other.[2]

Box 1.8 Conflict of Interest: MP's Speak

Chandan Mitra, MP (Rajya Sabha), Bharatiya Janta Party

In my opinion, voluntary declaration of interest is not enough by way of safeguards because their violation does not carry any punitive provision. Besides, businessmen MPs can get away by declaring only a few of their areas of interest and hide the rest. In other words, the current norms are not particularly effective…I suggest that MPs, upon being elected and before taking oath, be required to submit an affidavit regarding their business/professional interests just as they have to submit affidavits of property, convictions in criminal cases and so on, at the time of filing their nomination. Subsequent discovery of non-disclosure or revelation of inaccurate or inadequate disclosure should lead to disqualification proceedings.

E.M.S Natchiappan, Member of Parliament (Rajya Sabha), National Congress Party

Regarding 'conflict of interest', it is very much complicated with relevant to individual members and to the Party to which they belong. Hence the rule expects that if any member has come within the issue of conflict of interest they have to tell their interest in that particular issue and proceed with the debate…This is very complicated. Because every political party is having interest on certain issues. They are for that. Since the original role of Parliament to debate in open and known to everybody will itself protect the others as its a known fact. But now the various department related standing committees are taking crucial decisions in close door in camera meeting. Many of the MPs have taken membership in such committees just to protect their interest. Moreover some of them have come to Parliament just to promote their business and commercial interest. Hence there should be a new rule to stop such persons from using the committee system in their favour. Anyhow transparency in committee proceedings is the need of the hour.

Nilotpal Basu, Former Rajya Sabha Member, Communist Party of India (M)

This issue is, particularly highlighted in the involvement of Bellary Reddy Brothers in the mining business in Karnataka. The process of direct entry of corporate owners and their representatives in the political process is increasingly taking place. This can be seen from the huge leaps and bounds by which the number of legislators, both at the state and the national level, whose earnings and assets are astronomical, are going up. Virtually, all important sectors of the economy and their corporate brass are conspicuously visible in the political process. And, their entry into legislatures is also getting translated to their entry into the executive and levers of governance itself… They clearly influence government decisions. This phenomenon can be traced back to the acceptance of neo-liberal paradigm which endorses that government will allow free interplay of market forces and will not play any role in business and economy. But, in actual reality, it is the government which is acting on behalf of the corporate sector.

The growing importance of the committees and their role in the legislation can be seen in the steady increase of Parliamentary Committees. Lok Sabha has three Financial Committees, 16 Department-Related Standing Committees (DRSCs) and 20 other committees. Rajya Sabha also has 24 committees and eight DRSCs within its jurisdiction. Besides, there are 30 Consultative Committees attached to different ministries. Bills are increasingly been referred to the committees for further scrutiny. Similarly, the policy documents emanating from the committees are of great significance, The Public Accounts Committee for instance, has a credible record for producing such reports, which at time have been held responsible for the change of guard at Raisina Hill. However, if we look at the government's response to the reports generated by Standing Committees, is lukewarm at best as only 53 per cent of the recommendations were accepted in 2005–06 and in 2006–07 it was 53.56 per cent.

The role of the committees in legislation initially shows a decline from 46 bills being referred to the committees in the 1st Lok Sabha to 35 Bills in the 2nd Lok Sabha, 21 Bills in the 3rd Lok Sabha and 25 in the 4th Lok Sabha. Rajya Sabha showed similar declining trends. However, from the 10th Lok Sabha onwards, there has been a steady increase, from 1.4 per cent in the 7th Lok Sabha to 25.3 per cent in the 12th Lok Sabha and finally 68.84 per cent in the 14th Lok Sabha (see Table 1.7). The process is becoming more consultative as various stake holders including the state governments are presenting their case suo moto or on the behest of a committee (see Box 1.9).

Apart from making multilateral input to the bills referred, the committees also examine the demands for grants, policy and the working of ministries. They also come out with the Action Taken Reports (ATR) on the basis of the reports submitted earlier. In the 15th Lok Sabha, many committees have taken up the reports submitted by the committees from the 14th Lok Sabha, which may force the governments to take care of the recommendations of the committees even if the term of one Lok Sabha expires.

Table 1.7 Bills Referred to the Committees SCs/JSCs/DRSCs (5th to 14th Lok Sabha)

Lok Sabha	Bills referred to				Bills introduced	% of Bills to SCs/ JSCs (a+b/d)	% of Bills to DRSCs (c/d)
	(a)	(b)	DRSCs (c)	SCs+JSCs (a+b)	(d)		
5th/Congress	08	12	NA	20	378	5.3	NA
6th/Janata Party	00	10	NA	10	161	6.2	NA
7th/Congress-I	01	03	NA	04	290	1.4	NA
8th/Congress-I	00	02	NA	02	273	0.7	NA
9th/NF & SJP	00	00	NA	00	81	0.0	NA
10th*/Congress	00	06	37	06	248	2.4	14.92
11th/UF	01	02	09	03	67	4.5	13.43
12th/NDA	00	01	17	01	71	1.4	23.94
13th/NDA	00	02	86	02	252	0.8	34.13
14th/UPA	00	01	142	01	219	0.5	64.84

Source: Government Bills, Resume of work done by 5th Lok Sabha to 14th Lok Sabha, Each Session, New Delhi: Lok Sabha Secretariat, April 1971–April 2009. (Table compiled)

Notes: *DRSCs became operational from the sixth session of the 10th Lok Sabha.

SC = Standing Committees; JSC = Joint Standing Committees; DRSC = Department Related Standing Committees

Methodology: In case a Bill, passed by the Rajya Sabha and laid on the table of the Lok Sabha, was sent to the SCs, it was not included here for the purpose of calculation. Like in the third session of the 10th Lok Sabha, The Constitution (71st Amendment) Bill, 1990 was laid on the table of Lok Sabha after being passed by Rajya Sabha and referred to the Select Committee. Similar was the case of the Transplantation of Human Organs Bill, 1993 in the eighth session of the 10th Lok Sabha. They were referred to the SCs by the Lok Sabha, but they have not been included here. In case of reference to the JSCs and the DRSCs, only those Bills have been included which were introduced in the Lok Sabha. For instance, The Representation of the People (Amendment) Bill, 1990 and The Acquired Immune Deficiency Syndrome (AIDS) Prevention Bill, 1989 were introduced in the Rajya Sabha and referred to the JSCs during the 9th Lok Sabha, but they had not been included here. This has been done in order to make the data comparable.

Box 1.9 Standing Committees at Work in 15th Lok Sabha

- Standing Committee on Chemical and Fertilisers produced a report on the availability of medicine of Swine Flu. The Department of Pharmaceuticals had requested the drug firms to keep the price of Oseltamivir within a 'reasonable range', a term the Standing Committee has found too broad and vague that could be 'manipulated' by the pharma companies. It recommended that such drugs be brought under the price net (*Financial Express*, 18 December 2009).
- Committee on Defence has produced six reports till May 2010, four of them are ATRs on the recommendation made in the previous Lok Sabha. It is a good sign for continuity in the process of ensuring the accountability.
- Committee on Finance took up the issue of inflation and price rise in its sixth report. It asked the government to amend the Essential Commodities Act to check hoarding and speculation. 'The Ministry of Finance...has obviously failed to intervene timely and squarely address this burning issue [price rise] with due seriousness', the committee said and asked the government to, 'overcome its inertia and come to grips with the reality of unabated rise in the prices of essential commodities'. The committee asked the government to formulate a comprehensive food pricing management policy and create a separate index on essential food items—Food Price Index—to accurately reflect the prevailing price situation in essential commodities (*The Hindu*, 17 December 2009).
- Committee on Finance also scrutinised three Bills referred to it regarding LIC, SEBI and Indian Trusts. It has opposed a government proposal to reduce the distributable surplus to LIC policy-holders, stating that the planned change in surplus sharing formula would result in reduced returns to the policy-holders. The current norm of distributing at least 95 per cent of the surplus to policy-holders should be retained. The Standing Committee has also sought withdrawal of a provision that would pave the way for dilution/phase-out of the full sovereign guarantee currently available on LIC policies (*The Hindu*, 13 March 2010). In its meetings, sources said, not just the BJP and the Left parties, but even UPA allies like the DMK have opposed the government's move to expand the scope of foreign capital in the insurance sector. (Available online at: http://news.in.msn.com/moneyspecial/insurance/article.aspx?cp-documentid=3679682) Here, the minor ally in the governing coalition has used the committee site for pushing forward its point of view.
- The committee also recommended that the Ministry of Finance must intervene and resolve the standoff between the two financial sector regulators—Securities and Exchange Board of India (SEBI) and the Insurance Regulatory and Development Authority (IRDA) over the regulation of Unit-Linked Insurance Plans (ULIPs). The committee also urged the government to set up the Financial Stability and Development Council (FSDC) early to address such inter-regulatory issues.
- In an ATR on 'Credit Flow to Agricultural Sector', the committee found that 54 per cent of the recommendations were accepted by the government, whereas the government's response in case of 46 per cent of its recommendations were not acceptable to the committee.
- Till May 2010, the Committee on IT produced eight reports on demands for grants of different ministries/departments under its purview and next four reports were quick follow up ATRs of these reports.
  - The Committee on Installation of Portraits, Statues of National Leaders and Parliamentarians in Parliament House Complex, has decided to disallow further installation of statues and portraits in the Parliament to maintain its neat and spacious look (*The Hindu*, 4 April 2010). The meeting was attended by senior leaders of different political parties and the committee route seemed to be helpful in deciding a very contentious issue.
  - Questions have been raised about the quality of reports of these committees on demand for grants and the way the government treats their recommendations. 'The system of Standing Committees of Parliament examining these proposals may have harmed the process of scrutiny in two ways. One, the reports of these committees rarely get highlighted or debated in Parliament. Two, because the committees do the initial job of scrutinising the proposals, whatever attention members of Parliament would have otherwise paid in the earlier system also goes missing.' [A.K. Bhattacharya, 'The truth behind unread Parliament committee reports', http://business.rediff.com/column/2010/apr/13/the-truth-behind-parliament-committee-reports.htm]
  - The Committee on Science & Technology, Environment and Forest reviewed the Protection and Utilisation of Public Funded Intellectual Property Bill, 2008, which is also known as 'Indian Bayh-Dole Act' owing to its provision for exclusive commercial use of patents of state-funded institutions. A total of 52 amendments have been made to the original draft. Shamnad Basheer, a patent law expert and a Ministry of HRD chair at the National University of Juridical Sciences, Kolkata, hailed the Reddy committee's openness to hearing suggestions from a range of stakeholders. 'This was a truly revolutionary process in law-making and I was pleasantly surprised at the level of openness and consultation,' said Basheer, who represented the intellectual property law fraternity at the standing committee hearings.
    '[N]ever before in the IP [Intellectual Property] law-making history has there been such a meaningful consultative process, where a parliamentary standing committee took pains to understand the nuances of a technical legislation from a wide array of stakeholders', he said. (C.H. Unnikrishnan, 'House Panel Suggests Drastic Changes to Innovation Bill', *Mint*, 7 June 2010. Available online at: http://www.livemint.com/2010/06/07001522/House-panel-suggests-drastic-c.html)

In many cases, the committees have prepared ATRs of reports on demands for grants of different departments very quickly (see Box 1.9). In a socially diverse and developing country like India, the committees can make a meaningful contribution in making effective policies and keeping an eye on government spending. Over a period of time, the potential of the committee system has been tapped to some extent, but a challenging path lies ahead in terms of quality of report produced and impact made.

Inside the Committees

The figures are not very encouraging if we look at the average attendance of the 16 Standing Committees in the Lok Sabha. In 2005–06, the average attendance was 42 per cent (13 out of

Figure 1.4 **Draft Reports are Approved in a Single Session**

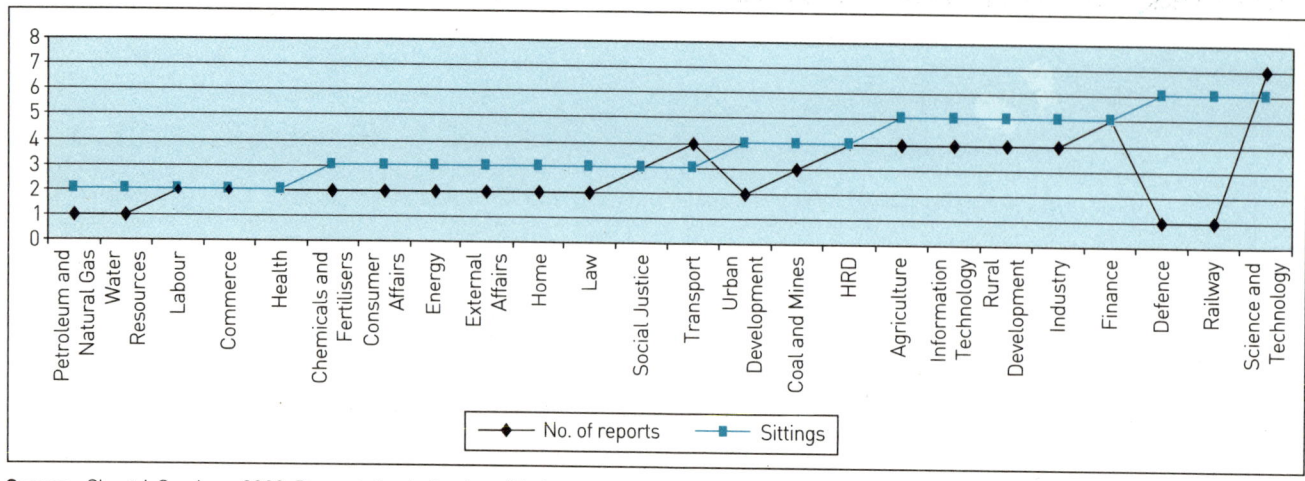

Source: Shastri, Sandeep. 2009. Presentation in Seminar 'Evaluating Parliamentary Committees and Committee System: Changing Contours of Governance & Policy', National Social Watch Coalition.

Table 1.8: **Average Per Cent of Attendance in Committees in 15th Lok Sabha**

Committee	Average % of attendance
Financial Committees	
Estimates Committee	36.6
PAC	52.3
CoPU	45
Standing Committees	
Agriculture	35
Chemical and Fertiliser	33.3
Coal and Steel	50
Defence	38.7
Energy	46.7
External Affairs	49.3
Finance	46.4
Food, Consumer Affairs and Public Distribution	51.1
IT	33.3
Labour	47.5
Petroleum and Natural Gas	50
Railways	46
Rural Development	39
Social Justice and Empowerment	56
Urban Development	58.6

Source: Resume of work done by Lok Sabha: 15th Lok Sabha, Third Session, T O No 3/15LS Vol. III. Available online at: http://164.100.24.207/resumeofwork/III/191LS.pdf

31) which increased marginally to 45 per cent (14 out of 31) in 2006–07.[3] In most of the committees, the average attendance was ranging from 14–16 members. Even the data of the 15th Lok Sabha (see Table 1.8) seem to follow this trend. No committee has witnessed even 60 per cent. Out of the 18 committees listed in the following Table, only six committees, i.e., one-third of them could register the attendance of 50 per cent or more. The attendance trends are dismal during the legislative business.

In the case of Department Related Standing Committees, most of the evidence is taken in one session and the draft is approved in the second session. The draft report in almost all the cases is approved in a single session. This clearly shows that the time devoted to the deliberations is not sufficient, especially in the light of some serious policy matters which are posed in the DRSC's. The role of DRSC's in the legislative functions is also undermined in the light of the fact that heavy workload is allotted to them and limited time devoted to the business hinders their working.

On an average, each committee spends 182 minutes to approve a draft, but in many cases it is less than 120 minutes which can be seen clearly from Figures 1.5 and 1.6. The approval of the final draft report in most cases is done in less than an hour and on seven instances, specifically in case of DRSC, the final draft reports were approved in less than 35 minutes.

CONCRETE PROPOSALS[4]

The utilitarian assessment of the committees in the Indian context can be erroneous and

Figure 1.5   Demand for Grants, 2007–08: Time Taken to Deliberate and Approve a Report

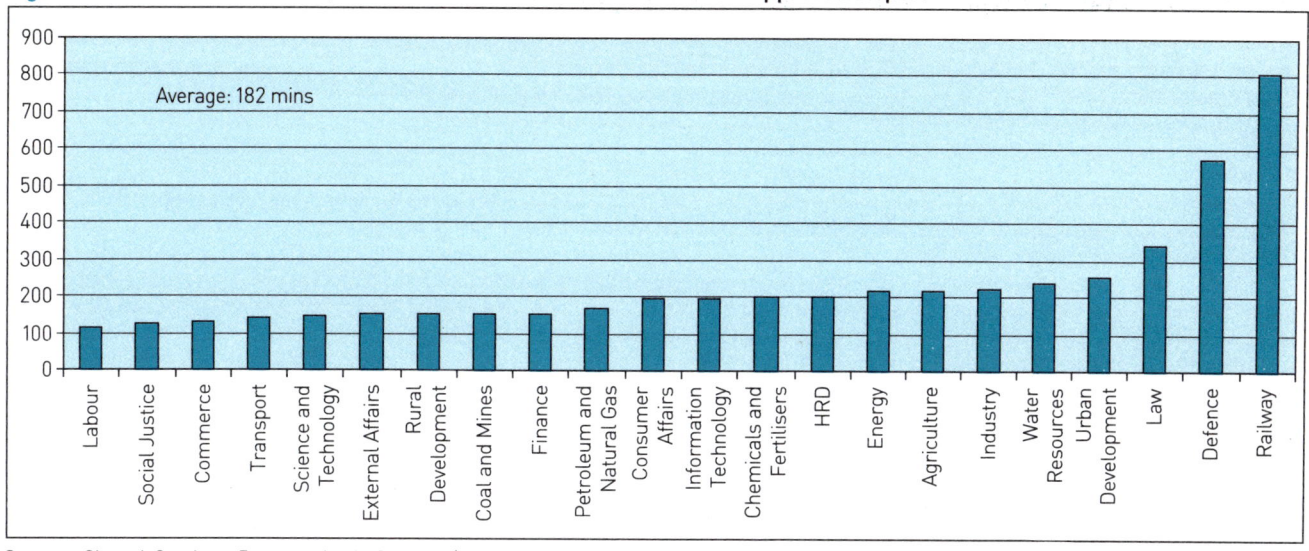

Source: Shastri, Sandeep, Presentation in Seminar 'Evaluating Parliamentary Committees and Committee System: Changing Contours of Governance & Policy', National Social Watch Coalition, 2009.

Figure 1.6   Demand for Grants, 2007–08: Time Taken to Approve the Final Draft Reports

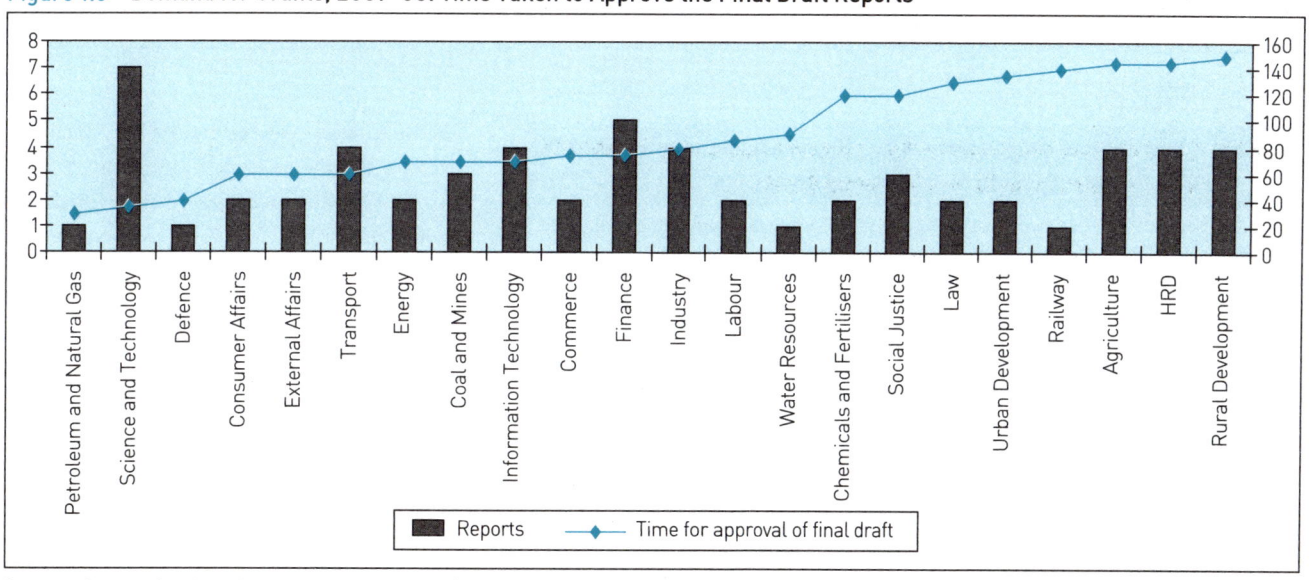

Source: Shastri, Sandeep, Presentation in Seminar 'Evaluating Parliamentary Committees and Committee System: Changing Contours of Governance & Policy', National Social watch Coalition, 2009.

they should also be looked at from the point of inclusiveness and legitimacy. The reform proposals made here is based on the premise of optimum utilisation of the potential and opportunities offered by existing committee system in the given political environment.

- Need for strict rationalisation of the committee system. The Consultative Committees should pack the bag. The Nodal Standing Committee on Economy should be introduced urgently. Gradually, the troika of financial Standing Committees may be phased out after making an assessment of the experience of the committee on economy for a while. Greater use of sub-committees should be made so that the demand of flexibility and changing environment can be met.

- The number of members in the Standing Committees and the Financial Committees

Box 1.10   15th Parliament and the Committee System: Some Emerging Issues

As the committee formation got delayed in the 15th Lok Sabha, the demands for grants of various ministries in the first budget were passed without any scrutiny by the Standing Committees. P.K. Bansal, the Minister for Parliamentary Affairs, explained that constitution of such a large number of committees prolonged the process. Second, the presence of 302 new MPs has been unprecedented (*The Indian Express*, 28 June 2009).

Fifty MPs from different parties belonging to the Other Backward Classes (OBCs) met Prime Minister, Dr Manmohan Singh and Lok Sabha Speaker, Meira Kumar on 23 July 2009, to seek the constitution of a parliamentary committee for OBCs to monitor implementation of reservation (*The Hindu*, 24 July 2009).

As a matter of convention, prestigious chairpersonship of the Public Accounts Committee (PAC) goes to the largest Opposition party in the Lok Sabha and senior BJP leader Jaswant Singh got this position following this formula, but the situation suddenly changed when he was expelled from the party on 19 August 2009 before the party's *Chintan Baithak* at Shimla without any show-cause notice being served. The party pleaded and appealed that he should step down as he got this post as the party nominee. Mr Singh however, argued that he had been appointed by the Speaker and it was the prerogative of the Speaker to remove him. Later, he convened the first meeting of the PAC, which was boycotted by the member MPs of the BJP and some of its allies. Speaker Meira Kumar refused to remove him by saying that the rule does not permit to sack a chairperson till he/she was 'unable to act'.

As the UPA-II is planning to give a boost to infrastructural projects, the government was reluctant to continue with leftist chairpersons of the Standing Committees dealing with infrastructural ministries. In a meeting called by Parliamentary Affairs Minister, P.K. Bansal, to sort out the formation of Standing Committees, Sitaram Yechury was told to either opt for Commerce, Industry or Science and Technology relinquishing his present responsibility of the Tourism, Culture and Transport but Yechury refused. 'They offered me alternatives. I said that since I have worked on this committee and have familiarity with the subject, I will continue to work here', he said (*The Times of India*, 26 August 2009).

The conflict of interest issue was raised by *Citizens' Report on Governance and Development 2008–09*, which reappeared in the initial days of 15th Lok Sabha. Three MPs from Andhra Pradesh—T. Subbarami Reddy (Promoter of Gyatri Projects), N. Nageswara Rao (Chairman, Madhucon Projects) and Rajagopal Lagadpatti (Promoter of Lanco Infratech) are members of CoPU. These three companies have 97 disputes with National Highway Authority of India (NHAI), involving around ₹10,000 crore. In a recent meeting, the committee reviewed the functioning of NHAI and questioned delay in projects. Some officials opined that membership of such a committee provides leverage to the companies promoted by them and parties in the disputes but N. Nageswara Rao argued that he was committed to the national interest as an MP over his personal business interest. 'We have a better understanding of the sector and can offer practical suggestions', he said ('Conflict of Interest in House Panel?', *The Times of India*, 21 September 2009).

The CIC held that the proceedings of a Parliamentary committee did not come within the ambit of the Right to Information Act and would remain confidential unless a report of its findings was on record before Parliament (*The Indian Express*, 30 December 2009).

Box 1.11   Concrete Recommendations during Keynote Address by the Hon'ble Vice President of India Shri M. Hamid Ansari

One can conclude that to a large extent, the Standing Committee system has improved Parliamentary debate through reports that have enhanced the information available in the public domain, has held officials to account, and influenced the government on major policy and legislative issues.

I offer three suggestions that could help improve the Standing Committee system:

- First, the lack of Ministerial participation in Department Related Standing Committees significantly curtails the efficacy and outcomes of the Committee process. While heavy demands made on the time of ministers is understandable, their contribution to the work of the Standing Committees would be very important because political inputs can only be provided at the ministerial level. Perhaps there is a case for looking at the British model and our own Parliamentary Select Committees and Joint Select Committees where ministers dealing with the subject matter are included as members.

- Second, we need to build a political consensus so that the room for political and policy expression in Parliament for an individual member is expanded. This could take many forms. For example, the issuance of a whip could be limited to only those bills that could threaten the survival of a government, such as Money Bills or No-Confidence Motions. In other legislative and deliberative business of Parliament, this would enable members to exercise their judgment and articulate their opinion.

- Third, every effort must be made to intensify public engagement and indeed, enchantment, with Parliament and politics. A recent poll in Britain undertaken by the Hansard Society has revealed that around two-thirds of the British population does not feel that they have a good understanding of how Parliament works and only half of the population recognises that Parliament and government are not the same entity. It is also significant that 54 per cent of those polled felt that the media had the most impact on the everyday lives of people whereas only 26 per cent cited the Westminster Parliament as having such an impact.

Source: Concrete Recommendations during Keynote Address by the Hon'ble Vice President of India Shri M. Hamid Ansari, inauguration of the seminar 'Evaluating Committees and Committee System: Changing Contours of Governance and Policy', National Social Watch Coalition, 18 November 2009.

can be further reduced to 20. The system of floating members should be introduced in the Standing Committees to scrutinise legislative proposals more effectively. Two experts on the Bill under consideration can be nominated to the concerned Standing Committee, who will not have voting rights.

- The Standing Committees, while scrutinising the Bills, should be like the Select Committee/Joint Select Committee in terms of procedure and reporting. Second, reading stage of the Bills can be conducted in the respective committees.

- Using BAC as a platform for coordination in more effective way. A sub-committee of BAC can be formed to streamline the legislative affairs in the parliament. Cross-membership in the related committees should be promoted.

- The deliberations and examination of witnesses can be opened for the public, but the finalisation of the report can be done in-camera. The reports of the committees should be open to discussion in the Houses under non-voting provisions.

- There is a need for dedicated research staff for each committee. Steps should be taken to tap the abundance of resources available with universities and civil society organisations. Close and continuous liaison with the university system must be developed.

- Some dedicated sittings (like PMBs) in each session for discussing the ATRs and implementation of the committees' recommendations are needed. Direction 73A needs to be adhered to strictly in letter and spirit.
- Making committee work attractive for the MPs with the help of mass media and civil society organisations.

CONCLUSION

The Parliament is an important institution which is supposed to play a crucial role in providing a clear cut direction and shape an appropriate trajectory for effective governance and democracy. The Parliament is there to uphold representative and participatory governance. What role then is Parliament supposed to play in a democracy? What is the pattern of its functioning? How well is it performing its function as a legislature? The task of the Parliament is to ensure good and effective governance. It performs this task through its representative, legislative and accountability functions, which are carried out on the floor of the two Houses, as well as in the Parliamentary committees. This institution is not only designed to be the body representing the people of India, but also expected to represent the rising aspirations of the billion plus nation. In this backdrop, this year's report has brought out many key issues which have been a matter of concern for some time among Parliamentarians, as well as those who have observed and followed the functioning of the Parliament closely.

The trend emerging from this year's analysis does not reflect favourably on the institutional aspect of the working of the Parliament. The time lost due to pandemonium and disruptions continues to be a worrying trend. Seriousness and commitment of the members themselves can be questioned especially in the light of the collapse of question hour. The lack of time devoted to the legislative business in both the Houses is also a matter of concern. Admittedly, while it is important to look at these trends, it

is equally prudent to dig deeper into these patterns and perhaps explore the reasons for these tendencies.

The potential of conflict of interest is one of the key issues. The study on this issue done in this report indicates how deep and wide this potential has assumed. The fact that over 20 per cent of the members of Lok Sabha are businessmen/industrialists/traders/builders is a revelation in itself. The Prime Minister himself has been concerned and going by the circular his office issued to the ministers, we are far from finding a satisfactory solution. Though one cannot jump to the conclusion that all of them will misuse their powers, both as members of the Parliament, and also on the various committees of Parliament, to their own personal advantage, the numbers certainly raises the issue of creating foolproof methods to avert any such misuse.

The Rajya Sabha has made some effort towards this aim, by insisting on members filling up a form known as the 'Register of Interest'. While it is certainly a welcome step, whether this in itself will be enough to arouse the confidence of the people that the matter has been taken care of, is doubtful.

On the other hand, the Lok Sabha, where the problems seem to be way more than in Rajya Sabha, has not come out with any mechanism, including even the 'Register of Interest', so far. It is also to be noted that just creating a 'Register of Interest' will not suffice, as the specific business and industry interests and their role in it, needs to be specified.

For instance, one of the problems noted is how some members have been nominated on to committees, where their personal business interests and the scope of the committee they are to represent are directly related. The onus is therefore directly on the political parties which nominate these members to be extra cautious while deciding on which members should be on which committees.

There is obviously a need for wider and broader consultation to evolve mechanisms to ensure that members' personal interests do not come into conflict with their public role. As this report indicates, there are examples from some of the western democracies which can be studied to evolve such mechanisms, as to ensure there is no conflict of interest. The committee system is another area which obviously needs a re-look. One of the key issues this report has brought about is the absenteeism in these committees. It has also revealed that in most of the Standing Committees as well as other committees, it is a handful of members who are active and take interest on the subject under discussions and contribute to the reports.

This has thrown up the question that whether the present practice of appointing a large numbers of members to these committees is really necessary. Another related question is whether all members should necessarily be nominated to one committee or another? It has been found that several times the chairperson of these committees has been forced to postpone meetings due to lack of quorum. Though a broadbased representation is always good in a democracy, in this particular case, whether it really serves the purpose is something which needs a wider debate.

The report has also indicated that the Parliament as a 'talking shop' has its own key role in such a democracy like ours, but it is also a fact that except in some rare cases, political parties have not made any serious effort to encourage specialisation of various subjects by its members. Whatever specialised view that emerges from the floor of the two Houses has been the result of personal interest and motivation displayed by members to study in depth on issues.

What this has resulted in is parliamentary debates meandering along most of the times, with members who have little in-depth knowledge generalising the issue and speaking only for the sake of it. So we have members, with clout within the party, bullying their way into the lists of speakers from their respective parties, regardless of the subject, and especially when the issue of a particular debate has attracted media interest.

This is another area in which political parties in particular and Parliament in general needs to apply its mind and evolve training programmes for its members who show interest in different subjects, and create specialists, instead of the present practise of 'generalists' abounding in every party.

In this year's report, we have made initial efforts to develop a methodology to assess the performance of the MPs within the Lok Sabha in the hope that it would encourage MPs to perform better. While this year's report has looked at the performance of members of the 14th Lok Sabha, in the coming years, our endeavour would be to also assess the performance of the members of Rajya Sabha , and also do an annual assessment of members of both Houses.

It is well acknowledged that in the Indian scenario, it is not just the performance of the members in the Parliament, but also their performance in their respective constituencies which has an equal, if not greater, impact on their popularity. In the coming years, we will be endeavouring to create methodologies which can stand the test of objectivity, to assess the performance of the MPs on the ground.

A blend of the two, parliamentary and ground level performance is sure to produce much more interesting results. However, the pioneering assessment done this year should make all our MPs and all those who follow their performance interested in looking forward to the future assessments.

NOTES

1 The title is inspired by the keynote address delivered by the Hon'ble Vice President of India Shri. M. Hamid Ansari on the occasion of the seminar titled 'Evaluating Committees and Committee System: Changing Contours of Governance and Policy' organised by the National Social Watch Coalition. For complete speech, visit: http://vicepresidentofindia.nic.in/content.asp?id=246.

2 Keynote Address by the Hon'ble Vice President of India, Shri M. Hamid Ansari at the inauguration of the seminar titled 'Evaluating Committees and Committee System: Changing Contours of Governance and Policy' organised by the National Social Watch Coalition on 18 November 2009.

3 A. Suryaprakash, Monograph on Parliamentary Committees, 2009.

4 Jha, Rajesh K. 2009. 'Evaluating Parliamentary Committees and Committee System: Changing Contours of Governance & Policy', Social Watch Perspective Paper, Vol. 2, *Social Watch India*, New Delhi.

ANNEXURE 1.1
Lok Sabha

	Constituency	Party	Profession	Committee membership	2009	2004
Andhra Pradesh						
Komati Reddy Rajgoppal Reddy	Bhongir	Congress	Business Person	Water Resources	19.88 cr. (1.41 cr.)	N.C
Kristappa Nimmala	Hindupur	TDP	Business Person	Health and Family Welfare	1.86 cr. (12.16 lakh)	N.C
Y.S. Jagan Mohan Reddy	Kadapa	Congress	Industrialist	Finance	77.40 cr. (6.63 cr.)	N.C
S.P.Y. Reddy	Nandyal	Congress	Industrialist	Water Resources	8.47 cr.	4.8 cr. (1.33 cr.)
M. Venugopal Reddy	Narasaraopet	TDP	Business Person	Commerce	93.35 lakh (51.96 lakh)	N.C
Magunta Sreenivasulu Reddy	Ongole	Congress	Industrialist	Finance, Estimates	18.67 lakh	14.17 cr.
Gaddam Vivekanad	Pedda Palli	Congress	Business Person	Coal and Steel	72.95 cr.	N.C
Sabbam Hari	Anakapalli	Congress	Business Person	Industry	8.55 cr. (4.75 lakh)	N.C
K.S. Rao	Eluru	Congress	Industrialist/ Engineer	Public Accounts, Energy	12.60 cr. (31.14 lakh)	11.18 cr. (1.91 lakh)
Rayapati Sambasiva Rao	Guntur	Congress	Trader	Finance and Ethics	14.71 cr. (4.52 cr.)	4.81 cr. (98.89 lakh)
Nama Nageshwar Rao	Khammam	TDP	Industrialist	CoPU, Transport Tourism and Culture	1.60 cr.	6.38 cr.
L. Rajgopal	Vijayawada	Congress	Industrialist	CoPU, Home Affairs	288.94 cr. (8.31 cr.)	9.25 cr.
Sai Pratap	Rajampet	Congress	Industrialist	Minister of State/Steel	71.33 lakh (6.05 lakh)	97.09 lakh (14.09 lakh)
Dr Jhansi Botcha Lakshmi	Vizianagaram	Congress	Business Person	Railways	2.90 cr.	2.61 cr.
Assam						
Badruddin Ajmal	Dhubri	AUDF	Industrialist	Industry	30.23 cr.	N.C 14.22 cr (March '06)
Raman Deka	Mangal Doi	BJP	Business Person	Home Affairs, DONER, Mines	72.89 lakh	N.C
Rajen Gohain	Naugaon	BJP	Business Person	IT	1.06 cr. (7.75 lakh)	37.04 lakh (3.36 lakh)
Bihar						
Uday Singh	Purnia	BJP	Vice Chairman/ CEO	Agriculture	43.86 cr. (14.10 lakh)	3.06 cr. (7.31 lakh)
Pradip Kumar Singh	Arraria	BJP	Business Person	Health and Family Welfare	2.57 lakh (7.64 lakh)	N.C 1.45 lakh (36000) Nov '07
Sushil Kumar Singh	Aurangabad	JD(U)	Industrialist	IT, Estimates	2.08 cr.	Not Available
Puranmasi Ram	Gopal Gunj	JD(U)	Business Person	Food, Consumer Affairs, Public Distribution	2.78 cr. (5.33 lakh)	N.C 17.73 lakh (2.73 lakh) Nov '07
Maheshwar Hazari	Samastipur	JD(U)	Business Person	Petroleum and Natural Gas	1.00 cr. (10.54 lakh)	N.C (Not Available)
Chhattisgarh						
Dilp Singh Judev	Bilaspur	BJP	Industrialist	Commerce	2.44 cr. (26.76 lakh)	N.C
Madhusudan Yadav	Rajnand Gaon	BJP	Business Person	Food Consumer Affair Public Distribution	11.99 lakh	N.C

(Annexure 1.1 continued)

(Annexure 1.1 continued)

	Constituency	Party	Profession	Committee membership	2009	2004
Goa						
Shripad Y. Naik	North Goa	BJP	Industrialist	Energy	1.09 cr. (9.82 lakh)	46.37 lakh (5.12 lakh)
Gujarat						
Darshana Jardosh	Surat	BJP	Business Person	IT	91.80 lakh (3.95 lakh)	N.C
C.R. Patil	Navsari	BJP	Business Person	Science and Technology/ Environment and Forest	25.61 cr. (4.22 cr.)	N.C
Dinsha Patel	Kheda	Congress	Business Person	Minister—Micro, Small, Medium Enterprise	2.76 cr. (88.76 lakh)	57.27 lakh (30.83 lakh)
Dinubhai B. Solanki	Junagadh	BJP	Business Person	Food Consumer Affairs, PD	1.95 cr. (59.45 lakh)	N.C 1.84 cr. Dec '07
Vikrambhai A. Maadam	Jamnagar	Congress	Builder	Petroleum and Natural Gas	1.60 cr. (4.0 lakh)	47.90 lakh (5.74 lakh)
Ramsinh Ratwa	Chhota Udaypur	BJP	Business Person	Industry	1.17 cr. (6.62 lakh)	31.12 lakh
Dr Tushar Chaudhary	Bardoli	Congress	Business Person	Minister—Tribal Affairs	20.72 lakh	12.82 lakh (34 lakh)
Mukesh Gadhvi	Banaskantha	Congress	Builder/Contractor	Petroleum and Natural Gas	2.10 cr.	N.C 1.68 cr. Dec '07
Bharatsinh Solanki	Anand	Congress	Trader/Engineer	Minister—Power	1.37 cr. (28.13 lakh)	9.96 lakh (1.18 lakh)
Haryana						
Avtar Singh Bhadana	Faridabad	Congress	Business Person	Transport, Tourism and Culture	4.28 cr. (1.22 lakh)	96.20 lakh
Naveen Jindal	Kurukshetra	Congress	Industrialist	Public Accounts, Home Affairs	131.09 cr. (4.26 cr.)	12.12 cr.
Himachal Pradesh						
Anurag Singh Thakur	Hamirpur	BJP	Industrialist	Transport, Tourism and Culture	2.47 cr. (25.04 lakh)	N.C
J&K						
Chaudhary Lal Singh	Uddhampur	Congress	Business Person	CoPU, Railways	17.89 lakh (4.00 lakh)	54.12 lakh (5 lakh)
Jharkhand						
Pashupati Nath Singh	Dhanbad	BJP	Business Person	Coal and Steel	39.90 lakh	N.C 55.99 lakh Feb '05
Ravindra Kumar Panday	Giridih	BJP	Business Person	Estimates Energy	3.27 cr. (33.17 lakh)	Not Available
Nishikant Dubey	Godda	BJP	Business Person	Finance	10.12 cr.	N.C
Madhu Koda	Singhbum	Independent		Chemicals and Fertiliser	1.37 cr.	N.C 13.31 lakh (1.2 lakh) Feb '05
Karnataka						
P.C. Mohan	Bangalore Central	BJP	Business Person	Urban Development	5.37 cr. (3.28 cr.)	N.C 2.73 cr. (1.93 cr.) April '04
H.D. Kumaraswamy	Bangalore Rural	JD(S)	Business Person	Rural Development	49.85 cr. (35.94 cr.)	N.C 3.06 cr. (21.13 lakh) April '04

(Annexure 1.1 continued)

(Annexure 1.1 continued)

	Constituency	Party	Profession	Committee membership	2009	2004
Suresh Angadi	Belgam	BJP	Business Person	HRD	22.54 cr. (4.34 cr.)	4.55 cr. (81.48 lakh)
Ramesh Jigajinagi	Bijapur	BJP	Trader/Industrialist	Estimates, Defence	1.17 cr. (39.02 lakh)	54.80 lakh (0.75 lakh)
Dhruva Narayan Rangaswami	Chamarajanagar	Congress	Business Person	Social Justice/ Empowerment	1.67 cr. (38.96 lakh)	N.C 16.34 lakh April '04
Nalin Kumar Kateel	Dakshina Kannada	BJP	Builder	Commerce	54.91 lakh (28.06 lakh)	N.C
G.M. Siddeshwara	Davanagere	BJP	Trader/Industrialist	Water Resources	14.28 cr. (5.03 lakh)	5.38 cr. (20 lakh)
Prahalad Joshi	Dharwad	BJP	Business Person	Railways	75.38 lakh (27.96 lakh)	71.79 lakh (3.15 cr.)
Shiv Kumar C. Udasi	Haveri	BJP	Builder	Water Resources, External Affairs	32.46 cr. (3.38 cr.)	N.C
Shivaram Gouda Shivanagouda	Koppal	BJP	Busines Person/ Industrialist	Commerce	1.40 cr. (34.44 cr.)	N.C
Pakkirappa	Raichur	BJP	Business Person	Labour	7.83 lakh (0)	N.C
B.Y. Raghavendra	Shimoga	BJP	Industrialist/ Business Person	Industry	6.57 cr. (42.34 lakh)	N.C
Anant Kumar Hegde	Uttar Kannada	BJP	Business Person	CoPU, Agriculture	65.38 lakh (59.55 lakh)	12.06 lakh (1.31 cr.)
			Madhya Pradesh			
Jyoti Dhurve	Batul	BJP	Business Person	PPG, Law and Justice	71.35 lakh (6.0 lakh)	N.C
Kamal Nath	Chhindwara	Congress	Industrialist	Minister	Not Available	4.31 cr.
Sajjan Singh Verma	Dewas	Congress	Builder	Water Resources	2.90 cr. (11.04 lakh)	N.C 39.00 lakh Jan '03
Prem Chandra Guddu	Ujjain	Congress	Business Person	Social Justice and Empowerment	10.57 cr.(15.0 lakh)	10.23 cr.
			Maharashtra			
Dilip Kumar M. Gandhi	Ahmad Nagar	BJP	Business Person	Petroleum and Natural Gas	1.34 cr. (9.55 lakh)	N.C
Sanjay Dhotre	Akola	BJP	Industrialist	Rural Development	2.02 cr. (22.21 lakh)	1.30 cr. (24.08 lakh)
Chandrakant Khaire	Aurangabad	Shiv Sena	Industrialist	Estimates, Coal and Steel	1.56 cr. (3.98 lakh)	93.33 lakh (59.59 lakh)
Praful Patel	Bhandara-Gondia	NCP	Industrialist	Minister	94.88 cr. (21.07 cr.)	Assets (NA), (1.31 cr.)
Pratap Rao Jadav	Boldhana	Shiv Sena	Business Person	HRD	1.32 cr. (45.14 lakh)	N.C 42.06 lakh (13.25 lakh) Nov '04
Anand Paranjpe	Kalyan	Shiv Sena	Industrialist	Railways	1.22 (38.71 lakh)	N.C
Jaywant Awale	Latur	Congress	Business Person/ Industrialist	Coal and Steel	3.04 cr.	N.C (Not Available)
Gajanan Babar	Maval	Shiv Sena	Business Person	Urban Development	6.78 cr. (78.42 lakh)	N.C
Sanjay Dina Patil	Mumbai-NE	NCP	Business Person	Commerce	46.23 lakh	N.C 8.80 lakh Oct '04
Milind Deora	Mumai-South	Congress	Business Person	Estimates-IT	25.86 cr.	4.98 cr.

(Annexure 1.1 continued)

(*Annexure 1.1 continued*)

	Constituency	Party	Profession	Committee membership	2009	2004
Bhaskar Rao Patil	Nanded	Congress	Industrialist	Defence	6.39 cr. (2.60 lakh)	4.27 cr. (12.76 lakh)
Sameer Bhujbal	Nashik	NCP	Business Person	Petroleum and Natural Gas	6.66 cr.	N.C
Suresh Kalmadi	Pune	Congress	Business Person	HRD, Ethics	12.81 cr.	8.04 cr. (17 lakh)
Dr Nilesh Rane	Ratnagiri-Sindhudurg	Congress	Business Person	Home Affairs	Not Available	N.C
Haribhau Jawale	Raver	BJP	Trader	Water Resources	81.29 lakh (6.29 lakh)	N.C 53.04 lakh (6.60 lakh) Oct '04
Pratik Patil	Sangli	Congress	Industrialist/ Business Person	Minister	2.28 cr. (13.58 lakh)	3.88 cr.
Shivaji Dattatray Adhal Rao	Shirur	Shiv Sena	Industrialist	IT	7.08 cr. (1.62 cr.)	5.86 cr. (1.23 cr.)
Bhavna Gawali	Yavatmal-Washim	Shiv Sena	Business Person	Transport, Tourism and Culture	3.35 cr. (24.30 lakh)	1.88 cr. (7.48 lakh)
Orissa						
Baijayant Panda	Kendrapara	BJD	Industrialist	CoPU/Urban Devt.	16.18 cr. (4.51 lakh)	N.C
Pradeep Majhi	Nabarangpur	Congress			9.70 lakh (3.45 lakh)	N.C
Punjab						
Vijay Singla	Sangrur	Congress	Business Person	Energy	3.47 cr. (3.74 lakh)	N.C
Rajasthan						
Harish Choudhary	Barmer	Congress	Business Person	Energy	57.53 lakh (12.95 lakh)	N.C
Dr Mahesh Joshi	Jaipur	Congress	Business Person	Transport, Tourism and Culture	1.12 cr.(9.16 cr.)	N.C (Not Available)
Devji Patel	Jalore	BJP	Business Person	Personnel, Public Grievances, Law and Justice	1.09 cr. (25,148)	N.C
Dushyant Singh	Jhalawar-Baran	BJP	Business Person	Transport, Tourism and Culture	6.41 cr.(27.75 lakh)	70.82 lakh
Khiladi Lal Bairwa	Karauli-Dholpur	Congress	Business Person	Railways	6.28 cr. (54.38 lakh)	N.C
Ijyaraj Singh	Kota	Congress	Business Person	Defence	17.54 cr.	N.C
Badriram Jakhar	Pali	Congress	Business Person	water resources	7.89 cr. (4.98 lakh)	Not Available
Gopal Singh Shekhawat	Rajsamand	Congress	Business Person	Railways	42.36 lakh (4.89 lakh)	N.C
Sikkim						
Premdas Rai	Sikkim	SDF	Business Person	IT, Ethics	1.86 cr. (8.41 lakh)	N.C
Tamil Nadu						
S. Jagathrakshakan	Arakkonam	DMK	Industrialist	Minister—Information and Broadcasting	5.31 cr.	N.C (Not Available)
Dayanidhi Maran	Chennai Central	DMK	Business Person	Minister	3.72 cr.	1.43 cr.
S. Alagiri	Cuddalore	Congress	Industrialist	External Affairs	1.18 cr. (7.82 cr.)	N.C
Helen Davidson	Kaniyakumari	DMK	Business Person	HRD	4.84 cr. (21.23 lakh)	N.C

(*Annexure 1.1 continued*)

(*Annexure 1.1 continued*)

	Constituency	Party	Profession	Committee membership	2009	2004
D. Napolean	Perambalur	DMK	Business Person	Minister—Social Justice and Empowerment	19.08 cr. (1.13 cr.)	N.C 1.4 cr May '06
J.K. Ritheesh	Ramanathapuram	DMK	Business Person	Water Resources	10.82 cr.	N.C
T.R. Baalu	Sriperumbudur	DMK	Industrialist	Railways, Ethics	7.84 cr.	2.69 cr.
J.M. Aaron Rashid	Theni	Congress	Business Person	Health and FW	Not Available	15.09 cr. (22.44 lakh)
S.R. Jeyadurai	Thoothukudi	DMK	Business Person	Health and FW, Power	29.98 lakh	N.C
Ramasubbu S.S	Tirunelveli	Congress	Business Person	Science and Technology/ Environment and Forest	4.20 cr.	N.C (Not Available)
Abdul Rahman	Vellore	DMK	Business Person	IT	1.25 cr. (32.97 lakh)	N.C
Uttar Pradesh						
Rakesh Pandey	Ambedkarnagar	BSP	Business Person	Rural Development	14.77 cr.	N.C (3.20 cr.) May '07
Maneka Gandhi	Aonla	BJP	Trader	Railways	17.60 cr.	6.32 cr.
Kamal Kishore	Bahraich	Congress	Business Person	Defence	11.81 lakh	N.C
Arvind Kumar Chaudhury	Basti	BSP	Transport/ Contractor	Food, Consumer Affairs, Public Distribution	1.94 cr.	N.C
Kamlesh Balmiki	Bulandshahr	SP	Business Person	Food, Consumer Affairs, Public Distribution	8.49 lakh	N.C
Gorakh Prasad Jaiswal	Deoria	BSP	Business Person	Petroleum and Natural Gas	2.04 cr.	N.C
Surendra Singh Nagar	Gautambuddha Nagar	BSP	Business Person	Agriculture	49.30 cr.	N.C
Usha Verma	Hardoi	SP	Industrialist/ Business Person	Rural Development	17.54 lakh	9.76 lakh (2 lakh)
Ghanshyam Anuragi	Jalaun	SP	Business Person	Water Resources	53.65 lakh	21.24 lakh
Dhananjay Singh	Jaunpur	BSP	Business Person	IT	50.07 lakh (6.78 lakh)	N.C 20.95 cr. (13.59 lakh) May '07
Shriprakash Jaiswal	Kanpur	Congress	Business Person	Minister	3.08 cr.	1.91 cr.
Rajendra Agarwal	Meerut	BJP	Business Person	Railways, IT	24.47 lakh (3.15 lakh)	N.C
Balkumar Patel	Mirzapur	SP	Business Person	Transport, Tourism and Culture	2.29 cr. (1.16 cr.)	N.C
Kadir Rana	Muzzafarnagar	BSP	Business Person	Urban Development	6.33 cr.	N.C 2.94 cr. May '07
Shafiqur Rahman Barq	Sambhal	BSP	Business Person	Labour	17.59 lakh	13.49 lakh
Annu Tandon	Unnao	Congress	Business Person	Water Resources	41.99 cr. (1.47 lakh)	N.C
West Bengal						
Adhir Ranjan Chowdhary	Baharampur	Congress	Business Person	Estimates, Energy	3.04 cr. (19.26 lakh)	1.90 cr.
Dinesh Trivedi	Barrackpur	AITC	Industrialist	Health & FW	2.72 cr.	N.C
S.K. Nurul Islam	Basirhat	AITC	Business Person	Agriculture	16.16 lakh (3,024)	N.C
Ambica Banerjee	Howrah	AITC	Business Person	Urban Development	6.29 cr.	N.C 23.18 lakh (2000) May '06

(*Annexure 1.1 continued*)

(Annexure 1.1 continued)

	Constituency	Party	Profession	Committee membership	2009	2004
Sudip Bandyopadyay	Kolkata Uttar	AITC	Business Person	Finance	44.30 lakh (1.96 lakh)	N.C 36.47 lakh May '06
A.H.K. Choudhary	Maldah Dakshin	Congress	Trader/Industrialist	Coal and Steel	1.32 cr.	N.C 81.49 lakh May '06
Suvendu Adhikari	Tamluk	AITC	Business Person	Industry	48.21 lakh	31.98 lakh
Sultan Ahmed	Uluberia	AITC	Business Person	Minister	60.26 lakh (36 lakh)	26.63 lakh (27.30 lakh)
Delhi						
Ajay Maken	New Delhi	Congress	Business Person	Minister	4.21 cr. (0.97 lakh)	2.95 cr. (6.50 lakh)
Mahabal Mishra	West Delhi	Congress	Petroleum and Natural Gas		6.12 cr. (9.89 lakh)	N.C 1.40 cr. (12.38 lakh) Jan '03
UT						
Natubhai Patel	Dadra & NH	BJP	Builder	Home Affairs	8.41 cr. (34.26 lakh)	N.C
Lalubhai Patel	Daman & Diu	BJP	Builder/Business Person	Home Affairs	3.44 cr. (21.35 lakh)	N.C

Source: Various.

ANNEXURE 1.2
Rajya Sabha

Name	Party	Profession	Committee membership	Assets libailities	Liabilities
Andhra Pradesh					
Dr T. Subbarami Reddy	INC	Industrialist/Trader	CoPU, S&T, E&F	272.64 cr.	9 cr.
Girish Kumar Sanghi	INC	Industrialist	Industry and Urban Development	1.01 cr.	
Assam					
Birendra Baishya	AGP	Businessman	CoPU, Transport, Tourism and Culture	35.11 lakh	
Bihar					
Prem Chand Gupta	RJD	Industrialist		5.48 cr.	
Gujarat					
Vijay Kumar Rupani	BJP	Industrialist	HRD and CoPU	1.62 cr.	
Nathuji Thakur	BJP	Businessman	Industry	81.13 lakh	
Jharkhand					
Parimal Nathwani	IND	Trader/Industrialist	Personnel, Public Grievances, Law and Justice	52.65 cr.	
Dhiraj Prasad Sahu	INC	Industrialist	Coal and steel	N.A	
Karnataka					
Rajiv Chandrasekhar	IND	Entrepreneur	Finance	34.61 cr.	
Dr Prabhkar Kore	BJP	Trader/Industrialist		N.A	
Anil Lad	INC	Businessman	S&T, E&F	188.09 cr.	46.26 cr.
Dr M.A.M. Ramaswamy	JD(S)	Industrialist	Health and Family Welfare	278.64 cr.	

(Annexure 1.2 continued)

(Annexure 1.2 continued)

Name	Party	Profession	Committee membership	Assets libailities	Liabilities
			Kerala		
Abdul Waheb Peevee	Muslim League	Industrialist/Trader	Social Justice and Empowerment	N.A	
			Maharashtra		
Rahul Bajaj	IND	Industrialist	Commerce	308.28 cr.	386.72 cr.
Vijay J. Darda	INC	Businessman	Finance	32.98 cr.	
Murli Deora	INC	Industrialist	Minister	24.54 cr.	
Rajkumar Dhoot	S.S.	Trader	IT	16.51 cr.	
Manohar Joshi	S.S.	Industrialist		5.23 cr.	
			Punjab		
Naresh Gujral	SAD	Industrialist	Transport, Tourism and Culture	N.A	
			Rajasthan		
Ram Das Agarwal	BJP	Businessman	Transport, Tourism and Culture	6.46 cr.	
			Uttar Pradesh		
Dr Akhilesh Das Gupta	BSP	Businessman/Industrialist/Builder	Industry	53.13 cr.	1.03 cr.
Mahendra Mohan	SP	Industry	Finance	110.62 cr.	
Ram Narayan Sahu	SP	Businessman	Food, Consumer Affairs and Public Distribution	18.28 cr.	17.99 cr.
Amar Singh	SP/IND	Industry	Health and Family Welfare, CoPU	79.51 cr.	
			West Bengal		
Swapan Sadan Bose	AITC	Businessman	Coal and steel	11.05 cr.	

Source: Various.

Notes: CoPU—Committee on Public Undertakings
S&T—Science and Technology
E&F—Environment and Forests
IT—Information Technology

ANNEXURE 1.3
Register of Members' Interest (Parliamentary Bulletin Part-II)

No. 46877   Friday, 19 February 2010   Ethics Committee Section
Register of Members' Interests

1. The Committee on Ethics in its Fourth Report presented to the Council on the 14th March 2005 and agreed to by it on the 20th April 2005 has *inter alia* identified the following five pecuniary interests and the ingredients thereof, in respect of which information is to be furnished by Members for registration in the 'Register of Members' Interests', under sub-rule (1) of Rule 293 of the Rules of Procedure and Conduct of Business in the Council of States, in the prescribed Form:

I Remunerative Directorship
- Name and address of the company
- Nature of company business
- Salary/fees/allowance/benefits or
- Any other receipts which are taxable (per annum)

II Regular Remunerated Activity
- Name and address of the establishment
- Nature of business
- Position held
- Amount of remuneration received (per annum)

III Shareholding of Controlling Nature
- Name and address of the company
- Nature of business of the company
- Percentage of shares held

IV Paid Consultancy
- Nature of consultancy
- Business activity of the organisation
- Where engaged as consultant
- Total value of benefits derived from the
- Consultancy

V Professional Engagement
- Description
- Fees/Remuneration earned therefrom (per annum)

2. The Committee also recommended that:

   (a) Every Member who has taken his/her seat in the Council before the date of adoption of the recommendations of the Committee regarding 'Registration of Interests', by the Council, shall furnish the information as per the prescribed 'Form', under Rule 293, within ninety days from the date on which the said recommendations are adopted/enforced.

   (b) Every Member who takes his/her seat in the Council after adoption of these recommendations by the Council, shall furnish the information as per the prescribed form, under Rule 293, within ninety days from the date on which he/she makes and subscribes oath or affirmation for taking his/her seat.

   (c) Every Member shall notify the changes, if any, in the information so furnished by him/her, as on 31st March every year, within ninety days from that date.

3. The aforementioned recommendations were enforced *w.e.f.* 2nd May 2005. Accordingly, all Members of Rajya Sabha are required to furnish information in respect of their pecuniary interests in the prescribed Form. **Members who have not done so, are requested to file the requisite information without further delay.** Members may kindly note that the information that they furnish has to be with respect to their pecuniary interests whether held within the country or outside it.

4. Copies of the prescribed Form are available in the Notice Office, Committee Section (Ethics) and can also be downloaded from Rajya Sabha website (rajyasabha.nic.in) under the links 'Downloads ? Parliamentary Notice forms ? Form for Declaration of Interests by Members'; and 'Downloads? Application Notice forms? Declaration of Interests'.

5. In this connection, provisions of Rule 294 of the Rules of Procedure are reproduced below:

   (a) Whenever a member has a personal or specific pecuniary interest (direct or indirect) in a matter being considered by the Council or a Committee thereof, he shall declare the nature of such interest notwithstanding any registration of his interests in the Register, and shall not participate in any debate taking place in the Council or its Committees before making such declaration.

   (b) On a division in the Council if the vote of a member is challenged on the ground of personal, pecuniary or direct interest in the matter to be decided, the Chairman may, if he considers necessary, call upon the member making the challenge to state precisely the grounds of his objection, and the member whose vote has been challenged shall state his case, and the Chairman shall then decide whether the vote of the member should be disallowed or not and his decision shall be final:

   Provided that the vote of a member is challenged immediately after the division is over and before the result is announced by the Chairman.

   Explanation: For the purposes of this rule the interest of the member should be direct, personal or pecuniary and separately belong to the person whose vote is questioned and not in common with the public in general or with any section thereof or on any matter of State policy.

6. Members may kindly note for information and compliance.

V. K. AGNIHOTRI
Secretary-General

Source: Parliamentary Bulletin Part-II. Available online at: http://164.100.47.5/newsite/bulletin2/Bull_No.aspx?number=46877

ANNEXURE 1.4
Parliamentary Performance: State and National Averages

State	Average debates	Average number of private member bills presented	Average questions	Parliament attendance %
Andaman and Nicobar	31	0.0	425	64
Andhra Pradesh	20	1.0	220	72
Arunachal Pradesh	74	2.5	179	86
Assam	25	0.0	117	72
Bihar	36	0.1	146	75
Chandigarh	63	6.0	107	95
Chhattisgarh	15	0.3	95	54
Dadra and Nagar Haveli	1	0.0	6	74
Daman and Diu	17	1.0	56	49
Delhi	41	0.9	76	82
Goa	18	0.0	73	63
Gujarat	28	0.5	249	69
Haryana	16	0.1	107	74
Himachal Pradesh	47	1.3	172	86
Jammu and Kashmir	37	0.2	99	68
Jharkhand	19	0.0	157	64
Karnataka	20	0.4	156	56
Kerala	67	2.5	186	79
Lakshadweep	6	1.0	118	72
Madhya Pradesh	25	0.0	166	72
Maharashtra	21	1.3	296	64
Manipur	43	0.5	82	93
Meghalaya	6	0.0	0	45
Mizoram	10	0.0	8	89
Nagaland	17	2.0	7	77
Orissa	50	0.2	271	72
Pondicherry	151	0.0	380	94
Punjab	21	0.0	61	63
Rajasthan	36	0.0	154	73
Sikkim	12	0.0	75	82
Tamil Nadu	34	0.3	122	71
Tripura	21	0.5	6	74
Uttar Pradesh	28	0.6	151	66
Uttarakhand	28	4.8	82	76
West Bengal	40	0.4	152	75
National Average/Total	30	0.6	169	69

Source: PRS Legislative Research, New Delhi, 2009.

ANNEXURE 1.5
Time Taken to Discuss Bills 2008–09

Introduced	House (introduced)	Passed by Lok Sabha	Passed by Rajya Sabha	Title	Time taken in Lok Sabha	Time taken in Rajya Sabha	Total time	Remarks
7 March 2007	Rajya Sabha	23 April 2008	29 April 2008	The Jawaharlal Institute of Post-Graduate Medical Education and Research, Puducherry Bill, 2007	3:31	0:31	4:02	
14 May 2007	Rajya Sabha	19 March 2008	27 February 2008	The Maternity Benefit (Amendment) Bill, 2007	2:20	0:06	2:26	
11 March 2008	Lok Sabha	17 March 2008	19 March 2008	The Sugar Development Fund (Amendment) Bill, 2008	2:39	1:40	4:19	
17 March 2008	Rajya Sabha	19 March 2008	19 March 2008	The Constitution (Scheduled Tribes) Order (Amendment) Bill, 2008	0:27	0:03	0:30	
10 March 2008	Lok Sabha	17 March 2008	18 March 2008	The Prasar Bharati (Broadcasting Corporation of India) Amendment Bill, 2008	2:20	1:05	3:25	
3 March 2008	Rajya Sabha	18 March 2008	13 March 2008	The Food Safety and Standards (Amendment) Bill, 2008	3:46	0:49	4:35	
3 March 2008	Lok Sabha	11 March 2008	18 March 2008	The Delimitation (Amendment) Bill, 2008	1:30	2:56	4:26	Discussed together
10 March 2008	Lok Sabha	11 March 2008	18 March 2008	The Representation of the People (Amendment) Bill, 2008	1:30	2:56	4:26	
3 March 2008	Lok Sabha	11 March 2008	13 March 2008	The Railways (Amendment) Bill, 2008	14:53	0:45	15:38	Discussed with Railway Budget 2008–09
22 May 2006	Lok Sabha	21 October 2008	15 December 2008	The National Jute Board Bill, 2006	1:42	1:22	3:04	Also discussed in Budget Session 2008 (30 April 2008)
13 March 2007	Lok Sabha	21 October 2008	24 October 2008	The Indian Maritime University Bill, 2007	1:46	0:28	2:14	
5 September 2007	Lok Sabha	22 October 2008	24 October 2008	The Airports Economic Regulatory Authority of India Bill, 2007	0:12	1:58	2:10	
8 December 2006	Lok Sabha	23 October 2008	24 October 2008	(i) The National Waterway (Talcher-Dhamra Stretch of Rivers Geonkhali-Charbatia Stretch of East Coast Canal, Charbatia-Dhamra Stretch of Matai River and Mahanadi Delta Rivers) Bill, 2006 and (ii) National Waterway (Kakinada-Pondicherry Stretch of Canals and the Kaluvelly Tank, Bhadrachalam-Rajahmundry Stretch of River Godavari and Wazirabad-Vijayawada Stretch of River Krishna) Bill, 2006	2:40	0:57	3:37	Two Bills Discussed together

(Annexure 1.5 continued)

(Annexure 1.5 continued)

Introduced	House (introduced)	Passed by Lok Sabha	Passed by Rajya Sabha	Title	Time taken in Lok Sabha	Time taken in Rajya Sabha	Total time	Remarks
11 March 2008	Rajya Sabha	23 October 2008	25 April 2008	The Central Universities Laws (Amendment) Bill, 2008	2:11	0:08	2:19	Passed by Rajya Sabha in Budget Session 2008
21 August 2007	Rajya Sabha	23 October 2008	21 October 2008	The Drugs and Cosmetics (Amendment) Bill, 2008	0:02	1:25	1:27	
10 September 2007	Rajya Sabha	17 December 2008	23 October 2008	The Unorganised Sector Workers' Social Security Bill, 2007	5:42	2:48	8:30	
24 October 2008	Lok Sabha	24 October 2008	16 December 2008	The President's Emoluments and Pension (Amendment) Bill, 2008	0:02	0:16	0:18	
24 October 2008	Lok Sabha	24 October 2008	16 Decemeber 2008	The Vice-President's Pension (Amendment) Bill, 2008	0:03	0:16	0:19	
24 October 2008	Lok Sabha	24 October 2008	16 December 2008	The Salaries and Allowances of Officers of Parliament (Amendment) Bill, 2008	0:02	0:33	0:35	
24 October 2008	Lok Sabha	24 October 2008	16 December 2008	The Governors (Emoluments, Allowances and Privileges) Amendment Bill, 2008	0:03	0:15	0:18	
15 Decemeber 2006	Rajya Sabha	12 December 2008	24 October 2008	The Limited Liability Partnership Bill, 2008	0:34	0:40	1:14	
23 October 2008	Lok Sabha	12 December 2008	19 December 2008	The Science and Engineering Research Board Bill, 2008	1:44	3:50	5:34	
16 December 2008	Lok Sabha	17 December 2008	18 December 2008	The National Investigation Agency Bill, 2008, The Unlawful Activities (Prevention) Amendment Bill, 2008	6:52	7:06	13:58	Two Bills discussed together
15 March 2007	Rajya Sabha	22 December 2008	17 December 2008	The Gram Nyayalayas Bill, 2008	0:03	4:02	4:05	
23 August 2006	Rajya Sabha	23 December 2008	18 December 2008	The Code of Criminal Procedure (Amendment) Bill, 2008	0:02	2:15	2:17	
24 October 2008	Rajya Sabha	23 December 2008	19 December 2008	The Post-Graduate Institute of Medical Education and Research, Chandigarh (Amendment) Bill, 2008	0:02	0:21	0:23	
17 March 2007	Rajya Sabha	23 December 2008	19 December 2008	The Collection of Statistics Bill, 2007	0:02	1:38	1:40	
27 November 2007	Rajya Sabha	23 December 2008	22 December 2008	The Constitution (Scheduled Tribes) (Union Territories) Order (Amendment) Bill, 2007	0:02	0:02	0:04	
18 December 2008	Rajya Sabha	23 December 2008	22 December 2008	The South Asian University Bill, 2008	0:02	0:03	0:05	
29 April 2008	Lok Sabha	22 December 2008	22 December 2008	The Supreme Court (Number of Judges) Amendment Bill, 2008	0:02		0:02	
15 December 2006	Lok Sabha	22 December 2008	23 December 2008	The Information Technology (Amendment) Bill, 2006	0:21		0:21	

(Annexure 1.5 continued)

(Annexure 1.5 continued)

Introduced	House (introduced)	Passed by Lok Sabha	Passed by Rajya Sabha	Title	Time taken in Lok Sabha	Time taken in Rajya Sabha	Total time	Remarks
22 December 2008	Lok Sabha	19 February 2009	24 February 2009	The High Court and Supreme Court Judges (Salaries and Conditions of Service) Amendment Bill, 2008	1:58	2:43	4:41	
17 February 2009	Lok Sabha	19 February 2009	24 February 2009	The National Capital Territory of Delhi Laws (Special Provisions) Bill, 2009	1:41	1:08	2:49	
17 February 2009	Lok Sabha	19 February 2009	24 February 2009	The Central Universities Bill, 2009	2:49	2:32	5:21	
21 December 2005	Rajya Sabha	20 February 2009	25 February 2009	The Prevention and Control of Infectious and Contagious Diseases in Animals Bill, 2005	0:43	3:04	3:47	Discussed and passed in Rajya Sabha on 16 December 2008, again passed on 25 February 2009 as amended by Lok Sabha
22 December 2008	Lok Sabha	25 February 2009	16 February 2009	The Agricultural and Processed Food Products Export Development Authority (Amendment) Bill, 2008	0:27	1:43	2:10	Also discussed in Monsoon 2008 (23 December 2008)
4 March 2007	Lok Sabha	30 April 2008	18 February 2009	The Carriage by Air (Amendment) Bill, 2008	3:22	0:24	3:46	Passed by Lok Sabha in Budget Session 2008
18 December 2008	Rajya Sabha	25 February 2009	19 February 2009	The Central Industrial Security Force (Amendment) Bill, 2008	0:43	1:29	2:12	
17 October 2008	Rajya Sabha	20 February 2009	19 February 2009	The Prevention of Money-laundering (Amendment) Bill, 2008	1:04	1:52	2:56	
15 December 2008	Rajya Sabha	4 August 2009	20 July 2009	The Right of Children to Free and Compulsory Education Bill, 2009	5:32	5:26	10:58	
30 July 2009	Rajya Sabha	4 August 2009	3 August 2009	The Constitution (Amendment) Bill, 2009 (Extension of Reservation of Seats in Lok Sabha and State Assemblies)	1:55	0:33	2:28	
4 August 2009	Lok Sabha	6 August 2009	7 August 2009	The Metro Railways (Amendment) Bill, 2009	1:05	1:02	2:07	
28 July 2009	Lok Sabha	24 November 2009	18 December 2009	The Rubber (Amendment) Bill, 2009	2:59	0:56	3:55	
7 August 2009	Lok Sabha	25 November 2009	1 December 2009	The Workmen's Compensation (Amendment) Bill, 2009	3:33	2:10	5:43	
24 November 2009	Lok Sabha	1 December 2009	7 December 2009	The Central Universities (Amendment) Bill, 2009	4:03	2:42	6:45	
24 October 2008	Rajya Sabha	9 December 2009	25 November 2009	The Representation of the People (Amendment) Bill, 2009	4:12	3:40	7:52	

(Annexure 1.5 continued)

(*Annexure 1.5 continued*)

Introduced	House (introduced)	Passed by Lok Sabha	Passed by Rajya Sabha	Title	Time taken in Lok Sabha	Time taken in Rajya Sabha	Total time	Remarks
4 December 2009	Lok Sabha	10 December 2009	16 December 2009	The Essential Commodities (Amendment and Validation) Bill, 2009	4:00	2:38	6:38	
11 December 2009	Lok Sabha	14 December 2009	16 December 2009	The Competition (Amendment) Bill, 2009	1:31	1:34	3:05	
4 December 2009	Lok Sabha	14 December 2009	18 December 2009	The State Bank of Saurashtra (Repeal) and the State Bank of India (Subsidiary Banks) Amendment Bill, 2009.	2:12	0:42	2:54	
24 October 2008	Rajya Sabha	18 December 2009	1 December 2009	The Legal Metrology Bill, 2008	0:03	2:00	2:03	
4 December 2009	Lok Sabha	16 December 2009	18 December 2009	The Payment of Gratuity (Amendment) Bill, 2009	0:02	1:29	1:31	
26 November 2009	Lok Sabha	16 December 2009	17 December 2009	The National Rural Employment Guarantee (Amendment) Bill, 2009	0:02	1:49	1:51	
17 February 2009	Lok Sabha	16 December 2009	17 December 2009	The National Capital Territory of Delhi Laws (Special Provisions) Second Bill, 2009	0:02	0:06	0:08	
23 November 2009	Lok Sabha	18 December 2009	22 December 2009	The Civil Defence (Amendment) Bill, 2009	0:02	1:18	1:20	
17 December 2009	Lok Sabha	18 December 2009	22 December 2009	The Salaries and Allowances of Ministers (Amendment) Bill, 2009	0:01	0:02	0:03	

Source: PRS Legislative Research. New Delhi, 2009.

Repositioning Public Policy: Balancing Growth and Equity

chapter 2

A thorough and systematic review of policy initiatives of the government provides us a useful window to view the state's will as well as its capacity, both political and administrative, to design and formulate viable and effective public policies. Examining such contours of public policy also provides us with a unique lens to evaluate the administrative capacity of the state to effectively carry out the policy initiatives in terms of its reach and delivery. In the light of this, a bottom-up perception of the policies provides a view from the other end of the spectrum, i.e., at the very end of the delivery chain.

While the current crises in the implementation of the key policies continue to plague the administrative apparatus, some new challenges have emerged at both the national and the global level such as the financial crisis, price rise and climate change. This section examines the health of the executive by evaluating the public policy response in key sectors of health, education and agriculture. The policy response of the government in tackling emerging challenges of price rise and climate change is also discussed. Accountability, transparency and effectiveness remain the fulcrum of our analysis and understanding of the entire public policy apparatus.

To what extent have the existing and the emerging patterns in public policy in the country been able to address the issues of growth and equity? Are these policies specifically directed towards the millions who are still in the periphery? How inclusive is our public policy in its design and implementation? These are some of the searching questions we have attempted to answer in the current section.

With the objective of supplying an informed input to the public domain especially to the civil society, policy-makers and citizens, this review of policy is divided in four sections. The first section provides an overview of fiscal issues and maps out the patterns in public expenditure, especially on the social sector. The second section evaluates the current policies on health, education, agriculture and rural development. Third section presents a comprehensive picture of the emerging issues of climate change and price rise by critically examining the policy response to smoothen out these emerging challenges. The last section looks at the implementation of the Right to Information (RTI) Act within the whole gamut of accountability and transparency, a prerequisite for an effective administration.

FISCAL ISSUES: PATTERNS OF PUBLIC SPENDING

Fiscal Stance of the Union Government

Over the last decade in the domain of fiscal policy, the union government has adhered to a conservative perspective. Its conservative fiscal stance has also been given legal teeth with the Fiscal Responsibility and Budget Management (FRBM) Act, 2003. The FRBM Act for the centre was followed by FRBM Acts for the states, which based on the recommendations of the 12th Finance Commission (2005–10), were almost imposed on them in 2005–06. These Acts required the union and the state governments to ensure that their respective budgets attain—zero revenue deficit[1] and fiscal deficit,[2] not higher than

3 per cent of GDP[3] (for the union government) or 3 per cent of GSDP[4] (for any state government) by 2009–10. These FRBM targets were pursued ardently by the union government, as well as several state governments up until 2007–08. In the absence of any substantial growth in the collection of public revenue, the reductions in deficits were achieved mainly by checking the growth of public expenditure.

However during 2008–09 and 2009–10, in order to deal with the problems emerging from the global financial crisis, the union government adopted an expansionary fiscal stance. As shown in Table 2.1, the total expenditure of the union government as a proportion of the GDP went up from 14.4 per cent in 2007–08 to 16.6 per cent in 2009–10 (RE).[5] A direct fallout of the financial crisis, that originated in the US, has been a global economic recession, which has affected not only the developed countries but also many developing and emerging economies across the world. The extent of the impact of this recession has varied across economies depending on their linkages with the global economy. However, it has been recognised unanimously as the worst ever crisis of capitalism since the Great Depression of the early 20th century. As a consequence, measures to deal with the recession have acquired centrality among the policy-makers across the globe.

In India too, one of the major challenges for the union government, as well as the state governments in the last two years has been to tackle the impact of the economic recession. The union government has responded to the economic downturn with its 'fiscal stimulus packages', which mainly comprise of various kinds of tax concessions to boost consumption expenditure so that the demand for goods and services in the economy increases. It also ensures large magnitudes of spending on infrastructure (in the Public-Private Partnership-framework) and some further increases in the budgetary spending on rural employment generation programmes (like MGREGS).[6]

Since late 2009 however, there have been indications of the economy reviving its growth. As a result, the union government has decided to revert to the path of fiscal conservatism and pursue the deficit reduction targets prescribed in

---

Box 2.1   People's Mid-Term Appraisal (PMTA) of 11th Five-Year Plan

The demand for a participatory planning process saw a positive move in form of the People's Mid-Term Appraisal of the 11th Five-Year Plan organised by the Centre for Budget and Governance Accountability, National Social Watch Coalition, Wada Na Todo Abhiyan and a number of other national, as well as regional civil society organisations and citizens groups.

The process was unique in so far as providing inputs to the planning process from both macro and micro perspectives. The process was three fold, (a) mobilise people's voice and assess from a people's perspective, the larger policy framework and the programmes/schemes in the 11th Five-Year Plan, (b) identify gaps, as well as the best practices in implementation through collating the existing empirical evidence and (c) substantiate the case with testimonies, case studies, and so on, from the community.

State level consultations were held in 10 states followed by regional consultations. The process culminated in the National Convention which involved policy-makers, Planning Commission members and the representatives of civil society organisations.

The consultation put together a series of policy suggestions and demands from the grassroots which were substantiated by thematic research papers on focus areas of the 11th Five-Year Plan. Special focus was paid to the issue of social exclusion.

In many ways, the process was unique as the policy-makers at the national level recognised the need for engaging with the targeted beneficiaries across the country in the planning process. Large number of participated in assessing the implications of public policies on their lives and livelihoods. Also, this is the first time that people from so many places prioritised their needs over the goals of the present development trajectory.

Outcomes

- A successful advocacy initiative where the findings that emerged out of the consultations and village process were shared with the Planning Commission;
- The process was carried out with the inputs and suggestions from various planning commission members;
- Increased awareness among the common people about the relevance of Five-Year Plans in their lives;
- Paved way for larger civil society engagement in the decentralised planning process.

Table 2.1   Total Magnitude of the Union Budget

Year	GDP at market prices [at current prices] (in ₹ crore)	Total expenditure from the Union Budget (in ₹ crore)	Total expenditure from the Union Budget as per cent of GDP
2004–05	32,39,224	4,98,252	15.4
2005–06	37,06,473	5,05,738	13.6
2006–07	42,83,979	5,83,387	13.6
2007–08	49,47,857	7,12,671	14.4
2008–09	55,74,449	8,83,956	15.9
2009–10 (RE)	61,64,178	10,21,547	16.6
2010–11 (BE)	69,34,700	11,08,749	16.0

Source: Compiled by Centre for Budget and Governance Accountability (CBGA) from *Economic Survey 2009–10*, Government of India and *Union Budget 2010–11*, Government of India.

Notes: RE: Revised Estimates; BE: Budget Estimates.
GDP figure for 2008–09 is the Quick Estimate by CSO; that for 2009–10 is the Advanced Estimate by CSO and that for 2010–11 is the figure projected by the Union Ministry of Finance assuming a 12.5 per cent growth in GDP in 2010–11.

---

the FRBM Act in 2010–11. However, instead of strengthening measures to expand the tax revenue base of the country, the government has adopted the approach of expenditure compression in order to reduce its borrowing in the said year. The union government's total expenditure as a proportion of the GDP is projected to shrink from 16.6 per cent in 2009–10 (RE) to 16 per cent in 2010–11 (BE).[7] In tandem with the compression of public expenditure, the fiscal deficit of the union government as a per cent of the GDP, is projected to fall from 6.7 per cent in 2009–10 (RE) to 5.5 per cent in 2010–11 (BE). Similarly, the revenue deficit is estimated at 4.0 per cent in 2010–11 (BE), significantly lower than the 5.3 per cent figure for 2009–10 (RE).

While the policy-makers at the centre would like us to believe that there is a consensus on the need for curtailing government borrowing in the country by all means including reductions in budgetary spending by the centre and the states, in reality, there is no such consensus on the implications of government borrowing on the economy. Rather, many progressive economists have emphasised on the need to expand the scope of government intervention in the country, if required with larger magnitudes of borrowing.

Public Spending on Social Sectors

The union government's overarching emphasis on expenditure compression is clearly reflected in the allocations for social sectors in the last two Union Budgets. Table 2.2 shows the trends in the total expenditure in Social Services[8] in the Union Budget from 2004–05 to 2010–11. It is evident from the table that the budgetary

allocation for Social Services out of the total budget expenditure was stepped up from about 8 per cent in 2004–05 to over 13 per cent in 2008–09, which translated in the budgetary expenditure on Social Services as a per cent of GDP rising from 1.2 per cent in 2004–05 to 2.1 per cent in 2008–09. Although this increase was nowhere close to what was promised by the UPA government for social sectors in their National Common Minimum Programme (NCMP) of 2004, it was still a welcome trend in the sphere of Union Budgets. However, the allocations made in the 2009–10 and 2010–11 budgets reflect that the present Congress-led government has grown complacent with regard to its budgetary priorities for the social sectors. The budgetary allocation for expenditure on Social Services has stagnated at 2.2 per cent of GDP in 2009–10 (RE) and 2010–11 (BE), which is only marginally above the 2.1 per cent figure recorded for 2008–09.

The increase in the budgetary expenditure on Social Services during 2007–08 and 2008–09 seems somewhat impressive. However, we must take into account the fact that state governments continue to bear a significant share of the country's overall public expenditure on social sectors and the total public expenditure on social sectors in the country does not reflect any such impressive rise. Table 2.3 presents the trend in total public expenditure on Social Services, (i.e., the combined expenditure of the centre and states on Social Services), since 2004–05.

According to Table 2.3, the overall fiscal policy space available to the government in our country has shown a small expansion between 2004–05 and 2008–09. The magnitude of total public expenditure in the country (i.e., the combined expenditure of centre and states) was less than 25.5 per cent of GDP from 2004–05 to 2006–07 and it hovered around 26 per cent of GDP in 2008–09 (BE). The priority accorded to Social Services within the total public expenditure has not been high and the combined expenditure of centre and states on Social Services has increased gradually from 5.5 per cent of GDP in 2004–05 to 6.6 per cent of GDP in 2008–09 (BE).

The combined expenditure of centre and states on 'Education, Health & Family Welfare,

Table 2.2 Union Budget Expenditure on Social Services

Year	Expenditure from the Union Budget on Social Services	
	as % of GDP	as % of total expenditure from the Union Budget
2004–05	1.2	7.9
2005–06	1.3	9.8
2006–07	1.3	9.5
2007–08	1.6	11.1
2008–09	2.1	12.9
2009–10 (RE)	2.2	13.1
2010–11 (BE)	2.2	14.0

Source: Subrat Das and Yamini Mishra. 2010. 'What Does Budget 2010 Imply for the Social Sector?', *Economic and Political Weekly, XLV* (13): 64–68.

Table 2.3 **Combined Expenditure of Centre and States on Social Services**

Year	Combined (total) expenditure of centre and states* as % of GDP	Combined expenditure of centre and states on social services# as % of GDP	Combined expenditure of centre and states on education, health & family welfare, and water supply & sanitation@ as % of GDP
2004–05	25.5	5.5	3.8
2005–06	25.2	5.6	3.9
2006–07	25.4	5.8	4.0
2007–08 (RE)	26.9	6.3	4.2
2008–09 (BE)	26.3	6.6	4.3

Source: Das, Subrat and Yamini Mishra. 2010. 'What Does Budget 2010 Imply for the Social Sector?', *Economic and Political Weekly*, *XLV*(13).

Notes: * This refers to the total expenditure from the Union Budget and the state budgets combined; without any double counting of the inter-governmental transfers like central grants and loans to the states.

  # This refers to the total expenditure on Social Services from Union Budget and state budgets combined, without any double counting of the fund transfers from centre to states.

  @ This figure is a part of the combined expenditure of centre and states on Social Services.

and Water Supply & Sanitation' has risen from 3.8 per cent of GDP in 2004–05 to 4.3 per cent of GDP in 2008–09 (BE). In this context, there can be little doubt that the public expenditure on these three important social sectors is woefully inadequate. Way back in 1966, the D.S. Kothari Commission had recommended that total public spending on education in India should be raised to the level of 6 per cent of the Gross National Product (GNP) by 1986. Since then, many political parties have reiterated their commitment to this issue in their respective election manifestos. The UPA too had promised in its NCMP of 2004 that the total public spending on education would be raised to 6 per cent of the GDP. Likewise, following the recommendations of the World Health Organisation (WHO) for developing countries, the UPA had made a commitment in the NCMP of 2004 that the total public spending on health would be raised to 2 to 3 per cent of the GDP. This was reiterated in the 11th Five Year Plan. However, the reality is that even in 2008–09 (BE), the total public spending in the country on education, health, and water and sanitation combined was as low as 4.3 per cent of the GDP.

Implications of the 13th Finance Commission Recommendations[9]

The 13th Finance Commission was appointed by the President of India on 13 November 2007, with Dr Vijay Kelkar as the chairperson and was required to give recommendations on specified aspects of centre–state fiscal relations for the fiscal years 2010–11 to 2014–15. The Commission submitted its report to the President on 30 December 2009, covering all aspects of its mandate.

Before going deeper into them, it must be pointed out that the recommendations of the 13th Finance Commission do not deviate from the path of fiscal conservatism laid out by the 11th and 12th Finance Commission. Rather, they go one step ahead to further restrict the space available to the states to determine their fiscal priorities.[10]

The 13th Finance Commission recommended the 'Post Devolution (i.e., pertaining to the situation after the devolution of shareable central taxes to all states) Non Plan Revenue Deficit Grant' for only eight states. This is because it requires the states, which did not incur any revenue deficit in the year 2007–08, to eliminate their revenue deficit and bring down their fiscal deficit to the level of 3 per cent of GSDP by 2011–12. The other general category states are required to eliminate their revenue deficit by 2013–14 and bring down their fiscal deficit to 3 per cent of GSDP by 2014–15. It has also recommended a separate path for fiscal consolidation for Kerala, Punjab and West Bengal, i.e., states with large fiscal deficits. However, several economists have pointed out in the past that such an exogenous ceiling on the borrowing of states is arbitrary. There are a number of adverse implications which could possibly arise from this rigid policy prescription.

The recommendations of the 13th Finance Commission would recreate the pressure on states to check the growth of their development spending (particularly because a large part of the budgetary spending in the social sectors is reported as revenue expenditure), which were also there in the first three years of the recommendation period of the 12th Finance Commission (i.e., prior to the onset of the economic recession in 2008–09). What this implies is that most of the states could find it very difficult to step up their expenditure on inclusive growth and development over the next five years. Thus, crucial public policy commitments like raising total public spending on education in the country to 6 per cent of GDP, that on health to 3 per cent or ensuring peoples' right to food, and so on, could remain elusive over the next five years.

Moreover, both the recommendations of the 13th Finance Commission (for the union government) and the 2010–11 Union Budget clearly indicate that the next five years will witness growing efforts by the union government towards elimination/reduction of deficits through compression of public expenditure. Consequently, any significant boost to the country's public expenditure on social sectors through significantly higher allocations in the Union Budgets over the next few years seems equally unlikely.

Revenue Foregone due to Tax Exemptions

As regard the usual argument pertaining to the question of resources available to the government, we need to pay close attention to the problem of a huge amount of tax revenue foregone due to the exemptions/deductions/incentives in the central government tax system. The union Finance Minister recognised in his 2009–10 budget speech that India's tax base continues to be low compared to other countries, mainly due to a plethora of exemptions/deductions/incentives in the central government tax system. Yet, there have been no corrective measures in this regard in the last two Union Budgets.

As presented in Table 2.4, the total magnitude of tax revenue foregone due to exemptions/deductions/incentives in the central government tax system has been estimated (by the union Finance Ministry itself) to rise from ₹4.14 lakh crore in 2008–09 to ₹5.02 lakh crore in 2009–10. What this implies is that if all exemptions/deductions/incentives (both in direct and indirect taxes) had been eliminated, even a liberal estimate of the amount of additional tax revenue which could have been collected by the union government in 2009–10 stands at a staggering 8.1 per cent of GDP. Now it must be understood that not all kinds of tax exemptions/deductions/incentives can be eliminated. There can be a strong case however, for eliminating those exemptions which benefit mainly the privileged sections of population.

Fiscal consolidation in terms of reduction in deficits in the union and state budgets, if indeed necessary at the current juncture, should be achieved through strong policy measures

Table 2.4 Tax Revenue Foregone in the Central Government Tax System due to Tax Exemptions/Incentives/Deductions

Items	Revenue foregone in 2008–09 (in ₹ crore)	Revenue foregone as % of aggregate tax collection in 2008–09	Revenue foregone in 2009–10 (in ₹ crore)	Revenue foregone as % of aggregate tax collection in 2009–10
Corporate Income Tax	66,901	11.08	79,554	12.60
Personal Income Tax	37,570	6.22	40,929	6.48
Excise Duty	128,293	21.25	170,765	27.04
Customs Duty	225,752	37.39	249,021	39.43
Total	458,516	75.95	540,269	85.56
Less (Export Credit Related)	44,417	7.36	37,970	6.01
Grand Total	414,099	68.6	502,299	79.5

Source: Receipts Budget, Union Budget 2010–11, Government of India.

that would significantly increase the magnitude of tax revenue of the government, but the union government has failed to take any such measure in the last few years and the goal of deficit reduction has been pursued mainly by checking the growth of public expenditure. The targets for deficit reduction prescribed by the FRBM legislations are not only arbitrary, but also regressive from the perspective of the rights of poor and deprived sections of the population. Rather than the FRBM legislations, there is a need for legislations that would make it mandatory for the union and state governments to implement the plans and strategies meant for the disadvantaged sections of population, like the 'Special Component Plan for SCs', 'Tribal Sub Plan' or 'Gender Budgeting'. Also, it should also be mandatory for the union government and state governments to provide adequate funds for the implementation of the Right to Education Act. However, the policy-makers at the centre as also in most states are unlikely to change their approach unless there is a significant level of public involvement in the affairs of budgets.

SECTORAL OVERVIEW: HEALTH, EDUCATION AND AGRICULTURE

Inequities in Health Sector of the Year Gone by

The abiding images related to the health sector in 2009 were the scenes outside Pune's public health facilities, where people caused a near-riot situation while queuing up to get themselves tested for the H1N1. Those images typified the state of public healthcare in the country and while the H1N1 pandemic seems to have passed without causing the anticipated effects, it has left in its wake some very serious questions related to the public health system in India.

There is very little that can be categorised as 'major achievements' of the health care sector in the past year. We shall look at some of the major developments in the sector and examine their implications for securing accessible health care for people in India.

State of the Public Health System

The Economic Survey, 2009–10 is candid in admitting:

> However, despite the progress, India fares poorly in most of the indicators in comparison with a number of developing countries like China and Sri Lanka. In addition, the progress in health indicators has been quite uneven across regions (large-scale inter-state variations), gender (male/female differences) as well as space (with significant rural-urban differences).

Five years ago, the first UPA government launched the NRHM, precisely to remedy the kind of situation that the recent Economic Survey has talked about and by all accounts, the functioning of the NRHM has resulted in some improvements in the functioning of the public health system. The improvements are however, uneven and fall far short of the desired goals. Thus, it seems likely that India will fall short of the health targets that were set as part of the Millennium Development Goals (MDGs). Among these were the targets to reduce the Infant Mortality Rate to below 30 per 1,000 live births and the Maternal Mortality Rate to below 100 per 1,00,000 live births by 2012. However, the latest data suggests that the Infant Mortality Rate stands at 53 and the Maternal Mortality Rate at around 250. In other words, given the rate of progress, we would have a realistic possibility of achieving the targets set for 2012 in 2020. This means that an additional 2.4 million children and 250,000 mothers are likely to die in the next decade because of our failure to reach anywhere near the targets set by our own planners.

The NRHM has promoted a modicum of streamlining of the health infrastructure. The Third Common Review Mission (CRM) for the NRHM notes, '[t]he trends in revival of the public health system, noted by the first two CRMs continue. Across the states, there is a continuing increase in utilisation of public services, primarily for deliveries but also for other health care.' Additional infrastructure creation and augmentation of human resources have led to a larger number of people starting to make use of public health facilities. However there continue to be major gaps and the improvements themselves reveal some new areas of concern.

The report of the CRM goes on to state, as regards augmentation of human resources in the public system,

> [d]ecisively therefore the tremendous 15 year stagnation on this front, which more than any other single factor, led to a crisis of the public health system is broken. Much of the increases seen in performance—in out-patient, in patient and delivery services have been enabled by and directly related to this incredible increase.

While there would be no quarrel with the contention that there is some movement forward in terms of strengthening of the public health system, it is difficult to agree that this can be termed as 'decisive' and 'incredible'.

Creation of new infrastructure is a feature of the NRHM's functioning. However, the existing gaps are still too large to claim that we have finally managed to turn around the corner. The Economic Survey, 2009–10, says in this regard:

> However, there is still a shortage of 20,486 SCs, 4,477 PHCs and 2,337 CHCs as per the 2001 population norm. Further, almost 29 per cent of the existing health infrastructure is in rented buildings. Poor upkeep and maintenance and high absenteeism of manpower in rural areas are the main problems in the health delivery system in the public sector.

According to the annual report of the Ministry of Health and Family Welfare (MoHFW), there are 1,46,036 Sub-Centres, 23,458 Primary Health Centres (PHC) and 4,276 Community Health Centres (CHC). If we account for population increase in the past decade, then the approximate shortfall in infrastructure would be as follows: 60,000 Sub-Centres, 11,500 Primary Health Cen-tres and 4,000 Community Health Centres.

Numbers of course, do not tell the whole story. Much of the existing infrastructure is in an appalling state of disrepair and neglect, and exists only in name. A sampling of earlier data (Rural Health Statistics, 2007, MoHFW) indicates this state of neglect and apathy:

- 4,711 Sub-Centres are listed as 'functioning' without the services of both Auxilary Nurse Midwife (ANM) and Health Worker Male.

- 68.6 per cent of PHCs are functioning with one or no doctor.
- 807 PHCs have no doctor.
- Shortfall of Lab Technicians and Pharmacists in PHCs is 41.1 per cent and 17.1 per cent respectively.
- Shortfall of Specialists in CHCs is 64.9 per cent.
- 1,188 PHCs and 1,647 PCS respectively are functioning without electric supply or without regular water supply.

While activities of the NRHM has led to an improvement in the situation, there are no indications of a dramatic reversal of the situation. The CRM report states in this context:

> However, especially in the poor performing states, such is the accumulated deficit and poor systems development of the past, which vacancy situations are still impermissibly high. Thus the Madhya Pradesh report from Chindwara states, that even after a contractual staff recruitment drive, and the introduction of a one year mandatory rural posting for graduate and postgraduates from government medical doctors, and the appointment of AYUSH doctors there is a 48.8 per cent vacancy in the 172 doctors posts and 46.5 per cent vacancy in the 243 nurse posts in the district. Shortfalls reported from districts of Uttar Pradesh and Bihar are even higher.

An emerging matter of concern is that while some vacancies in the health infrastructure have been filled, it has largely been through contractual appointments. There is a reluctance to increase the number of sanctioned posts to facilitate a long-term vision plan for human resource development in the public health system. Thus, much of the claimed increase of 1 lakh new personnel in human-power since the start of the NRHM comprises of people hired on contractual basis. These people are without any career advancement possibilities which naturally generate poor motivation levels. Moreover, much of the augmentation of human resources has been focused on the Janani Suraksha Yojana (JSY). The CRM report states in this regard, '[t]hough NRHM is about a commitment to comprehensive health care, increases in many states are still focused too narrowly on obstetric care aspect of IPHS (Indian Public Health Standards), or merely responsive to immediate pressures without a longer term direction and vision.'

Public–Private Partnerships

The other area of concern is the continued reliance on partnerships with the private sector in the form of Public–Private Partnerships (PPP). It relates to the state's ability to fund infrastructure creation in the health sector. It goes beyond ambulance services, and extends to in-patient and out-patient care, including hospital services. The argument laid out in favour of PPP is that a bulk of infrastructure in the health sector is today privately managed and a majority of people access health services from the private sector. In such a situation, the government should make a virtue out of necessity by not spending money to create public infrastructure but by utilising privately owned and managed infrastructure for provision of public services. This is the model that is being promoted through the Rajiv Gandhi Swasthya Bima Yojana (RSBY) and in several state level schemes. To buttress the arguments in favour of such models, examples are used of other countries such as UK, Brazil, Germany, and so on, where the government reimburses for care provided through private providers. Thus, the role of provisioning is sought to be separated from that of financing.

This argument is, however, flawed. Brazil, UK, Germany and others are examples of countries with urban population clusters, thus creating a situation where private facilities exist in large numbers in areas where the bulk of the population resides. The situation however, is quite different in India. There exist few private facilities in large parts of rural India except for RMPs, who are really untrained quacks, which means provision of sub-standard health service to the rural masses from public funds. Thus, what PPP in health service delivery in India would do is that it will strengthen the private sector, on account, of their access to public funds. We have already seen this happening with the liberalisation of norms for reimbursement for the Central Government Health Scheme (CGHS). On one hand, the public infrastructure of hospitals and dispensaries has been dismantled, and on the other hand, CGHS beneficiaries are encouraged to seek treatment in private institutions, for which they are reimbursed with public funds. This is the logic of neoliberal economics—public subsidy to strengthen the private sector.

The CRM report details an evaluation of the Chiranjeevi scheme, a PPP to promote institutional deliveries that is held out as an example by many. According to the CRM report:

> In Gujarat, the Chiranjeevi scheme has been examined and commented upon by the team. The team calls for a closer look at the scheme, pointing out to some serious cautions and lacunae in the programme design. For one, quality of care is a big issue and all the problems we report from other states in public facilities seem applicable here also. Even basic care for the newborn is missing. Government oversight is reported to be restricted to ensuring providers receive payments and handling patient complaints. Demand generation by public functionaries seems to have been skewed to the private sector and often at the cost of the government hospital. BPL women in Dahod are reported to be making payments albeit at lower rates as compared to non beneficiaries and this is attributed to lack of information of the details of the scheme.

The report further notes, 'ANMs, especially those who were young, preferred to refer women to Chiranjeevi providers even when they had the facilities and training to conduct (normal) deliveries themselves.'

While in the short term it may be necessary to create arrangements where private facilities are utilised to provide public health services, this can never be a long term solution or a panacea. In the long term, there is no alternative to creating public infrastructure in a country like India but for that to happen, it is necessary that health administrators are not completely seduced by the perceived virtues of PPP. It needs to be understood that a for-profit private sector, increasingly corporate managed and controlled as in India, cannot be relied upon as the solution to provisioning of public goods such as health care.

Access to Medicines

Since 2004, the government has periodically promised that essential drugs would be made

Box 2.2 The Story of an Unborn Child: Gopalapuram Village, East Godavari District, Andhra Pradesh

Like any other couple, Mummidivarapu Srinu and Mummuidivarapu Kumari were overjoyed when they first heard the news of Kumari expecting their first child. It was the silver lining in the cloud for the couple who depend on Srinu's meagre income as a rickshaw puller and Kumari's income from farm work for their subsistence. Due to abject poverty, they share with their parents their one room house, which has been built with a government grant.

Her pregnancy was confirmed at a private hospital, Vijaya Lakshmi Nursing Home, and Srini was instructed to take certain medicines. However, since they could not afford the medicines, she did not take them and did not undergo any further medical tests. Rightly, she turned to the local primary health centre in Ublanka and the Anganwadi centre for treatment and medicines. Neither of them gave her the much needed guidance and nutritional supplements. When she was eight months pregnant, her labour pains started and she was taken to Ubalanka PHC. Despite being in intense pain, she was refused treatment since the resident doctor had gone to a medical camp. She was referred to a private clinic 15 kilometres away in Ravulpalem. A further two hours were wasted in Srini running from pillar to post in order to gather 6,000 rupees for the operation, but in vain. Kumari gave birth to a stillborn baby.

Now in debt and in shock, the constant refrain on Kumari's lips is if only she had gotten the necessary medical attention and help in time, her baby would have been alive. A life was lost, a dream shattered only due to the negligence on the part of the health care system in this little village in Andhra Pradesh.

Source: People's Mid Term Appraisal of 11th Five-Year Plan, *Voices of the People*, February 2010.

available at reasonable prices. A number of government appointed committees have also suggested various methods to ensure affordability of essential medicines. However, the government continues to drag its feet on this issue and the list of medicines whose prices are controlled remains what it was in 1995, despite many of the 74 medicines in the list having become obsolete. The government's inability to take a clear position has resulted in a curious situation where the new drug policy was announced in 2006, but the section on price control is still to be announced.

A welcome recent development is the initiative to open *Jan Aushadhi* shops to make available certain essential medicines at affordable prices through the procurement of low priced generic medicines. The setting up of such shops in public health facilities suggests that the government proposes to abandon any commitment to the provision of essential medicines, free of cost through public health facilities. However, it must be understood that this initiative cannot be an alternative, but should only be a complimentary process to the imposition of a regime of price control and free provision of essential medicines.

One of the major promises made by the NRHM was that all essential medicines would be made available at all levels of public health facilities. However, the failure to make medicines available is the one of the commonest problems and this is one of the principal reasons for under utilisation of public facilities. At present, just about 8 per cent of all drug consumption in the country is provided through public facilities. In such a situation, the need is for a plan to be set in motion immediately, which ensures that all essential medicines are made available at public health facilities.

The anarchy availability of irrational medicines is another important issue that was brought into focus two years ago when reports became available that 294 irrational combination products were being sold illegally in the market, without having been provided permission by the Drug Controller General of India (DCGI). Curiously, the DCGI did not ban these irrational products summarily, and instead chose to negotiate with the erring companies. It is imperative that all illegal irrational medicines be identified and banned without any further delay. In a welcome development, the Medical Council of India (MCI) has initiated a process to put controls on unethical practices by drug companies to promote medicines. It is hoped that the moves that have been initiated will not be abandoned or be diluted because of pressures from the industry.

Education

While policy-makers agree that education is critical to the development of a well-functioning and vibrant citizenship, the seemingly unfocused and scant attention paid to this key sector in the last one-and-a-half years leaves a lot of scope for action. Two conflicting developments dominated most of 2009 up to mid-2010—the enactment of the 'Right to Free and Compulsory Education' at the elementary level and the acceptance of privatisation as a means to provide and finance education at various levels. On the one hand, the government has effected a legislation that, if implemented in the correct spirit, could be a tool to increase enrolment and reduce drop-out from schools. On the other however, the unabashed promotion and acceptance of privatisation of education in its many avatars, is disturbing, to say the least.

The usual argument of profit-making being the *raison d'être* of a private initiative notwithstanding, the need to view education as different from any commercial project (e.g., infrastructure, real estate) is vital. In this context, as has been recently reported by a leading daily, the second term of the Congress-led UPA government appears to have begun in a state of political complacency and neo-liberal conservatism[11] with precious little to spare for social development. In this regard, some of the major policy developments in education in the period between 2009 and mid-2010 are presented here, followed by a discussion on the trends in financing for education and some of the key issues with regard to implementation of government schemes and programmes for education.

Policy Developments

While there have been many policy-related initiatives and advances in the field of education in the past one-and-a-half-years or so, this piece restricts itself to outlining select policy developments from the standpoint of social justice and equity. Three inter-related developments taken up for discussion are (*a*) the enactment of the Right to Education Act, (*b*) the growing privatisation of education at all levels including adoption of PPP as a mode of financing and (*c*) the promotion of school vouchers as a specific illustration of the encouragement given to the process of privatisation of education.

Enactment of Right to Education Act

To quickly recap the recent steps in the journey of the Right to Education (RTE) Act, 2009, the 86th Amendment Act, 2002, made three specific provisions in the Indian Constitution to facilitate the realisation of free and compulsory education to children between the age of 6 to 14 years as a Fundamental Right. These were (*a*) adding Article 21A in Part III (Fundamental Rights), (*b*) modifying Article 45 and (*c*) adding a new clause (k) under Article 51A (Fundamental Duties), making the parent or guardian responsible to provide opportunities for education

to their children between 6 and 14 years. After much dithering for almost seven years, subsequent to the 86th amendment of the Constitution and several drafts later, the RTE Act, 2009, was notified by the central government on 1 April 2010.

Ostensibly, this delay has been because the 'model rules' required to operationalise the Act are yet to be formulated and so a committee has been constituted by the Ministry of Human Resource Development (MHRD), Government of India, to draft the appropriate rules. While this task is quite slippery in many ways, the commonly held perception is that the centre may continue to drag its feet or dilute the relevant provisions itself, largely on account of the financial burden to ensure that the Act delivers what it promises. It may be recalled here that the RTE Bill was passed by the Parliament without an accompanying financial memorandum and so the issue of sharing the requisite costs between the centre and the states has been an extremely contentious one.

With regard to financing the Act, there is no clarity on who will take the lead, the centre or the states. Ideally, the central government ought to be shouldering this duty in the light of the poor fiscal situation that prevails in most states. The Act acknowledges this reality and notes that the states may seek a pre-determined percentage of expenditure as grants-in-aid from the central government, based on the Finance Commission's assessment of additional resource requirements to any state. Be that as it may, the Act reveals the obvious contradiction when, on the one hand, it suggests both the union and state governments have concurrent responsibility to finance the Act,[12] with the centre preparing estimates of capital and recurring expenditure under the Act, while on the other, it unequivocally holds the state governments responsible to provide funds for implementation of the Act.[13]

In an attempt to arrive at specific numbers based on prevailing unit costs in education, the CABE Committee, 2005,[14] had estimated that in the six year period between 2006–07 to 2011–12, additional outlays to the tune of ₹4.36 lakh crore (teachers' salary as per Kendriya Vidyalaya norms) and ₹3.93 lakh crore (teachers' salary at prevalent scales), would have to be allocated to universalise elementary education. Sticking to the lower level of CABE projections, the additional required outlays are ₹3.93 lakh crore for a five-year period. In this regard, reports in the media that the required additional outlays amount to ₹1.78 lakh crore,[15] spread over a period of five years, as estimated by the MHRD, for implementing the RTE Act, seem extremely disorienting, if not mysterious.

Further, recent MHRD announcements on 'Sarva Shiksha Abhiyan' (SSA), a flagship scheme to universalise elementary education introduced in 2000 by the central government, as the means to operationalise the RTE Act in the country, also pose specific concerns with regard to financing. The increase in the budget for education is grossly inadequate keeping in mind the need for a complete revamp of the expenditure norms in SSA if the RTE Act is to be implemented properly. The MHRD budget at ₹49,904 crore for 2010–11 accounts for just 0.72 per cent of the GDP and is at the same level (as proportion of GDP) as in 2009–10 (BE). With the government mulling over the possibility of operationalising the RTE Act through SSA, it is unclear how increasing the outlays for SSA from ₹13,100 crore in 2009–10 (RE) to ₹15,000 crore in 2010–11 (BE) would help achieve universal access to education by all.

In this regard, proceeds from the education cess have been almost half of the total budget of the Department of School Education and Literacy since 2006–07 (see Table 2.5). To add to this, the annual growth in the outlay for the Department has been on a decline since 2005–06. It is apparent that outlays for elementary education are not moving in the direction of ensuring effective implementation of the RTE Act.

In the meanwhile, financing concerns would also need to address the considerable increase in recruitment of teachers that would be required for effective implementation of the RTE Act. Conservative estimates suggest that the government would need to recruit 20 lakh teachers to successfully operationalise the RTE Act.[16] In response to filling this critical gap, the MHRD seems to be taking recourse to the Information, Communication and Technology (ICT) mode. It is suggested that similar to the adoption of ICT mode for higher education, in the next three years, the government would bring broadband connectivity to schools, and by the end of the 11th Five-Year Plan, 22,000 colleges and 480 universities will be fully connected. The target for connecting all schools in a similar fashion has been set for the end of the 12th Plan. It seems to have escaped the purview of the policy-makers that e-learning centres are hardly the solution to educating the 'demographic dividend', when access to uninterrupted supply of electricity is itself uncertain in most parts of the country.

Increasing Privatisation in Higher Education

The unbridled growth of privatisation in education across all levels for the past couple of years is a clear sign of the government's unapologetic adoption of a neo-liberal policy stance. The statistics may vary depending on the source it emanates from, but private (recognised)

Table 2.5 Elementary Education and Trends in Financing by the Union Government

Year	Total for department of school education and literacy	Growth in outlay for department of school education and literacy	Education cess	Education cess as % of total outlay for department of school education and literacy
2004–05 (RE)	8,004			
2005–06 (RE)	12,536	56.6		
2006–07 (RE)	17,133	36.7	8,746	51.04
2007–08 (RE)	23,191	35.4	11,128	47.98
2008–09 (RE)	26,026	12.2	12,134	46.62
2009–10 (RE)	25,338	–2.6	12,257	48.37
2010–11 (BE)	33,214	31.1	14,433	43.45

Source: Compiled by CBGA from Union Budget documents, Government of India, various years.

schools in India account for approximately 15 to 25 per cent of the total number of schools. According to the District Information System for Education (DISE) data for 2007–08 that was released in November 2009, 14 per cent of the total schools in the country are under private, unaided management. The Annual Status of Education Report(ASER), 2009 finds that a little over 21 per cent of the children are enrolled in private schools and that more than one-fifth of the elementary schools in the country are under private management. Adding the unrecognised private schools for which data is hard to come by, the estimate of the percentage children enrolled in private schools could range anywhere in the range of 25–30 per cent. Access to fee-charging private schools, even in rural areas, has grown from 28 per cent in 2006 to 44 per cent in 2009.[17]

The statistics become more skewed as one goes up to the higher and technical education sub-sectors. This has happened consistently over a period of time. With economic reforms leading to severe cuts on the education budget, the government successfully directed a shift of resources from higher to primary level of education. This was evident even in the Approach Paper to the 10th Plan that rationalised the government's focus being limited to the expansion of primary education while asking universities to make greater efforts to supplement the resources provided by the government.[18] While primary education is vital, emphasis on higher education paves the way for a nation's economic and technological progress. Thus, ignoring one level of education as opposed to another would be counter-productive in the long run.

Moreover, with education being on the Concurrent List, the centre is equally responsible for its provision at all levels, not just at the elementary level. Thus, while government spending at the elementary level has been on the rise since 1980s, this is not the case for secondary and higher education. With the government's adoption of economic reforms, several policy alternatives for alternative sources of financing higher education such as student fees, student loans and privatisation have been suggested. A quick look at these alternative sources is worthwhile.

- *Student Fees*: Recommendations made by several committees set up by the University Grants Commission (UGC) for higher education suggest the need for an upward revision of student fees. However, there are several components within fees such as fees towards tuition, admission, examination, registration, hostel and development charges. It has been found that since 1990, there has been a significant rise in students' fees of various types,[19] which indicates that the fees are already high and nearing various committees' recommendations. A related development of shifting higher education from merit goods to the list of non-merit goods needs to be seen in the context of the neo-liberal ascendancy in government policy.

- *Student Loans*: The fundamental premise of promoting student loans is flawed. The objective of providing loan access to students from socio-economically deprived background is not matched by the imperfections that exist in the capital markets. The lack of collateral security limits the ability of poor students to borrow for education. To add to this, the present Student Loan scheme introduced in 2000 is found to have inherent weaknesses in its design, as neither does it take into account equity concerns, nor does it adhere to clear-cut parameters such as eligibility, interest rates, repayment terms and conditions.

- *Privatisation*: There has been a historical role of private players in the field of education. Beginning with social reformers like Raja Rammohan Roy in the 19th century and the more recent reform movements in 1960s such as the Kerala Shastra Sahitya Parishad (KSSP), the motive behind these was largely philanthropic. However with time, the motive has drastically changed and the earlier mottoes of 'social upliftment' and 'sustainable development' have given way to the newer mantra of 'profit maximisation' (see Box 2.3).

Thus, it is clear that these policy alternatives undermine equity of access to higher education, especially for secondary level students belonging to the socio-economically deprived sections.

Box 2.3 Private Equities Pump in USD 140 Million in Education since January 2010

Education has emerged one of the most lucrative sectors in India, and private equity investors have lined up in big numbers to get a slice of the USD 80 billion plus industry pie.

Numbers crunched by education-focused private equity fund Kaizen Management Advisors show that this year, venture capitalists and private equity players have already pumped in excess of USD 140 million, 50 per cent more than what they invested in the whole of 2009.

'We feel the education sector offers tremendous growth potential and is poised for rapid growth in the next few years', says Ramesh Venkat, Chief Executive of Reliance Equity Advisors, a private equity arm of Reliance Capital, which entered the segment a few months ago by investing about ₹100 crore in Pathways World School, a primary and higher secondary school.

Lack of regulation in the K-12 (kindergarten to class XII) segment and supplementary education has made education attractive for investors. 'Sectors such as vocational training, supplementary education, preschools, and ICT are appealing as these are relatively immune from regulatory uncertainty', says Raja Parthasarathy, Managing Director, IDFC Private Equity.

The education sector began heating up in 2005 and although the deal sizes in the sector are much smaller compared to sectors such as infrastructure, the private equity appetite for the industry has rapidly increased. Perhaps the biggest deal till recently was IDFC Private Equity's ₹135 crore investment in Manipal Education in September 2006.

That was surpassed this February when Manipal Education raised a second round of funding of more than ₹190 crore (USD 43 million) from Premji Invest.

Source: Chatterjee, Dibyajyoti. 2010. 'Private Equities pump in $140 million in Education since January 2010', *The Economic Times*, 19 May.

Among other developments in the sector, the Foreign Educational Institutions (Regulation of Entry and Operations) Bill, 2010, was introduced in the Lok Sabha. This Bill allows foreign education providers to set up campuses in India and offer degrees. The proposed law prescribes a time-bound format for granting approval to foreign educational institutions to set up campuses in India. They would be registered with the UGC or any other regulatory body, which will scrutinise proposals of aspiring institutions as per India's priorities and advice the government whether or not to allow the institute to operate in the country. The Bill has a provision under which the government can reject an application of a university if it feels that the venture will have an adverse impact on national security. It is felt that this would distort the already elitist educational structure and make education more commercial. The Bill would be detrimental to the interests of the states as education is in the State List.

Privatisation of education is also being promoted through adoption of the PPP model. It is not just the allocations, but also the mode of financing adopted by the government, that determine its priority, whether critical commitments are being financed through an approach based on entitlements for people or through low-cost provisioning for the poorest sections of the population. For instance, setting up 2,500 of the 6,000 Model Schools under the PPP model is disconcerting. The difference between a government-aided private-run school and a PPP school would relate to government control and the corresponding role of private management.[20] The PPP schools would be free to fix fee levels with the government having no role in determining either the fee levels or the expenditure of the schools. This would of course only be keeping up with the motto of a private player to 'invest for a reasonable return'.

School Vouchers: Panacea or Pandora's Box?

Years ago, when Milton Friedman shared his idea of vouchers in schools, it was based on his premise that liberalising the school sector would result in emergence of a new market with educational 'entrepreneurs' taking advantage of the opportunity to offer quality school services.[21] Simply put, the voucher is a payment made by the government to the parent directly than to the school. It is tax-funded and covers most of the tuition charges with the stated objective of allowing the parent to choose the school they would prefer for their children. Friedman had propounded a universal voucher system and to enabling development of a 'for-profit' private industry that would provide diverse learning opportunities and compete with the public school system.

At the very outset, the logic of the government paying a parent instead of strengthening the public school system is confusing and fundamentally erroneous. Second, the principle of a universal voucher system is being flouted with the government considering issuing vouchers only to the low-income families residing in neighbourhoods classified as falling in the lowest socio-economic strata.[22] This is clearly illustrative of the government promoting different layers of schools; voucher schools for the poorest, government-aided private-run schools for the middle-income group, elite private schools for the *crème-de-la-crème* and elite government schools (Kendriya Vidyalayas, Sainik Schools) catering to children of the government employees and other personnel. Promoting voucher system as a solution, while at the same time acknowledging that every child has a right to universal, free and quality education appears an extremely confusing policy stance. In this regard, it is worthwhile to also take note that the long-standing demand by educationists and activists across the country to introduce neighbourhood schools, as was envisioned through the Common School System, remains a demand.

Finally, the premise that such private-run, profit-making voucher schools would compete with the public school system is twisted to say the least. The government has systematically let the public school system crumble with adoption of poor quality indices (i.e., para-teachers, poor teachers' training programmes), setting unrealistic unit costs for running these schools (costs for building a *pucca* building, school toilet, and maintenance and monitoring allowances) and not resolving the implementation bottlenecks (low level of decentralisation and poor community participation). In such a situation, the proposal to allow private-run, low-cost voucher schools to compete with a resource-starved public school system is erroneous. Thus although the government claims to ensure universal and free education for all, its treatment of education as a commodity that can be bought and sold is discomforting. An overview of the public provisioning of education is surely in order.

Issues in Implementation

The Finance Minister in his Budget Speech of 2010 commended the progress achieved through SSA. However, government estimates tell a different tale. It is unlikely that the SSA can address concerns of poor teachers and weak student attendance levels, given that majority of spending has been on two areas, civil works and the recruitment of contract teachers. To mention an instance, in the budget approved for SSA for 2008–09, 28 per cent of total outlay was earmarked for civil works and 31 per cent for teachers' salary, while the components that could influence quality of outcomes such as teaching learning equipment, teacher training, innovative activities, community training and research and evaluation, account for very low shares.

Increase in the quantum of the budget does not necessarily translate into better development outcomes if the funds are not spent in a timely and effective manner. Average spending in SSA as a proportion of the total approved outlay for the country was only 29 per cent in the first half of 2008–09. Under-utilisation of funds in schemes like SSA is a key concern, which is due to the inefficient institutional and budgetary processes, and flaws in the scheme design. Setting low and unrealistic unit costs is an appropriate illustration of this. A grant of ₹5,000 per year for a primary school for replacement of non-functional equipment and other recurring costs is a pittance. Similarly, providing ₹100 per person per day for training of teachers would be hardly sufficient to conduct effective training. It is disconcerting that even though the government acknowledges the need to address weaknesses in government systems, it has not made much headway in actually dealing with these concerns.

To conclude, in principle, the Right to Education Act, with appropriate modifications and financial provisioning, offers a great opportunity to correct the anomaly of poor education outcomes and deliver on the long-standing commitment of providing basic and quality education to the so-called 'demographic dividend' of the country. Unfortunately, small term political gains and poor judgement on the part of politicians and policy-makers may continue to be major roadblock in accomplishing this critical goal.

Farm Sector Report Card: The Agrarian Crisis 2008–10

The crisis on the farm front runs unabated with official figures pointing out that 1,99,132 farmers have been driven to suicide between 1997 and 2008. As per the figures of the National Crime Records Bureau (NCRB), there were at least 16,196 farmers' suicides in 2008, i.e., two every hour, an average that has remained unchanged since 2003. The search for a solution to stem the agrarian crisis is growing increasingly desperate, as neither policy instruments nor technological interventions, appear to be working. Whether it is a loan waiver, infusion of massive doses of credit, pushing alien and untested technologies like biotechnology or enhancing the budgetary allocation towards agriculture for the period between 2003–04 and 2008–09 by 300 per cent, all attempts to stem the crisis on the this front have failed miserably.

Suicides are but a symptom of the malaise that has hit the farm sector of the country ranked second in the world in terms of output. Implanting Green Revolution technologies on unsound conditions coupled with domestic re-forms and trade liberalisation in agriculture is playing havoc with the lives of millions of farmers across the country.

The Green Revolution helped the country to achieve self-sufficiency in food grain pro-duction. However, this has severely eroded the natural resource base of the major food bowls across the country and production levels have either stagnated or declined for most crops. This clearly shows that while industrial agri-culture does have the potential to boost yields in the short run, it also leaves behind a trail of devastation.

This section examines the on ground per-formance of agriculture during 2008–10, con-sidered as a period when the farm sector ought to have outperformed the rest of the economy beleaguered by recession. Unfortunately, this did not happen.

Growth and Productivity

Apart from the heyday of the Green Revolution, the rate of growth of the agricultural sector has generally lagged behind the overall growth of the national economy. Stagnation set in over the decade and a half period beginning 1980, when the growth rate hovered around 3 per cent, and dropped to a mere 2 per cent for the period 1995–2005. This further nosedived to 1.6 per cent in 2008–09 and it is estimated to be negative for the year 2009–10 though an official confirmation is due. Yet, the 11th Five Year Plan envisages a 4 per cent annual rate of growth in agriculture, a difficult mission by all counts.

The growth in productivity of most of the important food crops like rice, wheat, coarse cereals and oilseeds was negative for the period 1996–2004 and the depressed yield levels continue today. The food demand is projected to touch 240 million tonne in 2010. However, production stood at less than 234 million tonne during the year 2008–09, 2009 being a drought year with considerably lower produc-tion. It therefore would not be far fetched to say that India indeed is on the brink of losing the status of being self-sufficient in food grain production.

Even as the contribution of agriculture to GDP has fallen from 37 per cent in 1983 to around 17 per cent at present, the share of workforce engaged in agriculture has hardly diminished. The numbers engaged in farming remain disproportionately high with the aver-age holding size standing at 1.06 hectare, a size on which industrial agriculture is unviable. As has been the experience worldwide, small farms can be viable when they grow different varieties of crops per unit area, a concept that is alien to the Green Revolution model of cul-tivating monocultures.

Impact of Implanting Unsound Technology

The first impact of growing monocultures has been on biodiversity. At the beginning of the 20th century, over 30,000 varieties of rice were cultivated across the country. Today more than 75 per cent of the rice comes from just 10 varieties. Prior to the Green Revolution, as many as 41 varieties of wheat and 37 of rice were grown in Punjab. Today, three varieties each of wheat and rice dominate. Likewise, a loss of biodiversity has been reported from most parts of the country where monocultures were introduced.

Shrinking farmlands and reduced size of landholdings coupled with flawed technology prescriptions, and pushing farmers towards markets is forcing them to produce more by adopting intensive agriculture practices. This in turn is putting enormous pressure on the na-tural resource base of the country and in many cases, the devastation is irreversible.

The figures are damning. More than 10,000 million tonne of fertile top soil is being eroded every year. As per the figures of the Department of Land Resources of the Ministry of Rural Development, nearly two-thirds of the country's agriculture land is degraded or sick. The deterioration of soil health is worse in the frontline Green Revolution states and granaries of the country.

This claim is backed by the latest 2009 atlas on Desertification Status Mapping produced by the Ahmedabad based Space Applications Centre which shows that around a quarter of the total geographical area of the country is desertified while soil fertility has declined across another 32 per cent. The atlas further shows that 69 per cent of the country is dry. Not only has the Thar Desert in Rajasthan expanded by almost 12,000 square kilometers in the last 13 years, parts of Eastern and Western Ghats and the western Himalayas are also going down the same road.

In January 2009, the Department of Agriculture of the State of Haryana warned that important nutrients like nitrogen, phosphorus, iron and zinc are heavily depleted in around 2,50,000 hectare of prime crop land, which in turn will impact the yield of wheat. The situation is no different in neighbouring Punjab, which produces 20 per cent of the country's wheat and 12 per cent of its rice. Almost 40 per cent of the soil in Punjab, a whopping 1.7 million hectare is degraded due to soil erosion, rising water table, salinity, overuse of chemicals, and so on. In Maharashtra, around 10.5 million hectare of crop land are under moderate to heavy chemical deterioration due to salinity. The report card on soil health for the rest of the country is just as dismal.

Sick soils have lost their ability to respond to inputs like fertilisers, a major reason for stagnating productivity. This decrease in response indicates that the organic carbon content and microbial activities in the soil, which are critical for crop development, have declined. While dying soils should have evoked concern decades ago, all that the government has come up with is a centrally sponsored scheme on management of soil health and fertility in June 2008. With an outlay of ₹ 4.3 billion, the scheme aims to promote the usual technological interventions that in the first place caused the problem, i.e., external input-intensive farming.

Along with the declining soil health, the issue of water scarcity and misuse is a cause for concern. With the bulk of water for irrigation being mined from beneath the ground, we are facing depletion of aquifers. Of the 7,928 blocks in the country, 673 have over-exploited their groundwater while 425 are in the dark zone, i.e., the aquifers are almost dead. The worst affected states are Punjab, Rajasthan, Tamil Nadu, Maharashtra, Haryana, Andhra Pradesh and Gujarat, incidentally among the main food producing states.

In September 2009, the National Geophysical Research Institute, Hyderabad, reported that approximately 54 cubic km of water is being extracted annually from a 2.7 million square km area extending from Delhi to Bangladesh. A similar account was given by NASA whose figures pointed out that 18 million cubic km of groundwater was being depleted annually from the frontline Green Revolution states of Punjab, Haryana and Rajasthan. These alarming declines in groundwater pose a threat to agriculture as bulk of the irrigation depends on underground aquifers. Clearly, India's groundwater use is already on the threshold of exceeding availability, yet a groundwater utilisation law does not exist.

Intensive application of chemical fertilisers on farm lands is resulting in a leaching of nitrates, chemicals that pollute surface and groundwater leading to serious health impacts. The groundwater in 11 states has a nitrate concentration higher than the permissible limit. Coupled with indiscriminate use of other chemicals like pesticides and herbicides, the rate of pesticide poisoning and cancer rates among farmers has reached alarming proportions.

Drought and Floods, 2009

The year 2009 was marked by a failed monsoon with an overall rainfall paucity as high as 23 per cent, which is worse than the 19 per cent of the 1987 drought. Monsoons were also the weakest since 1972. About half of the country was in the grip of a severe drought with the worst rainfall

---

Box 2.4   Fertiliser Subsidy Conundrum

The 2008–09 fertiliser subsidy Bill of ₹1 lakh crore raised quite a few eyebrows and there were debates in several quarters on the ways to reduce this. However interesting details on these subsidies emerge when one closely examines the figures of the Ministry of Chemicals and Fertilisers.

During *kharif* season of 2008 which produced a bumper crop, fertiliser sales stood at 127.92 lakh tonne. In the subsequent season, when bulk of the country was in the grip of a severe drought and cereal production was at an all time low, fertiliser sales ought to have been lower. However, available figures show that 330.74 lakh tonne of fertiliser were sold during April–November 2009, i.e., a massive 200 tonne more. Similarly, while the sales for *rabi* in 2008 stood at 138.55 lakh tonne, the assessed requirement for the 2009 season is 265.75 lakh tonne! Clearly, there is something out of ordinary here.

The only credible explanation for this is that huge quantities of fertilisers are being smuggled out to neighbouring countries, particularly Bangladesh (Nepal being another destination) whose per unit fertiliser application is over 55 per cent higher than that of India. While Urea is the only major fertiliser whose movement is controlled, the import, movement and distribution of di-Ammonium Phosphate (DAP), Muriate of Potash (MoP) and complex fertilisers were decontrolled in 1992. Although India spends a huge amount for importing fertilisers and the government and scientists blame farmers for their inefficient use, the fact is also that corruption, leakages and smuggling are responsible for inflating the fertiliser subsidy Bill.

This brings up a crucial question, should subsidies be doled out to fertiliser companies who sell it in the market at reduced price or transferred directly to farmers? A study by the National Institute of Public Finance and Policy (NIPFP) shows that around 38 per cent of the fertiliser subsidy is cornered by manufacturers. If farmers were to receive direct subsidy payments, they might also be able to exercise their informed choice to use or shun chemical fertilisers which are playing havoc with the natural resource base, besides inflating the cost of cultivation.

There are no subsidies available for producing and using non-chemical fertilisers. Fertiliser subsidies are meant to deflate the cost of production and thereby benefit farmers. Instead, they end up promoting business interests of fertiliser manufacturers.

---

deficit in north-west India at 36 per cent, while the southern part of the country was just 7 per cent below average. June was the driest month in previous 83 years.

To make things worse, rains returned to many parts of southern and western India by the end of September after an extremely dry period. The heaviest rains in more than a century hit parts of Andhra Pradesh and Karnataka between 29 September and 3 October 2009, inundating more than 4,800 villages and leaving over 1.5 million people homeless.

This climate quirk made things worse for agriculture. Take the case of north Karnataka which was reeling under drought and then was hit by floods. Prior to the floods, around 1.66 lakh hectare went unsown while the floods later wiped out standing crops across 22 lakh hectare. In Andhra Pradesh, the loss has been substantial with *kharif* food grain production and that of rice declining by more than 30 per cent each over last season. The overall food production of the country was hence badly hit.

Going by the 21 January 2010 update of the Ministry of Statistics and Programme Implementation, lower growth in farm sector due to drought and floods is likely to pull down economic growth in the third quarter of 2009–10 to 6–6.5 per cent. The farm sector will take a 6–7 per cent hit in production, which is significantly lower that the growth during the second quarter. As it is, the growth of agriculture and allied sector during the second quarter slipped below 1 per cent, which makes this drop in growth during the third quarter much more severe. Food grain production in this *kharif* season is likely to go down by 19–21 million tonne.

The shortfall in rice production that was earlier pegged at 15 million tonne has now been revised to 13 million tonne. This is on account of the near saturation of irrigation in the states that were most affected by drought in north-west India, Punjab, Haryana and west Uttar Pradesh, where harvests have been better than normal and procurement has been higher than last year. The prospects for wheat during the *rabi* season in these states is likely to be a bit gloomy as groundwater aquifers have been pumped dry during the *kharif* season. The cost of production of rice has also been substantially higher this year as farmers had to spend around 30–40 per cent more on diesel for energising pump-sets.

Reduced production of rice fuelled the speculations that India might resort to imports to meet the domestic demand and quell prices. This was despite the fact that in July 2009, when it became clear that the country is heading for a major drought, the buffer stock of food grains was more than 53 million tonne, almost double the stocking norms. Notwithstanding this, the Ministry of Agriculture built a case for imports and tenders were floated to import 30,000 tonne of rice.

Higher international prices forced the government to scrap the tenders. As of 1 December 2009, the national rice stock was 22.9 million tonne, four times higher than the buffer stock norm of 5.2 million tonne. This clearly demonstrates that as in the case of wheat imports during 2006 and 2007 that were unnecessary, import of rice at inflated prices was being pushed ostensibly for reasons that were not justifiable.

Agriculture versus Industrialisation

In last few years, there have been concerted moves to convert agriculture land for non-agriculture purposes. According to available official figures which are quite dated and do not reflect the true picture, 1.5 per cent of agriculture land has been lost between 1990 and 2003, though the actual diversion is much higher whereas in contrast, between 1990 and 2004, land under non-agricultural use has gone up by 34 lakh hectare. This present figure of agricultural land lost in percentage terms may not look big but in absolute terms, it translates to more than 21 lakh hectare. Putting just this much land under wheat cultivation would yield 57 lakh tonne of produce, enough to feed more than 4.3 crore hungry people every year and India would reduce the number of people going hungry by 12 per cent.

The issue of land acquisition for the setting up of Special Economic Zones (SEZs) brought national attention on the issue of loss of agricultural land. Addressing a National Development Council meeting on 23 December 2006, Prime Minister Manmohan Singh said:

> I agree that we must minimise the diversion of agricultural land and, given the choice, must opt for using wasteland for non-agricultural purposes. However, it must be kept in mind that industrialisation is a national necessity if we have to reduce the pressure on agriculture and provide gainful, productive employment to millions of our youth who see no future in agriculture.

It is obvious that the Prime Minister's statement was directed more at assuaging the violent opposition to the deprivation and displacement unleashed by land acquisition rather than at generating employment in non-farm activities for the rural youth. If this were not so, the government would have provided a figure on the threshold level for this diversion so that agricultural land is protected. In fact, the government itself does not know how much agricultural land has been diverted till date, as the Planning Commission's July 2006 report of

the Working Group on Land Relations for the 11th Five Year Plan made clear.

The reason for this lack of awareness is not difficult to figure out because both the government and the private sector have partnered in appropriating agricultural land to promote industry, real estate, infrastructure, highways, dams, and so on. All this is purportedly done to benefit the 'public', which somehow does not include people engaged in agriculture. The fact is that diversion of agricultural land for non-agricultural use will not only continue, but will also enjoy official sanction. As always, it is the poor who will pay in terms of livelihood loss and food insecurity.

This extensive diversion of farmland has been facilitated by the relaxation of land acquisition and ceiling regulations post-1991, and has resulted in the state itself turning into one of the largest real estate brokers and developers in the country. All that the centre did to protect agricultural land was to issue the National Land Use Policy Outline to states and union territories in 1986 and even there, instead of full implementation, the state-level Land Use Boards have redefined their role to coercing farmers to give up farmland.

Diversion of agricultural land for industry is frequently justified by pointing towards cultivable wasteland, around 132 lakh hectare, which can be developed and put under cultivation. However, cultivable wastelands have also declined by over 18 lakh hectare between 1990 and 2004. Further, even if these wastelands are developed and made cultivable, their productivity will remain abysmally low for several years.

Due to the increasing demand for land for industrialisation and urbanisation, not only is the area under cultivation shrinking, but the area irrigated is also declining mainly on account of a falling groundwater table and diversion of prime crop land. The country is barely self-sufficient in producing cereals and meeting the domestic demand for pulses and edible oils requires an additional 20 million hectare of land. Thus, diversion of farmland is making the country perpetually dependent on imports, yet it is being actively promoted.

Farming is also facing competition from industrial estates for the use of water. Barely 40 per cent of the country's agriculture is irrigated while the rest depends on unpredictable rain. This limited area, however, accounts for more than half the total value of output of the agriculture sector. Irrigation also has the potential to increase crop yield by 30 per cent and therefore its importance for ensuring food security cannot be stressed enough. However, water for irrigation is being diverted to meet the demand of industries across all major river basins of the country. Attempts are also being made to privatise irrigation facilities.

The experience of developed countries, where the population engaged in agriculture has slowly shifted out to other occupations, primarily to the manufacturing and services sectors, is routinely cited as an example that India ought to emulate. This is an extremely narrow view of the practice of agriculture in a country where a billion plus inhabitants need to be fed.

Reforms and Liberalisation

In this grim scenario where farm productivity and farmers' income have taken a hit, domestic reforms and liberalisation policies, and bilateral/multilateral trade agreements are additional dimensions that confront the farm sector. Beginning with economic reforms in 1991, a steady process of dismantling safety nets for farmers and making agriculture more market oriented has taken precedence over ensuring the country's food security and protecting livelihoods of farmers.

India is a net agricultural exporter with exports valued at USD 19.33 billion and imports valued at USD 7.5 billion in 2007–08, a reason that is oft touted to further liberalise this sector. Trade liberalisation however has not enabled India to expand export of agriculture and food products, which stands at a meagre 1.4 per cent of global trade.

Agriculture imports on the other hand, have gone up manifold, which has further depressed domestic prices and hit income levels of farmers. Ironically, India is importing commodities like pulses, vegetables and edible oils, which

have traditionally been grown by dry land farmers. These also are commodities that are comparatively less expensive to produce in India than in the countries from where they are imported.

Imports are growing and include vegetable oils, wheat, pulses, raw cashews, dry fruits, cotton, wool, hides and skins, and fruits and vegetables. India is the largest global importer of pulses (beans, peas and lentils) and soybean oil and the second largest importer of palm oil. In 2006–07, India emerged as the third largest importer of wheat in the world, with total imports of around 6.2 million tonnes. Imports declined to around 2 million tonnes in 2007–08.

On the multilateral front, WTO negotiations reached a stalemate in 2008 when developing and developed countries stood their grounds over a mechanism to shield the former from unforeseen farm imports. After Prime Minister Manmohan Singh formed his cabinet for the second term, the first step was replacing the hardliner Commerce Minister Kamal Nath with a much pliable Anand Sharma.

The first indication that India will play a proactive role, or rather, dilute its stand, to conclude the Doha Round was when India hosted WTO mini ministerial in September 2009. However, much to the consternation of the Indian negotiation team, despite putting forth a diluted stand, the US was not interested in reaching a deal. This was probably because President Obama had much more pressing issues to deal with back home on the economic front and trade remained at the bottom of his agenda as it still does.

The bone of contention a few years back, the agricultural subsidies in developed countries, goes unchallenged. Developing countries are required to offer greater market access than what was required under the Uruguay Round. Now, areas where India could have claimed modest success like flexibilities to prevent imports from impacting livelihoods of farmers are being watered down at the insistence of developed countries. Yet the Prime Minister and the Commerce Minister are routinely citing that the current negotiations will benefit India.

On account of the stalemate of negotiations at the multilateral forum, the march towards trade liberalisation in agriculture is being pursued through a slew of bilateral free trade agreements. One such agreement that India entered into with the ASEAN bloc of nations is set to negatively impact the plantation sector. Yet potential gains in the services sector propelled the centre to sacrifice the cause of plantation farmers. Another deal that is being negotiated with the European Union will seriously marginalise the dairy sector besides ushering in unfair intellectual property regimes. Again, India is going ahead with the deal.

Farm Income and Farmers' Welfare

Not only do fertilisers, pesticides and other chemicals cause adverse health impacts, they also increase the cost of cultivation. Subsidies for most inputs that drove the Green Revolution have been scaled down with the exception of fertiliser subsidy, 38 per cent of which in any case is cornered by manufacturers. With increased participation of the private sector in the production of critical inputs for farming, their costs have gone up. As groundwater aquifers drop steadily, farmers invest more money to dig deeper. Cost of power for energising pump-sets has gone up. Nevertheless, public investment in agriculture has almost dried up in the last two decades. All this and more has increased the cost of cultivation by leaps and bounds.

The prices of most agricultural commodities, on the other hand, have fallen or remained static since the trade liberalisation in agriculture, especially after our accession to the WTO in 1995. For instance, during the period 1996–97 to 2003–04, agriculture commodity prices relative to non-agriculture prices have fallen by 1.7 per cent every year, adversely affecting the income levels of farmers.

While there has been an upturn in agriculture prices in the last three years, owing to a global food crisis followed by runaway domestic food inflation, which forced a reluctant government to upwardly revise procurement price for several commodities, it appears unlikely that the increase will be sustained in the future. This is because once the food and price crisis is over and production levels for essential commodities improve, the terms of trade in a liberalised market scenario will bring domestic food prices down. In any case, announcing a higher procurement price does not always lead to enhanced income for every farmer—barely 30 per cent of the farmers in the country benefit from this policy. The majority of marginal and small farmers who do not produce for markets are therefore being further impoverished.

The marketing of agriculture commodities is in most situations a tough proposition for farmers. Despite more than 7,500 regulated markets and 21,000 rural periodical markets, the price received by farmers is a fraction of that paid by the consumer. Worse, about 72 per cent of the fruit and vegetable production in India goes waste because of lack of proper retailing and adequate storage capacity. Food processing industries are rarely to be found in rural areas.

To ensure that farmers get a fair price for their produce, as also enable government agencies to procure sufficient quantities to meet the food security concerns of the country, the government announces what is known as the Minimum Support Price (MSP) for 24 commodities and a Statutory Minimum Price for sugarcane, which serves as a ruling price for the public sector agencies engaged in procurement. While fixing the MSP, the various costs involved in the cultivation process are worked out by running trials at approximately 18,000 locations across the country. A nominal amount over and above the cost of cultivation is offered as procurement price to farmers.

However, neither is this a failsafe methodology nor is it fair. While working out the cost of cultivation, a farmer is considered an unskilled worker, lower than a Group D government employee, which depresses the assumed wage rate. In case the land is leased-in, the rent is taken into account but no such considerations are made for farmers who cultivate their own land. Many state governments instead of quoting the prevailing market rate of rent for land declare what is known as statutory rent, which is way lower. Some states have outsourced the crop trial experiments to private parties who have been accused of not carrying out the exercise properly.

Commissions and parliamentary panels have regularly recommended that farmers ought to be paid 50 per cent over and above the cost of cultivation, but to no avail. All this and more plague the process of working out a MSP that could help farmers receive a fair price for their produce. On the procurement front too there are glaring lapses and actual procurement is done for a select few. This forces farmers to turn to private traders who usually pay much less than the MSP.

In a response to a query in the Rajya Sabha on 18 December 2009, the Minister of State for Agriculture, K.V. Thomas produced some interesting figures on the cost of cultivation and net income from cultivation of selected cereals, wheat, paddy, sorghum (jowar) and pearl millet (bajra). In the case of paddy, the MSP (including bonus) went up marginally from ₹560 to 620 per quintal during 2004–05 to 2006–07. As a result, the net income for the cultivators did go up a bit but was negative for most states as can be seen from in Figure 2.1 for the top eight rice growing states.

On the other hand, the major hike in MSP from ₹640 to ₹850 per quintal (including bonus) for wheat during the same period translated to significant gains for farmers, as can be seen in Figure 2.2. Also, this substantial hike in MSP

has brought about a skewed distribution of benefits with certain states making the most of it at the expense of others. For instance, gain in income for north-western states like Punjab, Haryana, Rajasthan and Uttar Pradesh, where procurement agencies are more active, is higher than that of states like Bihar and Madhya Pradesh.

Since MSP is worked out based on the total cost of cultivation, a C2 cost in economic parlance, a higher procurement price for wheat and paddy is technically correct, as their cost of cultivation is high.

However, millets like *jowar* and *bajra* are dryland crops cultivated by millions across the country but whose support price is way too low and procurement more or less non-existent. They require less water for irrigation and virtually no chemicals for cultivation and are thereby more sound for agro-ecological reasons. These also are crops that can help meet the food and nutritional security requirements at the local and household levels. Being climate hardy and with much lower cost of inputs, as compared to the 'star' crops (wheat and paddy), they involve much lower risks in cultivation too. However, the potential of these to mitigate the current agrarian crisis is consistently ignored by policy-makers.

Figure 2.1 Net Returns from Paddy

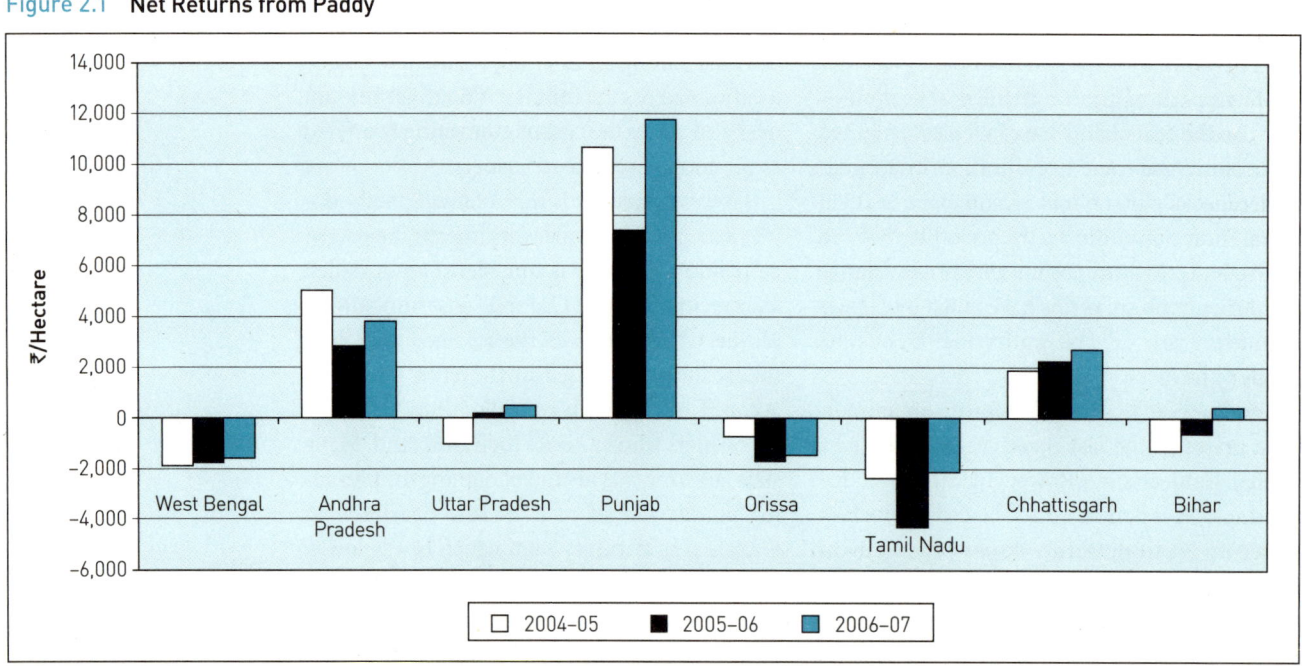

Figure 2.2 **Net Returns from Wheat**

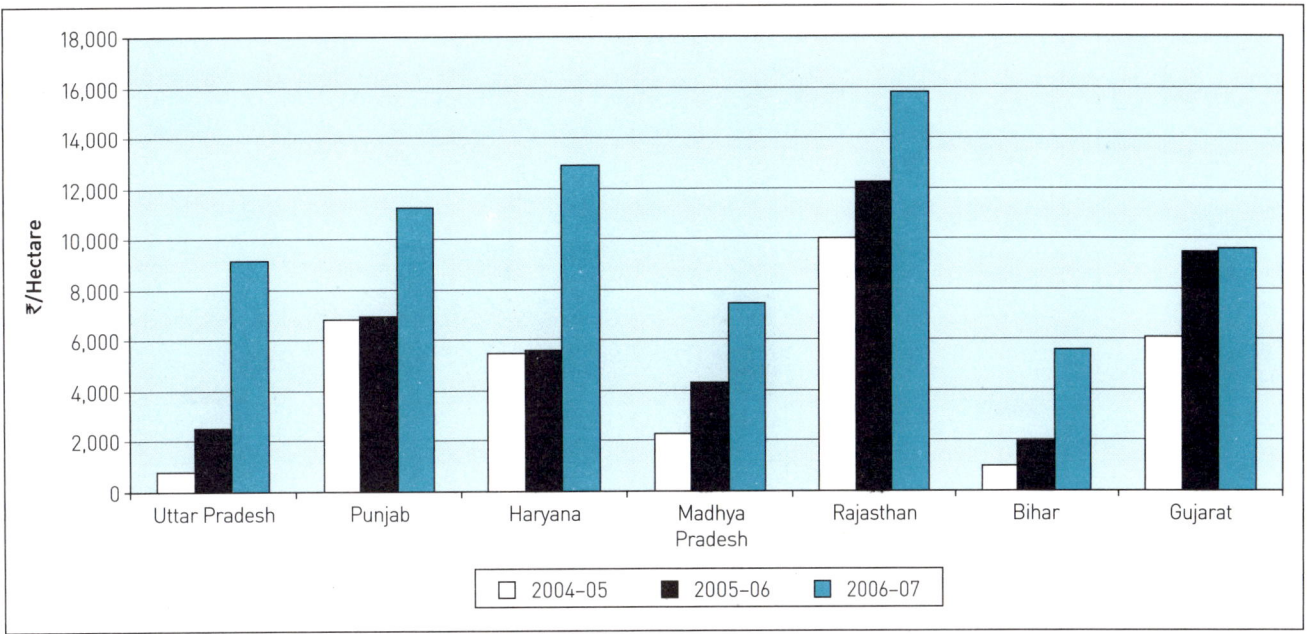

A comparison of the cost of cultivation, net income and MSP of these four crops in the highest producing states in the country is presented in Figure 2.3. It can be seen that income from dryland crops like millets are lower not due to lower levels of productivity alone as is usually believed, but also because of flawed pricing and procurement policies that fail to take into account suitability of a crop to a specific agro-ecological zone or the degree of risk involved in its cultivation.

This brings up the crucial issue of income from farming. Now while the real income of the country as a whole was growing at the rate of around 4 per cent every year for more than a decade, it grew at less than 0.5 per cent for rural India. No wonder a family of five in rural India had to subsist at an average income of ₹2,115 a month while the consumption expenditure was ₹2,770 during the year 2003, as per the National Sample Survey Organisation (NSSO). The NSSO further points out that as many as 49 per cent of rural households were indebted with an average debt of ₹12,585 during the year 2003, one-third of which was owed to moneylenders who charge usurious rates of interest. The vicious circle of debt and loss of assets (mainly land) is driving thousands of farmers to commit suicide every year. In fact,

more than 40 per cent of farmers want to quit farming.

Decreased real income levels have also impacted food grain consumption. For the year 2002–03, this stood at 155.7 kg per capita, which is lower than the figure during 1933–38. During the period 1993–94 to 2004–05, caloric intake in rural India declined by 5 per cent. In fact, two-third of the country is consuming less than the recommended nutritional intake and malnutrition in India is higher than even Ethiopia. It came as no surprise when the National Family Health Survey of 2005–06 pointed out that almost half of the children under the age of five years, a staggering 60 million, are stunted, which is an indicator of malnourishment, and that 43 per cent are underweight. In fact, every third malnourished child in the world is an Indian. Every year, 2.5 million children die in India, half of whom could be saved, if only they were well nourished.

Conclusion

Agriculture is and will remain the backbone of our rural economy. It will continue to employ the bulk of our population, as it should. All that is required is promotion of sustainable agriculture that is in harmony with nature, and desisting

Figure 2.3 **Comparative Parameters for Cereal Cultivation in Highest Producer States**

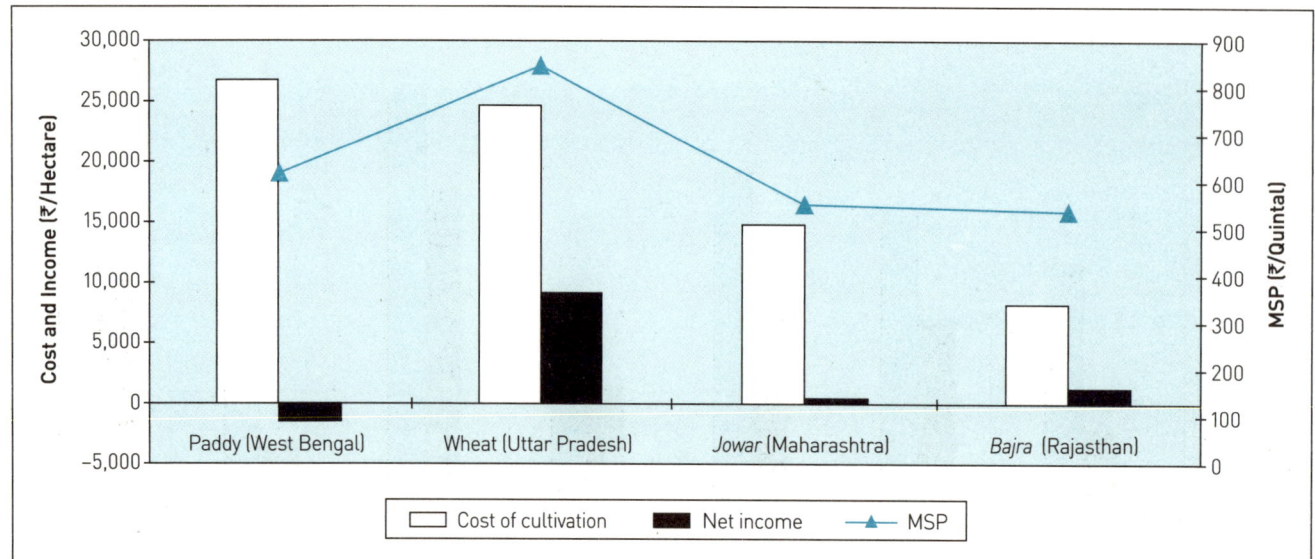

from policy prescriptions that depress farmers' incomes and force them out of farming. One must not ignore the reality that opportunities for economic engagement are limited in the rural areas and therefore pushing a farm exit policy for marginal and small farmers would be fraught with danger.

In policy-making circles there are however discussions on ushering in a 'second Green Revolution', and an 'ever-Green Revolution'. That is why there is an urgent need to draw a balance sheet of the Green Revolution, so that we know why and what went wrong and not to repeat the same mistakes in the future.

Our farmers have delivered much more than what was expected of them in the past and they alone have the ability and will to ensure that the nation remains food secure. It takes time to dismantle four decades of mistakes and application of flawed technologies. However, a beginning must be made. The sooner this happens, the better it would be for the country's food sovereignty and farmers' livelihoods.

Rural Employment and Livelihood Security

According to the 61st round of National Sample Survey (2004–05), a little over 73 per cent of the households in the country belong to rural India and constitute around 75 per cent

of the total population. With 73 per cent of the people living below poverty line residing in the rural areas (as per URP[23] consumption data), poverty in rural India is characterised by lack of gainful employment opportunities, hidden unemployment, large underemployment, low agricultural wage rate, uncertainty in getting employment due to seasonality of agricultural operations and declining agricultural productivity. As per the 11th Five Year Plan, the overall unemployment rate for the rural sector, as of 2004–05, was 8.28 per cent (as per current daily status), and particularly, the unemployment rate among the agricultural labour households had risen from 9.5 per cent in 1993–94 to 15.4 per cent in 2004–05. Underemployment had also been reported to be on the rise, given the widening gap between the usual status and current daily status measures of creation of incremental employment opportunities during the periods 1994–2000 and 2000–05. Low wage rate and exploitation also play a compounding factor in accentuating rural poverty. NCEUS[24] (2009) observes that share of wage workers securing wages below National Minimum Wage norm is significantly high across industries and in this context 85 per cent of all casual workers in rural areas received wages below the minimum wages.

Employment generation in the rural areas has been one of the major interventions by the government since long, and some of the prominent programmes/schemes have, in the past, focused on creating supplementary employment opportunities for the rural poor during lean seasons. These programmes and schemes were geared towards providing gainful employment, apart from creation of durable community assets, which would enhance productivity of the rural sector along with increase in demand for labour. However, the efficacy of these schemes in attaining the desired objectives was suspect due to several problems pertaining to implementation, transparency and awareness among potential beneficiaries.

The UPA government, in its first stint, had taken a host of progressive policy measures, landmark among which was the National Rural Employment Guarantee Act (NREGA), 2005 (named as the Mahatma Gandhi National Rural Employment Guarantee Act). NREGA was a considerable departure from the erstwhile programmes of employment generation. The Act guarantees at least 100 days of wage employment on demand, failing which the state government will have to pay an unemployment allowance. The Act also incorporates crucial features of transparency and accountability like mandatory requirement of social audits and payment of wages through bank or post office accounts rather than cash payments.

Mahatma Gandhi National Rural Employment Guarantee Scheme

The National Rural Employment Guarantee Act (NREGA), enacted in September 2005, was implemented from 2 February 2006 in 200 identified backward districts of the country in the form of NREGS, with the stated objective of providing at least 100 days of guaranteed wage employment to each rural household willing to do manual unskilled work. The coverage was increased to 330 districts with the addition of 130 new districts in 2007–08. The ongoing programmes of Swarnajayanti Grameen Rozgar Yojana (SGRY) and National Food for Work Programme (NFFWP) were subsumed under NREGS in these districts. The coverage of NREGS has now been extended to 615 districts

Box 2.5   The Story of a Helpless Father: Village Ajangaon, Nagpur, Maharashtra

Homdeo Narayan Pimple is a 38 year old father of three. He has been a resident of Village Ajangaon since he was born. The family's yearly income is 30,000 rupees. He had lived in poverty throughout his life and wanted to secure a better life for his children and provide them with better facilities so that they could lead a better life.

To increase his income and build a proper house, he applied for a loan under the Other Backward Classes Vitta Maha Mandal for goat farming in April 2008. He completed all formalities and also gave ₹4,000 to Meshram, the concerned official for the same. In due time, the application was forwarded to UCO Bank, Hingna for further processing and Homdeo received one copy of the approved loan. But after this, there was no progress in the matter. A harried Homdeo ran from pillar to post to enquire about the status of his approved loan. Finally, he was informed that his application had been rejected.

Today Homdeo is a broken man. He is under debt for a loan he had taken in order to improve his circumstances. He is under shock from the blow dealt to him by the failure and coldness of the government machinery.

Source: People's Mid Term Appraisal of 11th Five Year Plan, *Voices of the People*, February 2010.

(excluding the urban districts) in the country in 2008–09.

The novelty of the scheme compared to its precursors like SGRY and NFFWP are:

1. A paradigm shift to a rights based framework, which entails a legal guarantee of work unlike other programmes which could be withdrawn by a government at will;
2. Disincentive for underperformance as unemployment allowance will have to be paid by the state government within 15 days, if work is not provided within 15 days of demanding;
3. Resource availability under the scheme is demand driven and
4. Accountability of the public delivery systems through social audit.

Evidently, the scheme being demand driven, utilisation and in turn allocation depends on the actual demand for work by households.

The allocation for NREGS in the 11th Five Year Plan (at current prices), i.e., for the years 2007–08 to 2011–12, is tentatively provided at ₹1,00,000 crore. However, given that NREGS is a demand driven programme and the government is legally bound to provide employment mandated under the Act, the allocation is only indicative. The bulk of the financial cost for NREGS is to be borne by the central government, which includes (*a*) entire cost of wages of unskilled manual workers, (*b*) 75 per cent of the cost of material, wages of skilled and semi-skilled workers, (*c*) administrative expenses which will include, among others, the salary and the allowances of the Programme Officer and his supporting staff and work site facilities and (*d*) expenses of the National Employment Guarantee Council. The state government on the other hand bears the financial costs pertaining to 25 per cent of material costs, wages of skilled and semi-skilled workers, unemployment allowance and expenses of State Employment Guarantee Council.

Allocation and Utilisation of NREGS Funds

The extent of allocation and utilisation of funds under NREGS is dependent on the efficacy of its implementation, given that the scheme is demand-driven. The scheme in its initial phases witnessed certain inertia in implementation, owing largely to lack of awareness among functionaries and potential beneficiaries, which led to low allocation and utilisation across the states. However, over the financial years 2008–09 through 2009–10, the expansion in the coverage of districts and the concomitant financial allocation has been substantial with the budgetary allocation for the scheme, increasing manifold over allocations in 2006–07 and 2007–08. A noteworthy feature of the allocation and utilisation pattern of the scheme, even after phenomenal increase in coverage of districts and increased popularity and awareness about NREGS, is that the availability of fund per district has been hovering around ₹ 60 crore and utilisation per district varies between ₹ 44 crore

to ₹ 48 crore, showing very little improvement in the uptake of the scheme. Figures below provide the fund availability and utilisation patterns for various years. State level utilisation and availability can be seen in Figures 2.4, 2.5 and 2.6.

A major reason for the lack of improvement in the average uptake of the scheme is that majority of the states (barring a few like Andhra Pradesh, Madhya Pradesh, Rajasthan and Uttar Pradesh) have consistently been unable to improve upon the uptake. States like Orissa, Bihar, Chhattisgarh, Jharkhand, Assam, West Bengal and Maharashtra, despite having large proportions of their population living in rural poverty and significant extent of infrastructural backwardness in their rural areas, have failed to improve the performance of the scheme. While performance of the scheme in some states like Haryana, Punjab, Kerala, Karnataka and Gujarat has been comparatively abysmal owing to several factors, like the minimum wage rate under NREGS being lower than the market wage rate or works permissible under the scheme having little use for local area development.

The apathetic performance of NREGS in many states owes to several inimical factors, primary among which, is low capacity of functionaries at grassroots level to prepare a shelf of projects through which employment can be provided. Preparation of labour budgets for the proposed projects and their requisite administrative and technical sanctions continue to be very time-consuming due to unavailability of adequate human resources. In most of the cases, the *Gram* Panchayat secretary who is usually entrusted with the responsibility of implementing NREGS continues to be overburdened with responsibility of more than one *Gram* Panchayat and no mobility support to move from one work site to another. Additionally, in few states where implementation of NREGS could have been strengthened through convergence with other departments or other rural development schemes, such initiatives have not taken off due to lack of clear policy guidelines in this regard.

Impact of NREGS

Despite the poor performance of NREGS in many states, it has been successful in transferring

Figure 2.4 NREGS: Fund Availability and Utilisation

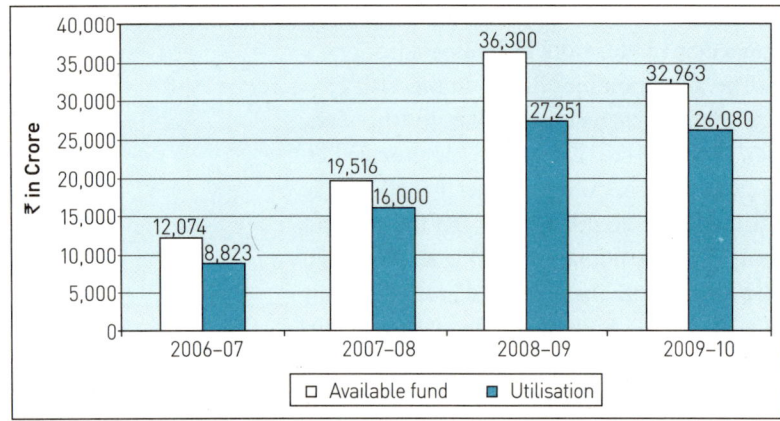

Source: NREGA. Available online at: www.nrega.nic.in
Note: Fund availability and utilisation for year 2009–10 is reported till December 2009.

Figure 2.5 **Performance of States 2008–09: Fund Availability and Utilisation**

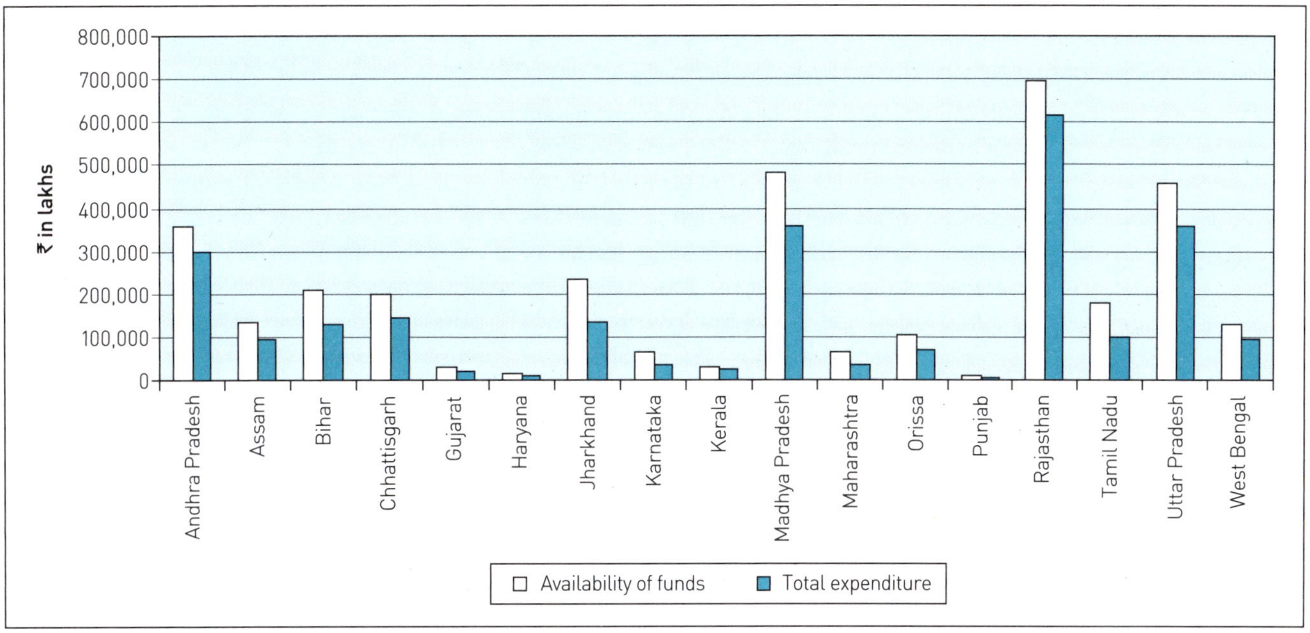

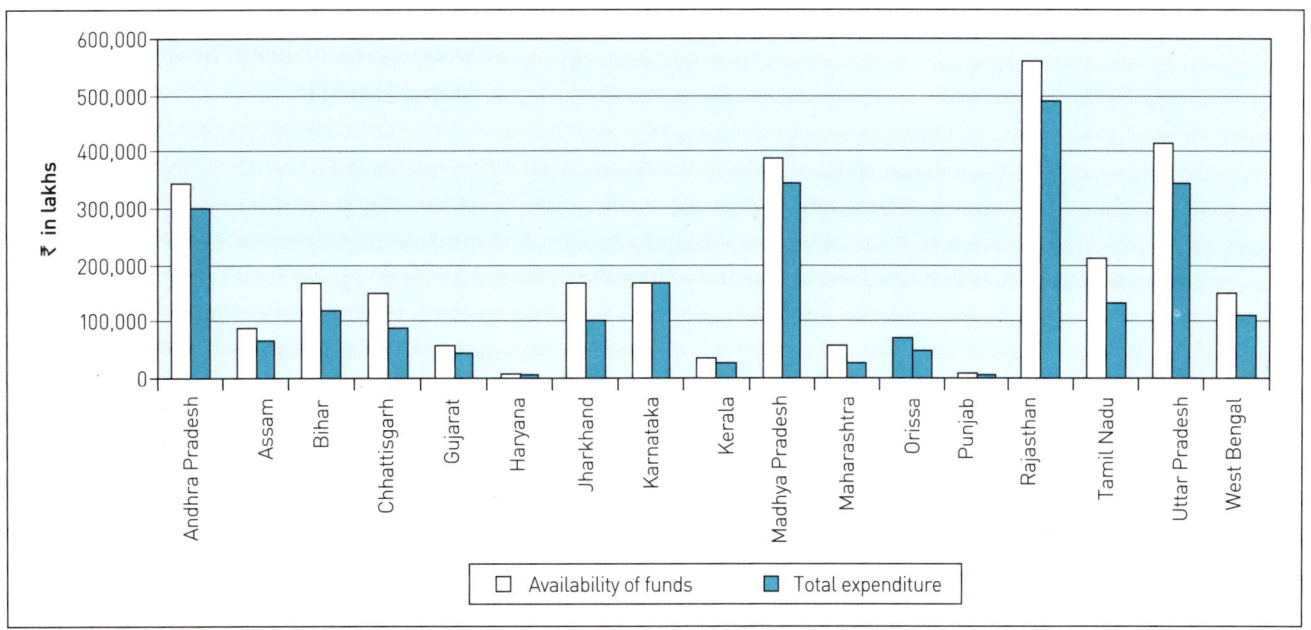

Figure 2.6 **Performance of States 2009–10: Funds Availability and Utilisation**

Source: NREGA. Available online at: www.nrega.nic.in.

resources to the poor who own neither capital nor any kind of skill. Other positive externalities of the scheme include, rise in the market wage rate leading to lesser exploitation of wage labour, better organisation of the rural poor into collectives, large number of women beneficiaries strengthening the potential of women's agency in the rural economy, creation of community assets having the potential of raising agricultural productivity and general economic well-being of the rural poor. The NCEUS (2009) reports that some of the other positive benefits of the scheme have been reduction in distress migration and improved food security with wages being channelled into incurring expenses on food, health, education and repaying of loans.

However, in terms of ensuring the basic entitlement of NREGS of providing 100 days employment to households demanding work, the performance of the scheme has been far from what is desirable. The state-wise implementation of NREGS reveals that apart from Rajasthan, no other state has been able to provide 100 days of wage employment to the significant portion of households (HHs). The striking feature of this phenomenon is that the poorer states like Bihar, Orissa and Jharkhand have performed worse than most other states. A GBPSSI (2009)[25] study of six north Indian states revealed that proportion of the sample workers who reported 100 days of work in the past 12 months was invariably very low: Chhattisgarh (1 per cent), Bihar (2 per cent), Uttar Pradesh (4 per cent), Jharkhand (9 per cent), Madhya Pradesh (19 per cent) and Rajasthan (36 per cent).

Given that the stated objective of NREGS is to provide livelihood security for the rural poor, its impact on the well-being of various socio-economic groups is important to assess its penetration. In this context, the performance of the scheme in providing a safety net to the disadvantaged section of the society has been fairly robust. As per the Ministry of Rural Development's Outcome Budget for 2009–10, the share of SCs in the person-days of job created under NREGS was 27 per cent in 2007–08, which increased to 29 per cent in 2008–09. For STs, the share of person-days of job created has been 29 per cent in 2007–08, which declined to 25 per cent in 2008–09, with the addition of 285 additional districts. The participation of women in the NREGS works have been significantly high with their share of person-days being 43 per cent which increased to 48 per cent in 2008–09. The overwhelming participation of socially disadvantaged groups in NREGS clearly underlines its necessity for these groups to attain basic sustenance in the face of multiple deprivations. The GBPSSI (2009)[26] study of six north Indian states found that 73 per cent of respondents who had worked in NREGS belong to the SC/ST families. It is also reported that often the participation of SCs and OBCs are higher than their respective shares in total households.

It has also been reported that the wages earned from NREGA is largely spent on food consumption and on health related issues. In many cases, it has also been reported that income generated from NREGS has allowed people to send their children back to school, repay past debts, and avoid migration and hazardous work.

Thus, the beneficial impact of NREGS on the rural poor clearly calls for the strengthening of its implementation. In this regard, necessary attention has to be given to the operational issues of the scheme, particularly in augmentation of human resources at the grassroots level and strengthening of accountability mechanisms, like social audits for better implementation and transparency in the operation of the scheme.

In addition to employment guarantee, the union government also implements a self-employment programme viz., Swarnajayanti Gram Swarozgar Yojana (SGSY) for enhanced livelihood security.

Swarnajayanti Gram Swarozgar Yojana (SGSY)

The Swarnajayanti Gram Swarozgar Yojana aims at bringing the assisted poor families above the poverty line by ensuring appreciable levels of sustained income for a period of time. This objective was to be achieved by organising the rural poor into Self-Help Groups (SHGs) through the process of social mobilisation, training and capacity building, and the provision of income generating assets. By design, the programme is meant to create widespread income generating activities through the empowering mechanism of SHGs, where group dynamics are expected to compensate for the basic weaknesses of the individual rural poor and present them as credit worthy and financially accountable units.

The funds for SGSY are provided by the centre and states in the ratio 75:25, except in the case of north-eastern states where the ratio is 90:10. As regards the target groups, the guidelines for the scheme require that at least 40 per cent of the beneficiaries should be women, SCs/STs should account for at least 50 per cent of the beneficiaries, religious minorities should account for at least 15 per cent and disabled at least 3 per cent. Over the five-year tenure of UPA-I, the budgetary allocation for SGSY had shown a gradually increasing trend (see Table 2.6). The allocation for SGSY in the 11th Five Year Plan (at current prices), i.e., for the years 2007–08 to 2011–12, is supposed to be ₹17,803 crore.

Budget Priorities for Rural Development

Starting from 2004–05, when the UPA-I took office, the union budgetary allocation for the rural development sector as a whole grew gradually until 2007–08. In 2008–09, the Union Budget allocation for rural development witnessed a quantum jump. The allocation for rural development in 2008–09 had been 79 per cent higher than that in 2007–08. However, the Union Budgets for 2009–10 and 2010–11 have almost reversed that trend of increasing allocations for rural development. The budgetary allocation for rural development sector stood at 1.1 per cent of GDP for 2010–11 (BE) compared to 1.2 per cent of GDP in 2009–10 (BE).

The last two budgets of the union government have been relatively disappointing. With the economy creeping out of recession and the rising commodity prices, the government should have stepped up the budgetary priorities for rural employment and livelihood security in 2009–10 and 2010–11. Also, the wide gaps in the attainment of physical targets set forth in the 11th Five Year Plan, which is nearing its completion, required larger magnitudes of public expenditure in rural development as a whole. However, the union government seems to have grown complacent about the adequacy of its interventions in the rural areas. In the latest budget, the allocation for NREGS has been increased by only 2.5 per cent from ₹39,100 crore in 2009–10 (RE) to ₹40,100 in 2010–11 (BE). The Union Budget allocation for the Department of Rural Development (under the Ministry of Rural Development) has registered small increases from ₹56,884 crore in 2008–09 (RE) to ₹62,201 crore in 2009–10 (RE) and then to ₹66,138 crore in 2010–11 (BE). Thus, the growth in the total allocation for the Department of Rural Development has been only 9.3 per cent

in 2009–10 and an even smaller 6.3 per cent in 2010–11. Given the high rates of inflation in the recent years, what this implies is the budgetary support for rural development provided by the union government has declined real terms in 2009–10 and 2010–11, as compared to 2008–09. Given that more the 70 per cent of Indian population resides in the rural sector and depends largely on a shrinking agrarian economy, a wage-led and inclusive growth of the overall economy would require larger priorities to be awarded to rural employment and development in the upcoming Union Budgets and the Five Year Plans.

EMERGING CHALLENGES

The Price Rise: Plight of the *Aam Aadmi*

Inflation in India has, somewhat paradoxically one may say, been much more in the news since the onset of the global economic crisis, than was the case in the boom years before that. The Indian economy's growth slowed down in 2008–09 after a five year phase in which it stayed at unprecedented 8–9 per cent per annum levels. In 2008–09 however, inflation rates also picked up after having remained subdued for a number of years (see Table 2.7). The increase in the monthly average of the Wholesale Price Index (WPI) in that year was 8.39 per cent. This was the highest level of increase in the annual average WPI since 1994–95, and was considerably greater than the

Table 2.6 Financial and Physical Progress of SGSY

	2004–05	2005–06	2006–07	2007–08	2008–09
Funds Available (in ₹ crore)	1,509.85	1,558.52	1,724.55	2,394.16	2,981.24
Funds Utilised (in ₹ crore)	1,290.88	1,338.77	1,424.19	1,965.97	2,198.08
% Utilisation	85.5	85.9	82.6	82.1	73.7
% Credit Disbursed	–	–	79.86	73.73	85.07
Swarozgaris Assisted (in lakh)	11.15	11.51	16.9	16.99	18.25
% of SCs	31.62	33.28	35.48	33.02	31.9
% of STs	13.36	14.37	14.26	14.82	14.6
% of Women	54.32	57.58	73.71	63.79	64.45
% of Minorities	–	–	3.58	8.38	14.83

Source: Compiled by author from Outcome Budget (various issues), Department of Rural Development, GoI.

Table 2.7 Annual Average Inflation Rates Based on Different Price Indices (per cent per annum)

Year	Wholesale price index	Consumer price indices		
		Industrial workers	Urban non-manual employees	Agricultural labourers
2001–02	3.60	4.28	5.12	1.31
2002–03	3.41	4.10	3.85	3.24
2003–04	5.46	3.73	3.70	3.76
2004–05	6.42	4.00	3.81	2.72
2005–06	4.49	4.23	4.59	3.82
2006–07	5.42	6.78	6.58	7.65
2007–08	4.66	6.40	5.97	7.63
2008–09	8.39	9.02	8.93	10.02

Source: Economic Survey, Government of India.

annual increases between 2001–02 and 2007–08. A similar story exists with the corresponding inflation rates based on the Consumer Price Indices (CPIs). All the CPIs showed increases of 9–10 per cent in 2008–09. However, annual average inflation rates measured in terms of the CPIs had started nudging up even earlier, from 2006–07 onwards.

The movement of the inflation rates based on the WPI and the CPIs in 2009–10 were even more sharply different in 2009–10. In the April–February period of 2009–10, the increase in the average WPI was only 3.12 per cent compared to 9.09 per cent for the same period in 2008–09. If the price situation still remained in the headlines, it was because no such reversal happened in the case of the rate of increase of the CPIs. On the contrary, inflation rate based on CPIIW (Industrial Workers) went up from 9.2 per cent to 12.1 per cent between April–February 2008–09 and April–February 2009–10, while that based on CPIAL (Agricultural Labourers) went up from 10.3 per cent to 13.7 per cent. These differences in the trends in movement of the WPI and CPIs are primarily on account of divergent price trends in food and other prices. In the WPI itself, food price inflation showed acceleration between 2008–09 and 2009–10. However, the weight of food in the WPI is much lower than in the CPIs. The WPI, in fact, is dominated by non-food manufactured products. The prices of fuel, power, light, lubricants and non-food primary articles including minerals

exhibited a flat or negative trend (deceleration) between 2008–09 and 2009–10. This compensated for the increase in food prices to keep the overall inflation rate measured in terms of WPI low. However, such compensation was not of the same order in the case of the CPIs. This was not only because weight of food items was much greater in them, but also because retail prices rose faster than wholesale prices.

The difference in the movement of food prices and other prices comes out even more sharply if we look at monthly year-on-year inflation rates. As can be seen from Figure 2.7, the movement in the overall monthly WPI, more or less reflects the movements in prices of manufactured products. The inflation rates in the prices of manufactured products remained at somewhat low levels for many years. An upward movement that began in late 2007 was cut short by the global crisis. Almost coinciding with the collapse of Lehmann Brothers, the inflation rate for manufactured products dropped sharply and even turned negative by mid-2009. Though it has picked up since then, the rise is on the low base of the previous year. In other words, the combined effects of the recession induced demand slowdown and the stimulus measures (tax cuts) of the government in response to that ensured that prices of manufactured product remained steady. It is however quite a different story in case of food prices, particularly foodgrains.

Foodgrain inflation rates measured in terms of the WPI had been rising steadily since the last quarter of 2004. The rise in the inflation rate subsided somewhat in end 2006, though it remained high. After temporarily reaching low levels towards the end of 2007, food price inflation started rising again along with that of manufactured products. Unlike in the case of manufactured products however, this trend of rise in food price inflation rates was not interrupted by the global crisis. If anything, the rise became even sharper following the crisis and the food price inflation rate has remained at very high levels since then.

Clearly therefore, the principal element of concern in the contemporary Indian price situation relates to the trend in food prices, which affect the poor more than anybody else.

Figure 2.7   **Monthly Inflation Rates, Year-on-Year, Based on WPI (January 2002 to February 2010)**

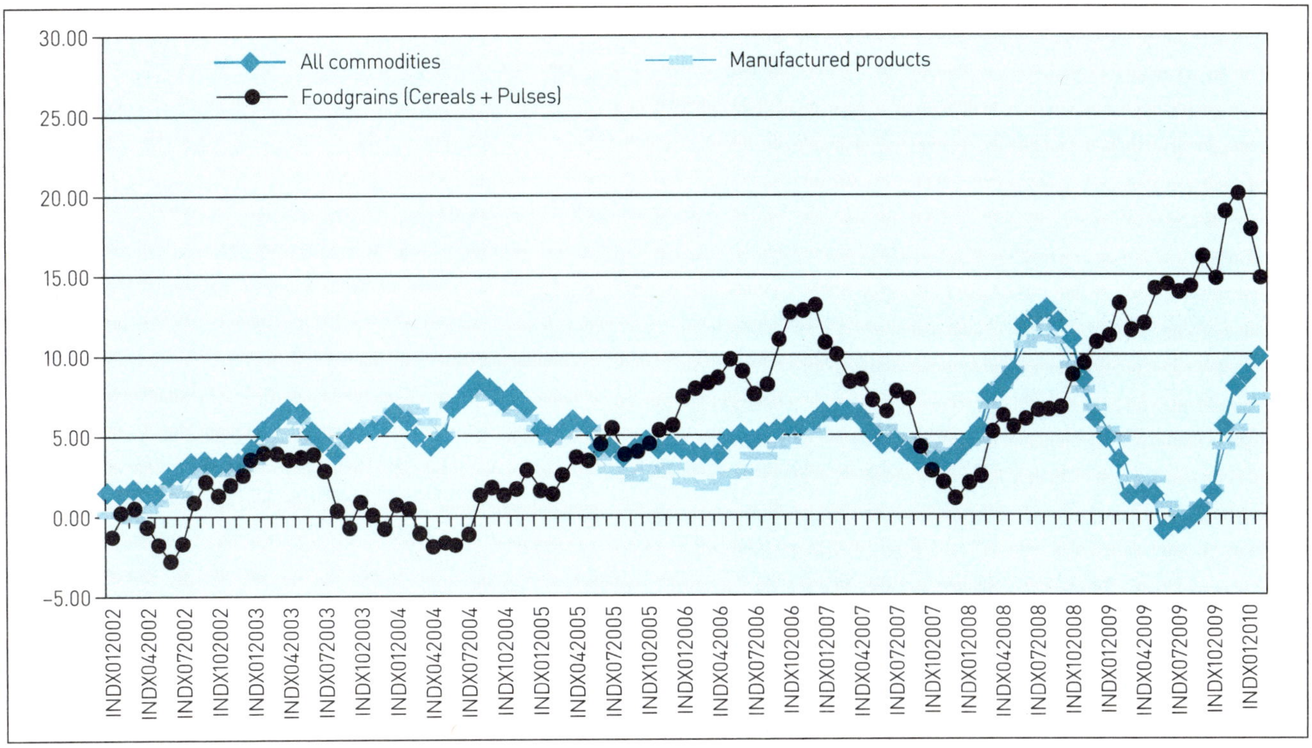

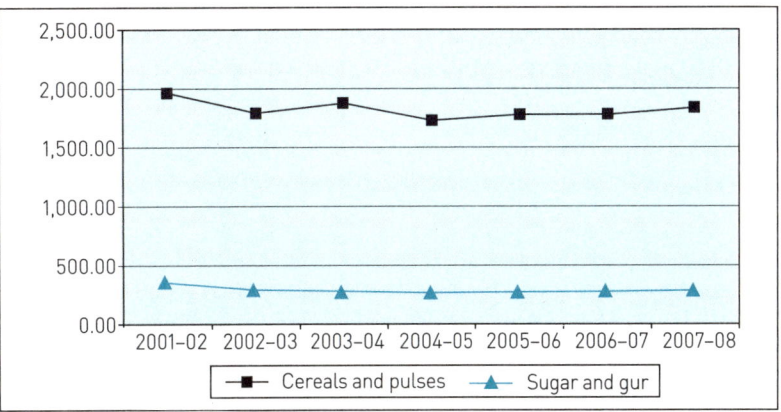

Source: Central Statistical Organisation.

In explaining the food price spike, the government is inclined to point towards temporary or short-term factors like the recent drought. The suggestion therefore, is that the price situation would automatically stabilise in time. This understanding however ignores the evidence which clearly indicates the existence of a systemic tendency for food prices to increase, with temporary factors inducing variations around that trend. If the real causes of food price inflation are to be understood, then the forces producing this systemic trend have to be identified. A demand-supply gap in food is clearly emerging. The peculiarity of this is that this is not because demand growth has been excessive in relation to supply growth, but because supply is tending to be inadequate even in relation to virtual stagnation in food demand.

Unlike what is believed by some, high growth in India has not led to galloping increases in food demand. In fact, even though overall real per capita expenditure on food has risen marginally, expenditure on basic food items has not increased at all despite the 6–7 per cent per annum rise in per capita income (see Figure 2.8). To put this level at which this expenditure has remained pegged in perspective, it may be noted that the average level of per capita expenditure on foodgrains in the boom years from 2004–08 was lower than in the first half of the 1960s (see Table 2.8). Net per capita availability of foodgrains during this period has also been lower than in the early 1960s.

Figure 2.8   Per Capita Consumption Expenditure on Selected Items at 1999–2000 Prices

Source: Central Statistical Organisation, National Accounts Statistics.

Table 2.8 Per Capita Availability of and Expenditure on Foodgrains

Period	Per capita net availability of foodgrains (Gram per day)	Period	Per capita annual expenditure on foodgrains at 1999–2000 prices (₹)
1961–65	461.1	1960–61 to 1964–65	1,893.49
2004–08	441.8	2003–04 to 2007–08	1,793.38

Source: Economic Survey and Central Statistical Organisation, National Accounts Statistics.

Box 2.6   Price Rise, Who Benefited?

The Wholesale Price Index (WPI) climbed to almost 20 per cent on 5 December 2009. However, the overall inflation fell across the year and even went negative during June. However, much need not be read into this paradox as food articles account for only 15.1 per cent weight in the computation of the WPI and can lead to misleading interpretations. Food prices were indeed on a record high in 2009 (they still are) and grew at the fastest pace in the last 11 years.

Prices of most agri-commodities have shot up. By December 2009, potato prices more than doubled from a year earlier, vegetable costs climbed more than 41 per cent, pulses were up by 40 per cent, while wheat gained 14 per cent. Clearly, such price rises are unprecedented. Also, such escalations could not have taken place overnight evading the government's notice.

It has been voiced in several quarters that the hike in MSP is a major reason for price rise. This is but partly true. Take the case of rice whose average retail price has risen from ₹16 to ₹23 per kg between 2007 and 2009. While every kilo of this rise in retail price is by ₹7, the MSP has gone up by ₹3. It is more or less the same for most commodities that witnessed significant hikes in MSP. Rather than a higher MSP and supply constrains, there are other factors that are playing a major role in the current range of prices.

Drought across half of the country followed by floods in several states is partly responsible for lower levels of production. This however ought not to have fuelled a crisis in food grain prices as buffer stocks levels are nearly double than what is the norm. Warnings on sugar prices were there for the government to act on for more than a year and a half. Potato prices, which doubled in 2009 over the preceding year, began to taper off by end of December owing to a record production which brought down the wholesale prices, but retail prices failed to abate. Retail prices of onions continued to rule high in December 2009, despite higher arrivals in markets and there were no shortages. The story is similar for most vegetables.

The fact remains that apart from a few commodities like sugar and pulses, there is no shortage of food in the country. Yet Food and Agriculture Minister, Sharad Pawar, has issued statements predicting shortage of commodities ranging from rice and sugar to milk over the last one year, which has fuelled speculations that India will import to meet the shortfall. International prices have immediately gone up and speculation by domestic players has contributed to domestic price rise.

Hoarding large quantities of commodities is rampant and has gone unchecked by the states. For instance, between January to October 2009, only 156 persons were detained for hoarding.

While food prices gallop, private companies selling agri-commodities and investors in such companies are reaping the benefit. As per a report by Ajay Modi published in the *Business Standard* on 21 December 2009, these companies have gained 150–340 per cent returns since April 2009 and have outperformed the broader market indices of stock exchanges. These companies and investors are the real gainers of the current price rise while farmers are merely the fringe beneficiaries. There are legal tools to regulate such profiteering but are not being employed by either the centre or the states.

Not only are the common citizens questioning the role of the government in fuelling price rise, the Comptroller and Auditor General (CAG) in December 2009, posed a question that the government has forever dodged that if there has been an unprecedented rise in retail food prices, why is it that the condition of farmers largely remains the same as before? To seek answers to this question, the CAG has decided to initiate a performance audit of the fertiliser subsidy regime and the Accelerated Irrigation Benefit Programme (AIBP) to ascertain whether farmers are actually benefiting or there are substantial leakages. In 2008–09, the Fertiliser Subsidy Bill was almost ₹1 lakh crore, while the allocation for AIBP stood at ₹20,000 crore. The CAG aims to table the audit report in the Parliament during the Budget Session.

Clearly therefore, the rising food prices are not due to the average Indian consuming more food as he/she is better off. On the contrary, food consumption levels have remained abysmally low. This is because the average Indian has been bypassed by the growth and only a small minority has experienced a rise in incomes. Rising food prices have reinforced this lack of inclusiveness in Indian growth. The real story of the tendency for food prices to rise therefore is on the supply side, with both production, as well as trade trends, contributing towards creating an adverse availability situation.

If we look at per capita production of foodgrains, the startling fact is that the per capita net production of cereals in 2002 was higher than in every year since then. The 2002 level itself was lower than in 1991, and similar to that achieved in 1995. This indicates that growth of foodgrain production levels tend to remain behind the growth of population. The effects of this have been aggravated by the fact that instead of supplementing limited domestic production of foodgrains, the trade in foodgrains has tended to accentuate the limited availability. Since 1995, India has been consistently a net exporter of cereals. Between 2001 and 2008, some 60 million tonne of cereals have been exported from India. Partly, the negative effect of this on availability was for some time compensated by a de-cumulation of government stocks of foodgrains. As on 1 January 2002, over 580 lakh tonne were held as stocks of foodgrains in the central pool. By 1 January 2008, this was reduced to less than 192 lakh tonne, which was below the minimum buffer norms. A similar situation had existed in 2006 and 2007 too (see Table 2.9). This process however could not continue indefinitely, and in 2008, the year which saw a relatively better per capita production level, some 17 million tonne were added to foodstocks. This, along with a 14.4 million tonne level of exports, aggravated the availability situation which took a turn for the worse. The industrial agricultural performance of 2008–09 and 2009–10 came in this background and triggered the sharp rise in food prices.

Even though food price inflation has not been a persistent feature of the period since Indian

---

Box 2.7   Price Rise: Case of Sugar and Pulses

Sugar: Engineering a Shortage

Sugar breached the ₹50 per kilo mark in 2009–10 wholly because of a deliberate inaction on part of the centre. In 2007–08, despite protests by sugarcane farmers, the Statutory Minimum Price (SMP) was not hiked at par with competing crops like wheat. As a result, there was a wholesale switch by farmers over to other crops. So much so that sugarcane lost more than a million hectare to other crops. Yet, the centre ignored the warning signals.

The problem of an impending shortage of sugar was obvious in mid-2008 when both the acreage fell and a lower sugarcane output was expected. Yet, not only exports continued but the centre also offered sops for the same. Come 2009 and drought compounded the problem of cane growers in India. At the same time, the world's largest sugar producer, Brazil, experienced too much rain which decreased the sucrose content on the cane and thereby dampened sugar production. Naturally, speculators in international commodity markets could smell an opportunity in the tight sugar market and drove up the prices to an all-time high in the last three decades.

Steps taken by the centre to address shortage of supplies and spike in price have been half-hearted to say the least. Future trading in sugar, which was driving up domestic prices, was curbed as late as May 2009. This allowed sellers to make windfall profits while buyers remained short-changed and again, contributed to the price rise. It tightened rules for exports as late as January 2009, despite which in the first six months of the sugar season (October–September), around 1.3 lakh tonne of sugar was exported (in 2008, India exported around 50 lakh tonne). At the same time, during the sugar season of 2008–09, more than 25 lakh tonne was imported.

To boost supplies, it asked three state-run firms to import one million tonne of duty free sugar in April 2009 but it was too late and the international prices were on a boil. Due to this delay, these firms were able to contract barely 25,000–30,000 tonne at a high price and by mid-January 2010, sugar prices had spiked to such an extent that imports became viable, i.e., domestic prices were matching international prices. Likewise, the list of omissions by the centre on sugar supply and price control is long.

The centre did take a belated step in January 2010 and released more than 1.4 million tonne of sugar in the open market which should have been sufficient to meet the demand for the month and ought to have quelled the prices. However bulk purchases were made by confectionary and other sugar-using industries and as a result, precious little was left in the market for the masses.

As in the case of other commodities, the blame for rise in sugar prices is being laid on farmers, especially those in Uttar Pradesh who hit the roads agitating for better prices. Sugar mills in the state have hiked the rate from ₹210 to ₹235 for a quintal of cane, which is the highest in the country. However, there is a catch: every quintal of cane yields around 9–10 kg of sugar. Therefore, if the price of sugar goes up by ₹10, sugar mills stand to gain ₹90 while farmers gain a meagre ₹25.

Meanwhile, sugar traders were busy hoarding stocks in the absence of any punitive action by the state governments. Few states were an exception. In August 2009, raids spread across five days in Madhya Pradesh yielded 4,000 tonne of sugar and immediately brought down wholesale prices from ₹3,300 to ₹2,800 a quintal. Had more states pitched in to unearth such hoarding, it is possible that the supply gap would have been considerably bridged. It however, did not happen.

Pulses: Killing Domestic Production

India is the largest importer of pulses in the world. Dried and shelled peas, Black Gram (*Urad*), Green Gram (*Moong*), Pigeon Pea (*Arhar*) and Garbanzos (Chick Pea) form the bulk of pulses imported by India. Most of these are imported from developing countries like Myanmar, Tanzania, Mozambique and developed countries like Canada, USA and Australia.

Pulses are rainfed crops and therefore of importance to marginal and small farmers. However, unlike wheat and paddy, pulses do not enjoy captive marketing support of the government. As a result, both area under cultivation and the yield of pulses has been stagnant for the last two decades. On the other hand, demand for this rich source of vegetable protein has gone up and necessitates costly imports to bridge the gap.

Large and bulk imports generally also carry a hefty price tag and as a result, pulses are turning unaffordable for the malnourished poor and its per capita consumption is declining. Rising international prices have also affected the import of pulses, which was 2.57 million tonne in 2008–09, down from 2.95 million tonne in the previous year.

In August 2009, Prime Minister Manmohan Singh announced the setting up of a mission on pulses. This was preceded by another mission that was set up way back in the late 1980s by the then Prime Minister Rajiv Gandhi, which was discontinued before it could achieve anything. Instead of importing pulses at a higher price, all that the government needs to do is offer a better price to farmers and ensure that procurement is actually done. In its absence, nothing much can be expected from the current mission.

It comes as no surprise that is exactly what is happening. The MSP for pulses are nowhere near the market price. For instance, currently when prices of pulses have gone through the roof and the retail price of, say, Pigeon Pea (*Arhar*) is around ₹10,000 per quintal, the MSP stands at ₹2,000–2,300 a quintal. Farmers are therefore reluctant to grow pulses.

The Planning Commission has pitched in with the idea of forming growers' federation who will trade on commodity futures exchanges. This is clearly a blinkered approach that completely ignores the reasons why pulses' farmers are a dying breed. Moreover, pulses are in short supply and prices are high. Therefore, they ought not to be allowed to be traded in futures markets. As of now, *Urad* and *Arhar* are the only pulses that are banned for trading at this platform.

---

liberalisation began in the early 1990s, but it created the conditions for its growth. Food price inflation finds it roots in that economic strategy. Fiscal constraints inherent in the strategy have led to a persistent neglect of the agricultural sector which has been starved of expenditures needed to improve agricultural productivity. At the same time, liberalisation in the trade of agricultural products has exposed Indian agriculture to the volatility in international prices.

Table 2.9   **Net Production and Availability of Cereals**

Year	Population (millions)	Net production (million tonne)	Net imports (million tonne)	Change in government stocks (million tonne)	Net availability (million tonne)	Per capita per year	
						Net production (kg)	Net availaibility (kg)
	1	2	3	4	2 + 3 – 4		
2002	1,050.6	174.5	–8.5	(–)9.9	175.9	166.10	167.43
2003	1,068.2	143.2	–7.1	(–)23.2	159.3	134.06	149.13
2004	1,085.6	173.5	–7.7	(–)3.3	169.1	159.82	155.77
2005	1,102.8	162.1	–7.2	(–)2.4	157.3	146.99	142.64
2006	1,119.8	170.8	–3.8	(–)1.8	168.8	152.53	150.74
2007	1,136.6	177.7	–7	(+)1.7	169	156.34	148.69
2008P	1,153.1	189	–14.4	(+)17	157.6	163.91	136.68

Source: Economic Survey.

One of the key consequences of these has been a deceleration in food production growth compared to the pre-liberalisation period. If this did not initially lead to a rapid rise in food prices, it was only because liberalisation also led to depressed incomes of the vast majority, particularly in rural India. The demand for food also consequently remained depressed. However, the declining trend in per capita production has now carried the situation to a point where even with low demand levels, production levels are inadequate. The problem of food production not keeping pace with the population growth is however not just an Indian, but also a global phenomenon. Global food prices are also therefore prone to sharp increases. The problem is compounded by the increasing role of speculative finance in global commodity markets. These have reduced the ability to check food price inflation through imports. Instead, given the large weight of the Indian economy in the global consumption of many commodities, domestic shortfalls in India tend to often get factored in by global commodity markets, leading to increases in global prices at the same time as India faces shortages. On the other side, high global food prices often aggravate domestic shortfalls by inducing exports from India. Trade channels, rather than checking food inflation, thus tend to work in the direction of transmitting global food inflation to India. Unless these structural features of India's food economy are addressed, the risk of food price inflation will remain a persistent one. The only way such inflation can be avoided is if India's economy moves towards a further squeezing of the already low food consumption levels of the *aam aadmi*, a direction which would be exactly the opposite of what is needed.

Climate Change: Challenges, Opportunities and Responses

There is a global consensus that climate change is happening. The earth's atmosphere acts like the glass in a greenhouse, allowing much of the sun's solar radiation to travel through unimpeded, but trapping a lot of the reflected heat trying to escape back to space. This process raises the temperature in the atmosphere just as it does in a greenhouse. Since industrialisation began, emissions of 'greenhouse gases' (GHGs), in particular, carbon dioxide, have significantly increased, primarily due to increased burning of fossil fuels, leading to the heating up of the globe. Average global temperatures today are 0.8° Celsius above pre-industrial levels and are further rising under the impact of human activity.

The core manifestations of climate change are gradual change in mean climate conditions (temperature and precipitation), increased seasonal and inter-annual variations (erratic rainfall and increasing temperature), frequent and intense extreme events (draughts, floods, and storms) and catastrophic transformations of ecosystems (sea level rise and water table changes). These will lead to greater exposure and sensitivity of poor through increase in environmental risks, reduction in livelihood opportunities, and thus, greater stress on existing social (and economic) institutions. Climate change is expected to widen up the 'inequality' between poor and rich, by doing 'injustice' to the poor, and thus, is expected to add to their vulnerability.

The adverse impacts of climate will be more striking in developing countries due to their geographic and climatic conditions, dependence on natural resources and limited capacity to adapt to the changing climate. Most serious impacts will fall on the poorest countries, while parts of the developed world may gain from climate change. There is a basic injustice in distribution of climate change impacts, that is, who will suffer worst and first. Climate change will have worst impacts on the poor, who have contributed the least to it and they will suffer first. It imposes a 'regressive tax' on the poor, where they pay for the deeds of rich. Climate change has a compounding effect on vulnerability; it will burden especially those populations who are already vulnerable by hampering their capability to adapt. The poor are most vulnerable to climate change impacts due to their geographic location (in developing countries), dependence on nature and low economic capacity (restricting adaptation). Climate change impacts will exacerbate the vulnerability of poor by deteriorating the ecological, as well as the socio-political-economic context they live in. On the other hand, it will push many people living at subsistence level to the poverty trap and thus, will make them vulnerable to future natural hazards.

Growing Climate Threats in India

The impact of climate change is already visible in India and it is affecting the economic performance of the country and the lives and livelihoods of the 836 million poor (77 per cent of country's population) that subsists on ₹20 a day or less. In last few years, frequent and intense disasters have caused severe damage to our agrarian economy, depleted natural resources, increased pressure on infrastructure, continued trends of decreasing country's GDP

and mounted pressure on the already vulnerable livelihoods of marginal and small entrepreneurs. Floods in Mumbai, cyclone in various parts, persistent droughts conditions in all agroecological regions are few indicators towards factors that increase vulnerability of already stressed poor population.

India continues to face fundamental constraints in its progress towards sustainable development, including inequitable economic growth, persistently low levels of human development; low status for women, the exclusion of majority of the population from decision-making and access to basic services, unabated environmental degradation, and failure of institutions to sufficiently integrate environmental and social development considerations into economic policy objectives. All these factors jointly complicate the overall national development. Added to this, climate change pressures on available resources, further nullify the outcome of the efforts being made for the social upliftment of certain sections of the society and poverty eradication amongst the rural poor. Climate change is hampering the achievement of many of the Millennium Development Goals (MDGs), including those on poverty eradication, child mortality, malaria and other diseases, and environmental sustainability; much of this damage would come in the form of severe economic shocks. In addition, the impacts of climate change will exacerbate existing social and environmental problems and lead to migration within and across national borders. Despite economic reforms and developments in environmental institutions, states will again be plagued by huge problems that have lead to a manifold increase the vulnerability of poor people towards any unprecedented disasters bringing cumulative impacts in terms of livelihoods, food, income and energy.

Though it is not a problem of India's making, yet the country is rapidly becoming one of global warming's victims. The Indian government estimates that dealing with the consequences of global warming is already costing the country more than 2 per cent of its GNP each year. According to the 2007 Pew Global Attitudes survey, 57 per cent of those polled in India said that global warming was a very

> **Box 2.8   Impacts of Climate Change: Insights from Panna District, Madhya Pradesh**
>
> Impacts of climate change are clearly visible and have been affecting livelihood in the district. The major visible impacts are:
>
> - Change in precipitation pattern: Not only the level of rain fall has declined over the period of last one decade, but also it has become irregular and erratic.
> - Change in pattern of cropping and reduction in yield: Due to erratic monsoon and depleting water level, there is forced change in cropping pattern and yield has also reduced.
> - Diversification in job and business: Reduced yield and income from farming has forced the local people to look for alternative source of income.
> - Climate change has also affected natural resource dependent livelihood.
> - There is visible decline in domestic animals in the villages and wild animals in forest.
> - As result of decline in farm income, most of the farmers are dragged into debt trap. Small farmers are forced to borrow from local money lenders at a very high rate of interest. At the same time, many of the farmers are migrating to urban areas to search for income.
>
> **Source:** Samarthan.

serious national problem. Only 47 per cent of Americans were that concerned. Climate experts think that the mean annual temperature in India could rise by as much as 2.7° F by the 2020s and by 8.1° F by the 2080s. This warming will vary widely depending on the season and region of the country. Hotter days will affect rainfall patterns. Central India, which is already arid, may see as much as 25 per cent less precipitation, but as much as 15 per cent more rain may fall during the intense monsoon periods. Lacking adequate reservoirs, many parts of the country may not be able to trap this runoff for use in drier months. The Tibetan glaciers act as a natural water preserve for the Indian subcontinent. Glacier melting, however, threatens to turn the Ganges, Indus and Brahmaputra rivers that crisscross northern India into seasonal waterways, adversely affecting agriculture, commerce and daily life. More erratic rainfall patterns and the periodic drying up of rivers will only aggravate current shortages caused by falling water tables. Thanks to over pumping to irrigate cropland, the World Bank estimates that three in five Indian aquifers could be critically short of water in less than a generation.

This double hit, i.e., climate change plus water shortages could undermine India's ability to feed itself. The greater the rise in future temperatures, the worse the future harvests. Between 2003 and the 2080s, agricultural output could fall by nearly 29 per cent, according to

William Cline, a senior fellow at the Centre for Global Development. If harvests fail, rural India will be hit hardest because that is where most of the country's poor live. A temperature rise of 6.3 degrees could cause a 25 per cent drop in net farm incomes, according to a modelling by the United Nations Development Program. At the same time, India's densely populated, low-lying coastal areas may be particularly vulnerable to the effects of climate change. A study by the Confederation of Indian Industry estimates that as many as one in four Indians may be exposed to increased risk of cyclones and floods, and one in five people living along the coastline may eventually be forced to migrate.

Country's Economic Imperatives of Energy Security for Sustainable Development

India faces formidable challenges in meeting its energy needs and providing adequate energy of desired quality in various forms to users in a sustainable manner and at reasonable costs. To deliver a sustained growth of 8 per cent through 2031, India would, in the very least, need to expand its primary energy supply by 3 to 4 times and electricity supply by 5 to 7 times the consumption today. Along with quantity, the quality of energy supply will also have to improve. The energy challenge is of fundamental importance to India's economic growth imperatives.

Efficient and reliable energy supply is critical for economic growth. The availability of conventional energy sources is limited and may not be sufficient in the long run to sustain the process of economic development. Further, the base of the country's energy supply system has steadily shifted from renewable to non-renewable sources. India meets about 30 per cent of its energy needs through imports. With the increasing share of fossil fuels in the energy supply/use, the share of imported energy may go up further. Development of newer energy sources thus gains importance. The challenge is to ensure adequate supply of energy at the least possible cost.

It is in India's interest to tap its renewable energy potential in order to achieve the most sought Energy Security Objective. The transition to green energy will also bring in economic benefits while playing an active role in mitigating the source of climate change. The potential is huge, and will ensure self-sufficiency in long run. India is endowed with abundant renewable energy sources, namely solar, wind and biomass and is ranked fourth globally in the generation of wind energy. India's installed wind power capacity was 6,315 MW in January 2007. Solar photovoltaic (PV) systems have emerged as useful power sources for decentralised applications such as lighting, water-pumping and telecommunications. The country has significant potential for ocean thermal, sea wave power and tidal power, which, however, have not yet been significantly utilised. Decentralised biomass-based power plants are a useful option where it is either too costly to extend the grid or the power demand is very low. Major biomass sources are crop residues and by-products of agro-processing industries.

Common but Differentiated Responsibilities and Respective Capability

The new science also shows that with any delay in action, the costs of mitigation and adaptation increases significantly. Delaying significant

---

Box 2.9   India in Copenhagen Summit

The world needed a climate treaty from the Copenhagen summit. All it got was an accord. There was no hiding the disappointment. The deal that emerged after more than a year of pre-summit negotiations and two weeks of face-to-face talks was merely, in Gordon Brown's terms, 'a first step'. According to Barack Obama, it was 'meaningful'. Given the scientific case for urgent action to mitigate the impact of manmade climate 'change, it was reasonable to expect something more substantial. But compromise is not the same as failure. Disappointment should not lead to despair.

So what is the significance of the accord?

It underlines consensus among world leaders that global average temperatures must not be allowed to rise beyond 2°C. It affirms that, to achieve such a target, there must be substantial cuts in carbon emissions and that the mechanism for achieving such cuts should not hamper economic progress in the developing world. In more specific terms, the deal includes the first formal financial commitment by richer nations to help poorer ones adapt to the threat of climate change. It establishes a fund with an initial annual outlay of USD 30 billion, rising to USD 100 billion by 2020. The accord also commits signatories to adopt, within six weeks, binding emissions targets, also for 2020.

But much of the text reads like the preamble to the treaty that was supposed to be agreed in Copenhagen, but was not. There is no headline global target for emissions cuts. National targets must be taken on trust. There are no incentives for countries to pollute less and no sanctions on those that pollute more. Many commitments are to be enacted 'as soon as possible'—not a phrase with much authority in international law. These gaps indicate more a failure of process than ambition.

India's Position

Prime Minister of India has unilaterally declared cut in carbon emission by 20 to 25 per cent. However, India has not claimed anything in return from the developed countries. It is to be noted that per capita carbon emission of India is much lesser than the United States of America and other industrialised countries. The declaration has brought large scale debate with in India. Jairam Ramesh, the Minister concerned, is questioned in the Rajya Sabha by the entire opposition. India always likes to occupy the high moral ground when it comes to multilateral agreements like the nuclear non-proliferation treaty, global trade talks and so on. But in the recent build-up to and during the Copenhagen summit, it abandoned any such pretence. It is making a point, as it always does, of safeguarding the country's interests, but two questions remain.

First, since when did India's interests diverge from those of other developing countries, the G77 group of 130 nations, as Environment Minister Jairam Ramesh is now explicitly stating? He has gone further to assert that India was not in Copenhagen to save the world or humanity. If India's interests coincide with those of the US, which orchestrated the suspect Copenhagen accord, or the recently cobbled together BASIC coalition (of 'the willing') consisting of Brazil, south Africa and China as well, all of whom comprise the biggest emitters of greenhouses gases in absolute terms, this is a drastic change in India's foreign policy, let alone environmental policy.

Second, and perhaps more insidiously, did Ramesh in his justification in the Rajya Sabha actually imply that India no longer cares for the 600 million nationals who have to make do without any commercial energy whatsoever, as well as 300 million of these who do not have access to electricity? This is the only inference one can draw from his statements: it means that the government is aligning itself with the well to do of the world.

To recap, India's interests are very much in line with what our negotiators—Saran and the former Environment Secretary made no secret of their antipathy to Ramesh's misguided moves—have been saying ad nauseam, over the past two years, from UN conferences at Bali to Bonn and Bangkok. Industrial countries must first commit to making 'ambitious' cuts in their emissions, failure to do so attracting penalties, as the Kyoto Protocol prescribes. This explains President Obama's allergy to the very mention of Kyoto. They must also commit funds and technologies to help developing countries adapt to climate change, for which the latter is not in any way responsible.

The Copenhagen 'accord' is a cop-out because it is not binding and does not address a single of these issues. Even the offer of USD 10 billion a year to developing countries from 2010 for three years and a USD 100 billion a fund from 2020 begs the question: what funding will be available between 2013 and 2020?

The harsh truth is that climate change is already upon us and cannot wait for industrial and other big emitters to safeguard their interests, leaving the poor in big countries, along with the most vulnerable in sub-Saharan Africa and small islands, to sink or be caught in the vice-like grip of perennial drought. Industrial countries have so far only pledged to cut their emissions by an average of 17 per cent by 2020—the US, a measly 4 per cent measured like the rest on 1990 levels—whereas the science insists that cuts of 40–45 per cent are required.

Source: Various.

actions by even 5–10 years undermines our ability to stay well below 2°C and severely undermines the effectiveness of long-term adaptive action. Further, addressing climate change in an inadequate or unfair way may also cause severe challenges to the poor and vulnerable communities. Efforts to address climate change must adequately reflect the right to sustainable development and also the principles of historical responsibility and common but differentiated responsibilities and capabilities as enshrined in the UN Framework Convention on Climate Change. Mindful of these principles, all countries must play a part in the global effort, with the developed countries taking the lead in combating climate change whilst economic and social development, and poverty eradication remain legitimate priorities of developing countries.

Consequently, a future climate agreement must be guided by the principles such as consistency, with a climate trajectory that gives us a high probability of keeping global warming well below the dangerous level of 2°C at least. Greenhouse gas concentrations would need to be reduced ultimately to 350 ppm CO_2, in the 22nd century. Global emissions must peak within the 2013–17 commitment period and rapidly decline to at least 80 per cent below 1990 levels by 2050. Regular scientific reviews, timed with IPCC reports, can trigger a process to strengthen reduction targets based on new scientific findings. The responsibility for such reductions should be shared equitably by developed and developing countries.

Considering the average temperature goal and the atmospheric CO_2 concentration, developed countries need to adopt an aggregate reduction target of more than 40 per cent below 1990 by the year 2020. National targets need to be driven from the aggregate target using objective criteria to measure historic and present, responsibility and capability. The calculations of national targets, ensuring that the mitigation effort is shared fairly amongst developed countrie , should include all developed countries, including the United States which has not ratified the Kyoto Protocol. The developed countries need to make efforts to meet the large majority of their national emission reduction targets domestically, with limited flexibility to, through offsets, or credits from, developing countries. A dual target system, delineating clearly between a country's domestic and international mitigation commitments, can create a clearer, more robust, and fairer system for international effort sharing. As long as developed countries fall short of ensuring that domestic emissions are reduced by at least 30 per cent below 1990 levels by 2020, there is no room, or indeed need, for offsets.

Though, it is acknowledged that the developed countries have drawn too heavily on a shared atmospheric resource, giving rise to the majority of current levels of global warming and significant future warming, developing countries must also now develop under the twin burden of mitigating and adapting to climate change. The developing countries need to pitch in their fair share to address the global challenge through domestic action, with highly advantageous co-benefits. Developing countries need to put in place plans and actions to achieve their sustainable development objectives, while at the same time also achieving a substantial deviation of their emission trajectory below the business-as-usual growth trajectory, supported by financing, technology, and capacity from developed countries. These actions must be developed at the national level, with implementation supported by positive incentives. These action plans will outline Nationally Appropriate Mitigation Actions (NAMAs) that are integrated and consistent with their wider sustainable development strategies. The aim is to set a clear long-term vision for national development in a low carbon world and to facilitate the policies and measures needed to implement this vision. This overarching vision, placing NAMAs in the context of sustainable development, could be materialised through the development of NAMA plans. NAMA plans should include the top emitting sectors and be informed by technology needs assessments.

Climate 'Responsible' India: A Drive towards Clean Energy

Acknowledging its responsibilities, most of the key developing countries have announced voluntary reductions of energy or carbon intensity in coming years supporting the effort to achieve the globally accepted average temperature goal of 2° C. Like other key developing countries, Brazil, South Africa, China, of the BASIC group, India committed to reduce the emissions intensity of its GDP to 20–25 per cent below the 2005 level by 2020. Such mitigation however, will not apply to the agriculture sector. In other words, for every unit of GDP recorded, Indian economy will target to spew 25 per cent less greenhouse gases. This indicates that though climate change has been country's priority for last few years, an active engagement has been observed on the global problem in the national policy agenda only recently.

The issues were publicly debated in the Indian parliament and the Indian Prime Minister has subsequently set up a council on climate change in which prominent experts from various ministries and external experts, such as, Nitin Desai, one of the authors of the Brundtland report and the General Secretary at the WSSD in Johannesburg, Dr R.K. Pachauri (Executive Director TERI and Chairman IPCC) and Sunita Narain (Director, Center for Science and Environment), are members. The Indian government has also engaged other ministries like the Ministry of External Affairs for all diplomacy, Ministry of Science and Technology for research and development and the Planning Commission to integrate climate change actions in future national plans, with regard to the decision-making processes related to climate change action. The highest decision-making body is the Prime Minister with total coordination and representation through his Special Envoy on Climate Change (SEPM), Mr Shyam Saran, who is a former Foreign Secretary and a seasoned diplomat. The composition of institutional structure in India on addressing climate change reflects the seriousness of Indian government. In 2008, PM's Council on Climate Change drafted 'National Action Plan on Climate Change' that clearly outlines the vision of addressing climate change through various measure that will increase emphasis on mitigation and adaptation in key sectors like energy, transport, agriculture, water, forests, and so on.

Prime Minister Manmohan Singh argues that the industrial nations, which together account for more than half of the cumulative CO_2 emissions in the past century, should act first, not India alone, which produces mere 2 per cent of atmospheric greenhouse gases. He couches his argument in a call for 'climate justice'. In addition, the Indian government contends that rich countries should provide India with the technology it requires to curb emissions. On equity grounds, the Indian argument can be hardly disputed. The west has been belching CO_2 into the atmosphere since the 19th century. However, one must consider the science here. Every additional tonne of carbon warms the atmosphere, whether it was released in Pittsburgh decades ago or in Mumbai last month. Forestalling global climate change can be achieved only by capping total emissions from all sources, not by finger-pointing.

When it comes to climate change, China, Europe and the United States have attracted the public's attention of late. India's emissions, however, are growing at a faster pace than almost any other major countries. At the United Nations' December 2009 international climate change conference in Copenhagen, that was intended to create a regime for controlling greenhouse gases, India, along with other BASIC countries, faced a new pressure to do its part to combat global warming.

Home Work: In Process through Domestic Actions

Though unsustainable consumption patterns of the rich industrialised nations are responsible for the threat of climate change, only 25 per cent of the global population lives in these countries. Yet, they emit more than 70 per cent of the total global CO_2 emissions and consume 75 to 80 per cent of many of the other resources of the world. In per capita terms, the disparities are also large. While an Indian citizen emits less than 2 tonnes of carbon per year, a citizen of USA emits more than 20 tonnes. Despite the nation's relative poverty, the mushrooming Indian economy is already changing the climate. India has passed Japan to become the world's fourth-largest emitter of CO_2, the principal greenhouse gas that most scientists now think, is trapping the earth's heat in the atmosphere. By 2015, India will surpass Russia to become the third-largest source of CO_2 emissions, trailing only China and the United States. 'India is on an unsustainable energy path', the International Energy Agency's 2007 World Energy Outlook concluded.

India has proceeded rapidly and is detailing its comprehensive National Action Plan on domestic measures to curb its GHG emissions as a home work and is following up by outlining various 'Mission' documents by its ministries which will be implemented as India's domestic climate legislation in the future. Yet, India's domestic climate policies are driven more by adaptation imperatives and less by mitigation efforts. India, in alignment with G77 and China position, expects the developed world to agree to a 40 per cent reduction in GHG emissions from 1990 levels by 2020, so that developing countries get the appropriate atmospheric space required to develop. Furthermore, technological and financial support for its own mitigation

and adaptation efforts is a must to cope with the scope of challenges that the country is facing with regard to global warming (see Table 2.10).

India has proposed to establish eight separate missions to deal with climate change. First among them, the solar mission is already launched with an ambitious target. Other missions have been approved by the cabinet and draft mission documents are prepared for most of the missions and are under consultation. In addition to the Missions, the actions on climate change are being steered by Prime Minister's Office (PMO) through its council that will ensure wider engagement and highest political attention. It is expected that soon the crucial Mission documents will be released by PMO that will adequately reflect the high level of ambitiousness of Indian government in combating climate change. However, it is not yet clear whether the Indian negotiators will use these missions and offer them as the deviations that India is willing to bring in its projected GHG

Table 2.10 **National Action Plan on Climate Change**

Missions	Objectives of Mission	Ministry Concerned	Status
National Solar Mission	20,000 MW of solar power by 2020	Ministry of Non-Renewable Energy Source	Jawaharlal Nehru National Solar Mission launched in November 2009
National Mission for Enhanced Energy Efficiency	10,000 MW of energy saving through energy efficiency by 2020	Ministry of Power	Mission yet to be launched Prime Minister has approved the mission and Consultation is being sought on the draft plan for the initiative
National Mission for Sustainable Habitat	Energy efficiency in residential and commercial buildings, public transport, solid waste management	Ministry of Urban Development	Mission yet to be launched Mission approved and draft plan prepared
National Water Mission	Water conservation, river basin management	Ministry of Water Resources	Mission yet to be launched Draft plan prepared and under consultation
National Mission for Sustaining the Himalayan Ecosystem	Conservation and adaptation practices, glacial monitoring	Ministry of Science and Technology	Mission yet to be launched Mission approved and draft plan prepared
National Mission for a Green India	6 million hectares of afforestation over degraded forest lands by the end of 12th plan	Ministry of Environment and Forests	Mission yet to be launched Mission approved and draft plan prepared Under consultation
National Mission for Sustainable Agriculture	Drought proofing, risk management, agriculture research	Ministry of Agriculture	Mission yet to be launched
National Mission on Strategic Knowledge for Climate Change	Vulnerability assessment, research and observation, data management	Ministry of Science & Technology	Mission yet to be launched

Source: *National Action Plan on Climate Change*, Government of India.

growth trajectories in Copenhagen. Though there are no official goals of GHG reduction laid down by India so far, the numbers may be tabled formally very soon after other missions are launched. The Minister of Environment and Forests has already claimed that India will build a mandatory fuel efficiency standard by law by 2011. Furthermore, it is aspired that 20 per cent of its electricity will be supplied by renewable energy by 2020. India also aims to reduce its energy intensity by 15 to 20 per cent within the next 20 years and increase the area under forest or tree cover by 15 per cent for GHS sequestration. This, in total, will result in more than a 9 per cent deviation compare to the business-as-usual scenario as calculated by a few NGOs in India.

Adaptation is priority for 500 million vulnerable people living in drought or flood prone areas. Still due to international pressure, most of the policy-making capital and negotiations are being spent on evolving actions to mitigate emissions from sectors like small and medium enterprises where technology cooperation holds the key. India does not have any firm position on adaptation so far and has failed to represent the most vulnerable communities, already facing the wrath of climate induced disasters. In the field of adaptation, India needs serious action aimed towards afforestation, drought proofing, flood protection and the need to protect coastal areas and glaciers that feed India's river systems.

Recommendations: Climate Policy Framework for Policy-makers

- The policy-makers need to mainstream climate actions in development initiatives rather then re-inventing the wheel.
- Make a detailed assessment of energy efficiency potentials at state level supporting efforts of central government in the country.
- Incentivise renewable energy entrepreneurs through tax holidays, subsidies, enabling market conditions, soft loans from financial institutions, and so on.
- To integrate climate risk management in existing national development plans and processes should be the main approach for adaptation.

Funding mechanisms to be developed under the post-2012 agreement should prioritise this approach over 'stand alone' funding and projects.

- Prepare State Adaptation Action Plans and engage impacted communities and civil societies in its formulation and implementation.
- Sensitise the State Planning Commission and establish a multi-donor coordinating committee to facilitate climate actions on mitigation and adaptation.
- While accessing funds, it is necessary to ensure that the most vulnerable communities are at the centre of and benefit from their adaptation policies, and that these policies reflect the needs and interests of both women and men. This is a key part of fulfilling commitments they have made to secure basic human rights of their citizens, such as the rights to food, health, water and shelter.
- Effective Disaster Risk Reduction should remain based on local knowledge, and build upon local level participatory analysis of vulnerabilities and capacities, but scientific climate information should be brought to the service of communities, in an accessible form, to inform their analysis and support the identification of sustainable solutions.

ACCOUNTABILITY AND TRANSPARENCY

Right to Information[27]

In about four-and-a-half years of its working, the Right to Information (RTI) Act 2005, has fundamentally changed the power equation between the government and the governed, between those who wield power of the state in any form on the one hand, and millions of those who are affected by the decisions and working of the state machinery on the other. Thanks to the RTI Act, in India, the 'Public Servants' are finally being forced to recognise their real master, the common people. No other law on India's book of statutes gives citizens so much power, so simply, to question any public authority in the country.

Across the country, a growing number of people are using RTI applications as a weapon to fight corruption and demand their rights. RTI is enabling people to say no to bribes. RTI has been used to bring about policy changes, as well as to feed hungry mouths. It is an all encompassing Act with consequences that have prompted some to say that it is the most important legislation since independence.

Despite the power of RTI to transform Indian democracy, the Act faces stiff opposition from many sections of the government, particularly the bureaucracy. For example, many officers are not performing satisfactorily. Some Information Commissioners, who are the final adjudicating authority under the Act, are perceived to be sympathetic to bureaucrats.

Sword of Amendment

Government has been systematically trying to dilute the Act since its inception. It is learnt from media sources that the Prime Minister is himself keen to amend the RTI Act and he is trying to convince the UPA Chairperson Smt. Sonia Gandhi in order to do this. If this Act is amended, it would be a major setback for the whole struggle to make the governance transparent and accountable to the people. The possibility of such an amendment is yet to be decided and public of this country does not have any option other than wait and watch; but during this year, the functioning of Information Commissioning emerged as the biggest roadblock in making the system transparent.

Government's Attitude: Denial of Information

The RTI Act provides a list of items in section 8 on which information should not be provided. In addition to the grounds mentioned in section 8, the following also emerged as important reasons for rejection.

Definition of Information

If the information sought does not fall within the definition of 'information' under the RTI Act, it can be rejected. This seems to be becoming a major cause for denial of cases.

Interestingly, different practices are being followed by different commissioners within the same commission. While Mr Shailesh Gandhi, Mr A.N. Tiwari and Mr M.M. Ansari of CIC rejected large number of cases on this ground, Mr Wajahat Habibullah and Mr O.P. Kejariwal from the same commission have allowed information and have denied very few cases on these grounds. Mr R.N. Das of Gujarat and Mr Vijay Kuvalekar of Maharashtra have not only entertained such requests for information and ensured that information is provided, but have also gone out of their way to get the grievances redressed. Mr M.M. Ansari rejected 134 cases on this ground, almost 8 per cent of the total cases decided by him. However, he has allowed information in some such cases by resorting to section 4(1)(d).

Missing Records

Many PIOs report 'missing records', 'records lost', and 'not traceable' as reasons for denying information. This trend seems to be on the rise, depending upon the response of Information Commissioners to such pleas.

Voluminous Information

PIOs have been rejecting applications on the ground that the information sought is voluminous. The RTI Act however, does not allow such rejection, and the Kerala High Court has clearly said in a judgement (*Canara Bank v. CIC*) that the RTI Act does not talk of 'voluminous information'. If the appellant is prepared to pay fee for information, he/she should be provided the same.

Pending Investigations

Many PIOs have refused to provide information on the ground that the investigation is pending. However, the Delhi High Court has clearly said in the case of *Bhagat Singh v. Income Tax Department*, that mere pendency of a case is not sufficient for denial of information. The public authority would need to establish how the disclosure of that information would impede investigations.

Box 2.10 Information Commissioners: The Biggest Roadblock

Public Cause Research Foundation (PCRF), set up by well known social activist Arvind Kejriwal, has studied the functioning of Information Commissions. This study was conducted to award the better performing Information Commission. For this purpose, the performance of each commissioner was studied in great detail. The study reveals a highly uneven implementation of RTI Act across the country. It also highlights best practices, which some commissioners may like to emulate.

For the purpose of this study, orders passed in 51,128 cases during 2008 by 72 Information Commissioners and 14 combined benches from 25 Information Commissions (barring Uttar Pradesh, Tamil Nadu and Sikkim) were analysed. It was found that in 35,930 cases (i.e., 68 per cent), orders were passed in favour of disclosure. Letters were written to these 35,930 appellants. Many of them were interviewed on phone. All of them were asked whether they did finally get the information after approaching the information commission. 8,400 appellants gave feedback and shared their experiences. The following are observations from some of the crucial issues in this regard.

1. *Orders in Favour of Disclosures*: Nationally, for every 100 appeals and complaints filed in Information Commissions, orders in favour of disclosure were passed in 68 cases. Information was denied in 22 per cent cases and 10 per cent cases were remanded back.
2. *Compliance of Orders*: A favourable order from the Information Commissioner does not necessarily translate into information. Nationally, only 38 per cent of the pro-disclosure orders were implemented. In the remaining 62 per cent cases, the people did not get information despite a favourable order.
3. *Non-compliance*: Many commissioners close a case after passing orders in favour of disclosure but without ensuring compliance thereof. The appellant has to often struggle with the public authority for a few months to get the order implemented. After writing several letters and making several visits to the public authority, if the order is still not complied with, he/she makes a complaint to the commission.
4. *Continuing Mandamus*: Some states follow the practice of 'continuing mandamus'. They do not close a case after passing orders but hold hearings subsequently for compliance thereof. Thus, the case is not closed till the appellant reports satisfaction. However, the problem with most of them is that barring a few, they are quite soft with officers. Repeated non-compliance is ignored. As a result, in some cases, several hearings take place spanning over several months, which leads to attrition and tires out appellants. When appellant stops coming, the cases are closed with the assumption that the appellant might have received all information. Therefore, continuing mandamus needs to be coupled with strict enforcement.
5. *Arrest Warrants*: Arunachal Pradesh is the first and the only information commission in the country to have issued bailable arrest warrants under section 18(3) of RTI Act for non-compliance of commission's orders. Non-compliance of their orders is treated as a complaint under section 18 of the RTI Act which empowers the commission to issue bailable arrest warrants and seek production of documents. Arunachal Pradesh has used this section quite effectively to get its orders implemented. Other commissions across the country may also like to invoke their powers under this section to improve compliance.
6. *Disposals*: Mr Vijay Baburao Borge and Mr Naveen Kumar have disposed the maximum number of cases, 383 and 333 per month respectively. However, they achieved this disposal by rejecting or remanding back almost 80 per cent of their cases without hearings. Mr Shailesh Gandhi stood out by disposing 270 cases per month in the first few months and more than 400 cases per month later. He could bring down his backlog from 12 months to less than 2 months. At the lower end are north eastern states, who disposed very few cases because they received few appeals. However, there are some commissioners who disposed very few cases despite many pending cases. Commissioners who disposed less than 10 cases per month despite huge pendencies are Mr Dileep Reddy of Andhra Pradesh, Mr Arun Kumar Bhattacharya of West Bengal, late Sh G.G. Kambli of Goa and Mr R.K. Angousana Singh of Manipur.
7. *Imposition of Penalties*: The RTI Act mandates that every violation of the Act 'shall' be penalised unless there was a reasonable cause on the part of the PIO. The penalty has to be deducted from the PIO's salary. However, just 2.4 per cent of the recorded violations across the country were penalised. In 74 per cent cases of recorded violations, the Hon'ble Information Commissioners did not even question the PIO whether there was a 'reasonable cause' or not. The PIOs were questioned in just 26 per cent cases through show cause notices. However, as many as 65 per cent of these show cause notices remained pending at the end of the year. 23 per cent notices were dropped because the commissioners found the explanations and excuses presented by PIOs in these cases as 'reasonable'.
8. *Withdrawal of Penalties*: Some commissioners withdrew penalties after imposing them. Mr B.K. Gohain of Assam imposed a penalty in just one case and subsequently withdrew it. Mr P.N. Narayanan of Bihar imposed penalties in 280 cases, but withdrew penalties in 244 of them (87 per cent). Dr Shakil Ahmed of Bihar imposed penalties in 65 cases but withdrew them in 28 (43 per cent).
9. *Pending Show-cause Notices*: Many commissioners issue show-cause notices but keep them pending and sometimes, no action is taken on them for years. Allegations were made by some people that this creates possibility for wrongdoing by staff as they could negotiate with guilty officers to misplace their files, and so on. While the possibility of this cannot be ruled out, one could not find any specific evidence of this. More than 70 per cent of the show-cause notices issued by the following commissioners remained pending at the end of the year (Table 2.11 does not include those commissioners who joined during the year and worked only for a few months or those who retired during the year).
10. *Pendencies*: Huge pendencies have become such a severe problem in some states that it takes more than a year for a case to come up for hearing if it were filed at the present date. Some urgent steps need to be taken to address mounting pendencies.
11. *State of Records*: In many commissions, the state of records is not very healthy. Many commissions did not even know for certain how many cases they have disposed. At different times, they gave different figures of disposals. Many commissions did not have copies of all orders. Uttar Pradesh claimed to have passed 22,658 orders during 2008. However, they said that they did not maintain copies of all orders. Tamil Nadu said that they had passed more than 40,000 orders but could only provide 900 orders.
12. *Missing Records*: The trend of PIOs reporting records to be missing or lost seems to be on the rise. In many cases, this is treated as a legitimate excuse for denial of information. However, in some parts of the country, when the commissioners threatened police action, suddenly records came out, which meant that 'missing records' was merely an excuse given by the PIOs to deny information.

Table 2.11 Disposals and Pendencies of Information Commissions

Commission	Total number of orders passed	Number of man months (based on number of ICs)	Number of orders per commission per month	Pendency of commission on 31 December 2008
Maharashtra	13,477	72	187	14,307
Bihar	5,951	34	175	4,884
Karnataka	6,041	36	168	4,887
Rajasthan	2,005	12	167	1,041
Gujarat	1,443	12	120	4,561
Central Information Commission	7,626	69	111	9,593
Chhattisgarh	1,272	14	91	984
Uttarakhand	1,048	12	87	0
Orissa	643	18	36	3,973
Andhra Pradesh	1,685	48	35	1,867
Punjab	3,207	96	33	0
Kerala	1,560	53	29	953
Madhya Pradesh	1,633	60	27	3,841
Haryana	1,586	68	23	409
Assam	230	12	19	42
Jharkhand	897	78	12	502
Himachal Pradesh	272	24	11	48
Goa	254	24	11	112
West Bengal	102	12	9	856
Tripura	88	12	7	13
Manipur	82	12	7	75
Meghalaya	52	12	4	5
Arunachal Pradesh	43	12	4	0
Nagaland	12	12	1	3
Mizoram	10	12	1	2

Source: PCRF Report.

CONCLUSION

The realities of the emerging patterns in the current public policy paradigm belie the objective of 'inclusive growth' and fail to address the issues of growth and equity. While the public expenditure in key social sectors are still largely insufficient, the flagship programmes themselves have not been able to fine tune themselves to the myriad of problems of implementation at the grassroots. A prudent fiscal policy and an effective administrative apparatus would facilitate in turning these flagship programmes into reality. Paradoxically, the crises in agriculture deepened with the plight of the farmers while the rise in the prices of essential commodities has continued unabated. Climate change has added to the challenge which is not only a stand alone problem but has a multidimensional effect on other sectors as well. In this light, there is an urgent need to mainstream the climate issues in the public policy priorities. Right to Information, heralded as the most powerful and potent tool to ensure administrative accountability has no doubt empowered the citizens as can be seen in the growing number of RTI applications. However, in addition to some inherent systemic problems, there have been attempts to dilute the spirit and content of the Act.

There is an urgent need to make the policy process more participatory starting from the formulation right up to the implementation. The recent People's Mid-Term Appraisal of the 11th Five Year Plan by civil society organisations is a case in point. The state has to reorient its policy direction in order to fulfil the global commitments made in form of the Millennium Development Goals and its own commitments in the 11th Five Year Plan.

NOTES

1 Revenue Deficit captures the extent by which expenditure exceeds receipts in the revenue account of the government's consolidated fund.
2 Fiscal Deficit captures the extent by which total expenditure exceeds total receipts (excluding borrowing) in the government's consolidated fund, which is also equivalent to the amount that the government needs to borrow in a financial year.
3 Gross Domestic Product is the measure of the size of a country's economy.
4 Gross State Domestic Product is the equivalent of the GDP for a state, i.e., a measure of the size of a state's economy.
5 Revised Estimates refer to the estimates of budgetary receipts/expenditure for an entire financial year that have been revised by the government based on the actual receipts/expenditure in the first half of that financial year.
6 National Rural Employment Guarantee Scheme (now renamed as Mahatma Gandhi National Rural Employment Guarantee Scheme).
7 Budget Estimates refer to the estimates of budgetary receipts/expenditure for an entire financial year that have been prepared by the government before the financial year commences.

8 This includes the following services: Education; Youth Affairs and Sports; Art and Culture; Health and Family Welfare; Water Supply and Sanitation; Housing and Urban Development; Information and Broadcasting; Welfare of SCs, STs and OBCs; Labour and Labour Welfare; Social Welfare and Nutrition; and Other Social Services.

9 In order to address the imbalance between the states' expenditure needs and their powers to raise revenue, the Constitution of India has provided for the sharing of the proceeds of centrally levied taxes with the states and making grants to the states from the consolidated fund of the union government. The Finance Commission, appointed by the President of India (once every five years or earlier), determines the overall share of states in the central taxes, as well as its allocation among different states and recommends grants to states in need of assistance.

10 R. Ramakumar. 2010. *The 13th Finance Commission: Fiscal Roadmap or Fiscal Roadblock?*, Research Brief 2, Project on Monitoring and Analysis of Budgets in Maharashtra State, Tata Institute of Social Sciences.

11 'Drift, Dissonance, Disappointment', *The Hindu*, 25 May 2010.

12 Sections 7.1–7.4, RTE Act 2009.

13 Section 7.5, RTE Act 2009.

14 Report of the Central Advisory Board of Education (CABE) Committee on Free and Compulsory Education Bill and Other Issues related to Elementary Education Spending, June 2005, Ministry of Human Resource Development.

15 Mukul Akshaya. 2009. 'Cost of Right to Education: ₹ 1.78 lakh crore', *The Times of India*, 29 September.

16 See '20 lakh teachers needed to implement RTE Act: Sibal', *The Hindu*, 19 May 2010.

17 Kaushik, Amit. 2010. 'Private Sector and Quality Concerns', *Annual Status of Education Report (Rural) 2009*, Mumbai, 15 January 2010.

18 Rani, P. Geetha. 2009. 'Economic Reforms and Financing Higher Education in India', NUEPA.

19 Tilak, J.B.G. and G. Rani. 2002. 'Changing Pattern of University Finances in India', *Journal of Services Research*, 2(2).

20 Tilak, J.B.G. 2010. 'Public-private partnership in education', *The Hindu*, 25 May.

21 As quoted by Amit Kaushik, op. cit., from Milton Friedman. 1955. 'The Role of Government in Education', in *Economics and the Public Interest*, Robert A Solo (Ed.), New Brunswick, NJ: Rutgers University Press.

22 Weidrich, Eva. 2009. *Education Vouchers: Is there a Model for India?*, Centre for Civil Society.

23 Uniform Recall Period.

24 National Commission for Enterprises in the Unorganised Sector (NCEUS). 2009. *The Challenge of Employment in India: An Informal Economy Perspective*, Government of India, New Delhi.

25 Ibid.

26 Ibid.

27 This section is primarily drawn from the Public Cause Research Foundation (PCRF) Study.

State of the Indian Judiciary: Issues and Aspects in Judicial Performance and Judicial Accountability

chapter 3

A judiciary of undisputed integrity is the bedrock institution essential for ensuring compliance with democracy and the rule of law. Even when all other protections fail, it provides a bulwark to the public against any encroachments of its rights and freedoms under the law. . . The greatest strength of the judiciary is the faith people repose in it.

Delhi High Court, January 2010

The present review comprises of two broad parts. The first part deals with specific cases, issues and proposals on judicial accountability and reforms. The key issues in this part include, transparency and judicial corruption, proposals of the Law Commission of India on restructuring of Courts, law reforms for the 'have-nots', and on mending practices of lawyers. It also includes new proposals of the Ministry of Law and Justice on judicial reforms, and regulation of the instrument of public interest litigation by the Supreme Court. The second part of the review maps out a range of positive pronouncements by the High Courts and the Supreme Court in the last one year on areas of civil liberties, social and economic rights, environment and development, and on issues regarding rural and urban self governance. At the end, some inferences and conclusions that arise out of the discussions in the two parts are presented. The two broad parts of the review are presented under Section I and II in the chapter.

I

SPECIFIC CASES, ISSUES AND PROPOSALS ON JUDICIAL ACCOUNTABILITY AND REFORMS

Issues in Judicial Corruption and Transparency

The Supreme Court is Subject to the Right to Information: A Review of the Landmark Decisions of the Central Information Commission and the Delhi High Court

On 6 January 2009, the Central Information Commission (CIC) upheld the request of a public individual for the supply of information concerning the declaration of personal assets by the Judges of the Supreme Court. In an appeal before the Delhi High Court, the Central Public Information Officer (CPIO), Supreme Court of India was quick to question the correctness and legality of the said order. However, in a landmark verdict delivered on 6 September 2009, Justice S. Ravindra Bhat of the Delhi High Court ruled that the CIC was correct in its order dated 6 January 2009. In the subsequent appeal, a three judge bench headed by Justice A.P. Shah of the Delhi High Court, in a verdict delivered on 12 January 2010, held that the judgement delivered by Justice Bhat in September 2009 was correct thus confirming and amplifying his findings.[1] Meanwhile, in a separate case before it, the CIC held on 24 November 2009, that the appointment of judges was a 'public activity', which the Supreme Court could not withhold from disclosure.

In view of their far reaching importance, each of the verdicts is discussed in brief, in the overall context of the facts that are essential to understand the case.

The Facts and Subject Matter of Controversy

The genesis of the dispute at hand relates to two resolutions: first, a resolution dated 7 May 1997, of the Full Court of the Supreme Court ('the 1997 Resolution') and second, the Re-statement of Values of Judicial Life (Code of Conduct), adopted unanimously at the Conference of the Chief Justices of the High Courts held in the Supreme Court on 3 and 4 December 1999 ('the 1999 Resolution'). Through the 1997 Resolution, Hon'ble Judges of the Supreme Court resolved that every Judge should, within a reasonable time, make a declaration of all of his/her assets in the form of real estate or investment held in own name or in the name of a spouse or any person dependent, and thereafter make a disclosure whenever any acquisition of a substantial nature is made. The 1999 Resolution referred to the 1997 Resolution and the draft Re-statement of Values of Judicial Life, prepared on the basis of inputs received from various High Courts and an earlier committee, as also resolutions passed in the Chief Justices' Conference held in 1992. The Code of Conduct thus finalised, came to be adopted and is also referred to as the 1999 Judicial Conference Resolution.

In the back drop of the two resolutions discussed earlier, an RTI activist made an ap-plication under the act to the CPIO, Supreme Court of India, on 10 November 2007, making a two-fold request. These are:

1. To furnish a copy of the 1997 Resolution of the Full Court of the Supreme Court; and
2. Information on any such declaration of assets and so on, ever filed by Hon'ble Judges of the Supreme Court and further information

if High Court Judges are submitting any declaration of their assets and so on, to the respective Chief Justices in the states.

The first request was granted by the CPIO and a copy of the 1997 Resolution was made available to the applicant. The CPIO vide order dated 30 November 2007, however, informed the applicant that the information sought under the second head was not held under the control of the registry (of the Supreme Court) and therefore, could not be furnished. The matter eventually came before the CIC. In the appeal before the CIC, the CPIO, Supreme Court took several defences including the submission that the Registrar of the Supreme Court did not hold the information and that the information sought related to a subject matter which was an 'in-house exercise' and pertained to material held by the Chief Justice of India (CJI) in his personal capacity. It was also submitted that the declarations made by the Judges of the Supreme Court had been furnished by them to the CJI on a voluntary basis and as per the terms of the 1997 Resolution, in a 'fiduciary relationship'. On the basis of the last said submission, it was also contended before the CIC that the disclosure of such information would be a breach of the fiduciary character attached to the material and therefore, contrary to the provisions of Section 8(1) of the RTI, 2005.

January 2009 Decision of the CIC

The CIC in its order dated 6 January 2009, rejected the contentions of the CPIO. He reasoned that Supreme Court is a 'public authority' within the meaning of the RTI (Section 2[h]), since it has been established under the Constitution of India.[2] The CIC pointed out that the information in question was maintained like any other official information available for perusal and inspection to every succeeding CJI and therefore, cannot be categorised as 'personal information' held by the CJI in his personal capacity. It was argued before the CIC that the CJI and Supreme Court of India are two distinct public authorities. This contention was repelled with a further observation that the Registrar and CPIO of the Supreme Court are both part of the

Box 3.1 What is Expected of a Judge

Restatement of the Values of Judicial Life

On 3 and 4 December 1999, the Conference of Chief Justices of the High Courts was held in the Supreme Court premises in which the Chief Justices unanimously resolved to adopt the 'Restatement of Values of Judicial Life' (Code of Conduct). The Delhi High Court in its landmark January 2010 decision held, 'It is a complete code of canons of judicial ethics.' The restatement is extracted below:

1. Justice must not merely be done but it must also be seen to be done. The behaviour and conduct of members of the higher judiciary must reaffirm the people's faith in the impartiality of the judiciary. Accordingly, any act of a Judge of the Supreme Court or a High Court, whether in official or personal capacity, which erodes the credibility of this perception, has to be avoided.
2. A Judge should not contest the election to any office of a club, society or other association. Further, he shall not hold such elective office except in a society or association connected with the law.
3. Close association with individual members of the Bar, particularly those who practice in the same court, shall be eschewed.
4. A Judge should not permit any member of his immediate family, such as spouse, son, daughter, son-in-law, daughter-in-law or any other close relative, if a member of the Bar, to appear before him or even be associated in any manner with a cause to be dealt with by him.
5. No member of his family, who is a member of the Bar, shall be permitted to use the residence in which the Judge actually resides or other facilities for professional work.
6. A Judge should practice a degree of aloofness consistent with the dignity of his office.
7. A Judge shall not hear and decide a matter in which a member of his family, a close relation or a friend is concerned.
8. A Judge shall not enter into public debate or express his views in public on political matters or on matters that are pending or are likely to arise for judicial determination.
9. A Judge is expected to let his judgements speak for themselves; he shall not give interview to the media.
10. A Judge shall not accept gifts or hospitality except from his family, close relations and friends.
11. A Judge shall not hear and decide a matter in which a company in which he holds shares is concerned unless he has disclosed his interest and no objection to his hearing and deciding the matter is raised.
12. A Judge shall not speculate in shares, stocks or the like.
13. A Judge should not engage directly or indirectly in trade or business, either by himself or in association with any other person. (Publication of a legal treatise or any activity in the nature of a hobby shall not be construed as trade or business.)
14. A Judge should not ask for, accept contributions or otherwise actively associate himself with the raising of any fund for any purpose.
15. A Judge should not seek any financial benefit in the form of a perquisite or privilege attached to his office unless it is clearly available. Any doubt in this behalf must be got resolved and clarified through the Chief Justice.
16. Every Judge must at all time be conscious that he is under the public gaze and there should be no act or omission by him which is unbecoming of the high office he occupies and the public esteem in which that office is held.

These are only the 'Restatement of the Values of Judicial Life' and are not meant to be exhaustive, but only illustrative of what is expected of a Judge.

Note: Extracted in full by the Delhi High Court in Secretary General, *Supreme Court of India v. Subhash Chandra Aggarwal*, LPA No.501/2009.

said institution and are thus, not independent or distinct authorities. On this finding, it was held by CIC that the CPIO is obliged to provide the information to a citizen making an application under the Act unless the disclosure was exempt.[3] The CIC in its order dated 6 January 2009, thus directed the CPIO,

> to provide the information asked for by the appellant in his RTI application as to whether such declaration of assets etc. has been filed by the Hon'ble Judges of the Supreme Court or not within ten working days from the date of receipt of this decision notice.

Delhi High Court's September 2009 Decision

The CPIO, Supreme Court of India questioned the correctness and legality of the order dated 6 January 2009, in an appeal to the High Court. On 2 September 2009, Justice S. Ravindra Bhat in a landmark verdict ruled that the CIC was right. The Court held, 'The CJI is a public authority under the Right to Information Act and holds the information pertaining to asset declarations in his capacity as the Chief Justice.' It was held that the office of the Chief Justice of India is 'public authority' under the Act and is covered by its provisions. It was also added, 'The second part of the application of the RTI activist (which relates to declaration of assets by the Supreme Court Judges) is "information" within the meaning of the expression defined in Section 2(f) of the Act.' The plea of the CPIO that the information contained in said asset declarations are held by the CJI in 'fiduciary capacity' and are therefore exempt from disclosure was held to be 'insubstantial'. Accordingly, it was held that the CJI does not hold such declarations in a fiduciary capacity or relationship. In view of these findings, the learned single Judge directed the CPIO, Supreme Court to reveal the information sought by applicant about the declaration of assets made by Judges of the Supreme Court within four weeks.

Delhi High Court's January 2010 Decision on Appeal

The High Court's decision of September 2009 was further appealed against by the Secretary General, Supreme Court of India. A three-judge bench headed by Justice A.P. Shah pronounced the verdict on the appeal on 12 January 2010, and held that Justice Bhat had been correct in his

September 2009 judgement and thus confirmed his findings.[4]

Amplifying the reasons laid out in the September 2009 decision of the High Court, the Division Bench observed as:

> The CJI cannot be a fiduciary vis-à-vis Judges of the Supreme Court. The Judges of the Supreme Court hold independent office, and there is no hierarchy in their judicial functions, which places them at a different plane than the CJI. The declarations are not furnished to the CJI in a private relationship or as a trust but in discharge of the constitutional obligation to maintain higher standards and probity of judicial life and are in the larger public interest. In these circumstances, it cannot be held that the asset information shared with the CJI, by the Judges of the Supreme Court, is held by him in fiduciary capacity, which if directed to be revealed, would result in breach of such duty.[5]

Finally, an oft quoted phrase in the media, 'sunlight is the best disinfectant', taken from the January 2010 verdict by the Delhi High Court was in fact part of the epilogue to the verdict and is worth extracting in full here:

> It was Edmund Burke who observed, 'All persons possessing a portion of power ought to be strongly and awfully impressed with an idea that they act in trust and that they are to account for their conduct in that trust.' Accountability of the Judiciary cannot be seen in isolation. It must be viewed in the context of a general trend to render governors answerable to the people in ways that are transparent, accessible and effective. Behind this notion is a concept that the wielders of power—legislative, executive and judicial—are entrusted to perform their functions on condition that they account for their stewardship to the people who authorize them to exercise such power. Well defined and publicly known standards and procedures complement, rather than diminish, the notion of judicial independence. Democracy expects openness and openness is concomitant of free society. Sunlight is the best disinfectant.[6]

CIC Decision that Appointment of Judges is a 'Public Activity'

While the above judgement of the High Court was a landmark one, the Chief Information Commissioner, Mr Wajahat Habibullah, held in another significant decision of the CIC on 24 November 2009, that the appointment of judges is a 'public activity' which cannot be withheld from disclosure, directing the Supreme Court to make public the records of appointing three justices of the Apex Court who superseded their seniors.[7]

All the above judgements of the CIC and the High Court of Delhi have put to rest the Judges' asset declaration controversy that hogged the headlines throughout the last year. If the Supreme Court had not appealed against the first decision of the CIC, the matter would not have attracted unnecessary attention. The RTI application on the issue was 'seemingly innocuous' and could have been duly responded by the CPIO, Supreme Court.[8] As Justice Krishna Iyer puts it:

> This information ('assets, accumulations and the methodology of acquisition of wealth by judges') should not be a secret that is hidden among the judges, for that could provoke suspicion. Suspicion is the upas tree under whose shade reason fails and justice dies. Judges, great in status and mighty in their majesty, should be, like Caesar's wife, above suspicion.[9]

One can only add that at the end of the day the law has been read right and it is now obligatory that every judge of the Supreme Court, and indeed all Courts in the country, makes a public disclosure of his/her assets. This timely corrective had purely come about because credibility of the higher judiciary and public confidence in it was directly at stake.

Justice Dinakaran Controversy

Last year presented another major test for the credibility of the higher judiciary when several serious allegations were made against the Chief Justice of the Karnataka High Court, P.D. Dinakaran, after it became known that he had been recommended for appointment to the Supreme Court of India. The breaking out of the entire controversy, the critical role of senior lawyers and the Forum for Judicial Accountability with the Committee on Judicial Accountability (COJA) in it, and the grave nature of charges against Justice Dinakaran are all well put in the following words of senior public interest lawyer Prashant Bhushan, especially as he himself (along with the Campaign for Judicial Accountability and Reforms) followed and contributed to taking the issue to its logical course. In his words:

> The Hindu newspaper got wind of the 5 appointments recommended by the Supreme Court Collegium (5 senior judges of the Supreme Court who have been assigned the power to select judges of the Supreme Court) which included the name of Justice Dinakaran. Soon after that, in September 2009, the Forum for Judicial Accountability, comprising of several senior and responsible lawyers of Chennai... as well as several other senior and respected lawyers of Tamil Nadu approached the members of the Committee on Judicial Accountability (COJA) expressing serious misgivings about the integrity of Justice Dinakaran. COJA (in particular, Ram Jethmalani, Shanti Bhushan, Fali Nariman and Anil Divan, all very senior and eminent jurists) wrote to the Collegium seeking a meeting with them. The Chief Justice (then) met Fali Nariman and Shanti Bhushan where they apprised him of the complaints against Justice Dinakaran and handed over a detailed representation of the Forum for Judicial Accountablity to the CJI... The Forum also wrote to the Law Minister and the Prime Minister as did COJA, asking them for a comprehensive and credible investigation into the charges. One of the charges was of him having acquired more than 300 acres of land in 3 villages of Tamil Nadu in his name, the name of his wife, daughter, and 4 companies. All these were incorporated on August 23, 2001, with his wife, daughter and other close relatives as the shareholders. It is also alleged that he has encroached upon another 150 acres of village common land as well as government land meant for distribution to landless dalit families. He had put more than 450 acres of land under a common fence.[10]

In addition to the above, there were also are several allegations about the manner in which Justice Dinakaran had dealt with a number of cases before him at the Karnataka High Court.[11] The media also investigated the veracity of charges against the Judge and presented detailed stories and findings on the issue.[12] Together with the Judges' asset declaration controversy, the Justice Dinakaran imbroglio did acquire a lot of media space and contributed to bringing some core judicial accountability issues from the margins to the mainstream, so to say.

It cannot be easily understood why the Supreme Court persisted with the elevation of Justice Dinakaran to Supreme Court for a long time in spite of growing evidence of impropriety on part of the judge. As eminent lawyer Fali Nariman said, 'In view of the materials, Justice Dinakaran ought to have been dropped like a hot cake!' But the Court insisted on his elevation until the government had to intervene to make clear that Justice Dinakaran would not be elevated.

One may also add here that it is also dangerous to see the entire issue as a limited controversy around a one judge. The Supreme Court had observed in ringing words in 1991 that a judicial scandal around a single dishonest judge (unlike a scandal involving a legislator or an administrator) can potentially endanger the foundation of the State. The Supreme Court observed then:

> ... A single dishonest judge not only dishonours himself and disgraces his office but jeopardizes the integrity of the entire judicial system. A judicial scandal has always been regarded as far more deplorable than a scandal involving either the executive or a member of the legislature. The slightest hint of irregularity or impropriety in the court is a cause for great anxiety and alarm. A legislator or an administrator may be found guilty of corruption without apparently endangering the foundation of the State. But a Judge must keep himself absolutely above suspicion; to preserve the impartiality and independence of the judiciary and to have the public confidence thereof.[13]

Corruption By and Within Lawyers: A Sting Case Reveals All!

The year 2009 carried with it a shock for the legal fraternity when two Senior Counsels at Delhi High Court were shown by NDTV in a national telecast—as part of a 'Sting Operation'—being involved in influencing and winning over a witness for one of the parties to the litigation.[14] The Defence Counsel, Sr Advocate Mr R.K. Anand, his associate, Mr Shri Bhagwan, on the one hand and on the other hand, the Special Public Prosecutor, Mr I.U. Khan were involved in such a contemptuous act, yet none of them tendered any apology or expressed regrets or contrition. *Suo motu* cognizance was taken by the High Court and in ultimate analysis, held the contemnor's guilty of charges levelled against them and in exercise of power under Article 215 of the Constitution of India, prohibited them by way of punishment, from appearing before the Delhi High Court and all the courts subordinate to, for a period of four months from the date of judgement. However, they were left free to carry on their other professional legal work, amounting to, 'consultation, advises, conferences, opinions, and so on'. Further, both the Counsels had to forfeit their designation as Senior Advocates and the Full Bench was recommended to divest them of the honour.

Under the circumstances, the Supreme Court noted that a senior defence counsel seen trying to suborn a witness was a particularly vile way of interfering with due course of a judicial proceeding. The Court also noted the obstructive measures adopted before the High Court in the form of a petition, 'requesting' the presiding Judge on the Bench dealing with the matter, to recuse him from the proceedings, as the Counsel had the feeling that he was not likely to get justice at the hands of said Judge. Supreme Court harshly commented that the contempt matter itself was reprehensible enough, but the Counsel's conduct before High Court aggravated the matter manifold and thus directed to issue a notice to him for enhancement of punishment.

The Supreme Court also took up the opportunity to give remarks on media reporting and commenting in a matter sub judice before court. It held that media cannot be left free to deal with a sub judice matter as they please. However, in the present matter, the telecast was held to be in the larger public interest, which served as an important public cause. It, in no way interfered with or obstructed due course of any judicial proceedings, rather, it was intended to prevent an attempt to interfere with or obstruct the due course of law. Finally, the Court also noted at some length the general erosion of professional values among lawyers at all levels and impressed upon the immediate need to arrest and reverse the trend, lest it would have very deleterious consequences for administration of justice in the country. This absolutely remarkable case on corruption, by and within lawyers, does not need any special comment. The facts speak for themselves.

Law Commission Reports on Restructuring Supreme Court, Judicial Reforms and Implementation of Human Rights

The 19th Law Commission was constituted through a government order with effect from 1 September 2009.[15] It will have a three-year term ending 31 August 2012. The Reports of the Law Commission are considered by the Ministry of Law in consultation with the concerned administrative Ministries and are submitted to the Parliament from time to time.[16] In a recent vision statement, the Ministry of Law and Justice pointed out that the Office of the Attorney General and Solicitor General has already embarked on a task of identifying all relevant recommendations from various Law Commission reports, which require implementation. This target was expected to be achieved by 31 December 2009. A report was then to be submitted to the Law Minister and the Prime Minister to take forward such amendments, as are necessary and which were approved by the Law Commission. Three of the significant reports of the Law Commission of India from the last year throw light on the state of the legal system and judiciary, and in view of their significance, they are discussed in some detail in the following sections.

Report 1: The Idea of Splitting the Supreme Court of India: Law Commission Raises the Issue Again

In a significant report in 2009, the Law Commission of India examined a question that it described as being 'of fundamental importance for the judicial system of the country.'[17] The all important issue was: whether the Supreme Court should be split into Constitutional Division and Legal Division for appeals, the latter with benches in four regions—North, South, East and West. In other words, the Report considered the question as to whether there is need for creating a Constitutional Court or Division in our Supreme Court that shall exclusively deal with matters of constitutional law and four separate Benches one each in the four regions for appeals from the Courts below it.

The question that whether India needs a separate constitutional court, as is the position in about 55 countries of the world, merits a close and serious consideration.[18] The Law Commission was of the view that questions and controversies involving constitutional law merit separate focus and attention and further added:

> Constitutional adjudication or determination of constitutional controversies by the Supreme Court has its own importance. This includes the authority to rule on whether or not laws that are challenged are in fact unconstitutional. All sorts of facts and their consequences, and the values we attach to them, the questions of economics, politics, social policies etc. going beyond purely legal disputes, are for determination by the Court.

Besides the constitutional controversies requiring a separate Constitutional Court, the idea of splitting the Supreme Court into various Courts of Appeal as outlined by the Law Commission holds considerable attraction given the size of the country and the backlog of cases before the Apex Court. This appeal can be best put in the following words used by the Chairperson of the Law Commission in his letter forwarding the report to the Union Law Minister:

> We are today also in dire search for solution for the unbearable load of arrears under which our Supreme Court is functioning as well as the unbearable cost of litigation for those living in far-flung areas of the country. The agonies of a litigant coming to New Delhi from distant places like Chennai, Thiruvananthapuram, Puducherry in the South, Gujarat, Maharashtra, Goa in the West, Assam or other States in the East to attend a case in the Supreme Court can be imagined; huge amount is spent on travel; bringing one's own lawyer who has handled the matter in the High Court adds to the cost; adjournment becomes prohibitive; costs get multiplied.

All of the above reasoning then forms the basis of the recommendation of the Law Commission, that a Constitution Bench be set up at Delhi to deal with constitutional and other allied issues, and four Cassation Benches be set up in the Northern region at Delhi, the Southern region at Chennai/Hyderabad, the Eastern region at Kolkata and the Western region at Mumbai, to deal with all appellate work arising out of the orders/judgements of the High Courts of the particular region.

The above recommendation to have regional Benches of Appeal of the Supreme Court would make eminent sense, if you put it together with the findings of a researcher:

> While on an average, nationally, there was about a 2.5 per cent chance in 2008 that a case will be appealed from a High Court to the Supreme Court, in States close to Delhi such as Punjab, Haryana and Uttarakhand, the appeal rates were more than double this. In Delhi itself the appeal rate was 10 per cent, giving credence to those who dub the court the 'Supreme Court of Delhi' for its proclivity for taking up cases from the national capital. Meanwhile, in the four southern States there was only a 1.7 per cent appeal rate, and in Tamil Nadu it was about 1 per cent...

The findings lead him to the logical inference that the farther one is from Delhi, the more expensive it becomes to bring a case, and many potential litigants simply cannot afford that cost. Orissa, for example, has the lowest appeal rate, at less than 1 per cent, seemingly the result of a combination of the State's low income levels and distance from the national capital.[19] It thus comes as no surprise that Justice Krishna Iyer has supported the idea of benches of the Supreme Court in different parts of the country. In his words, 'A vibrant democracy must have a circuit system of administration of justice. Alternatively, Benches in different parts of the country will make the court accessible to all.'[20]

The reference to arrears and backlogs as forming part of the reason for the Law Commission to *suo motu* take up the subject for consideration is interesting. While assessing the judicial system vis-à-vis the challenge of arrears to it, one can safely conclude that there are both structural and management inadequacies which affect the Court. The management factors include things like dilatory lawyering habits, nature of regulations on pleadings, extent of computerisation, and so on. Increasing the number of Appellate Courts is a response to just the structural problems of the judiciary.

Judicial reforms ultimately require effective and result oriented responses to both these inadequacies. Acting merely on one front, while not addressing the other, would have a limiting impact. However, in all fairness one may concede that there is no need to have an 'either this or that approach' to the problem. Rate of pendency and disposal together with their analysis and credible management responses to them, still does not take away from the need to think through a restructuring of the Courts.

Arguments For and Against Division of Supreme Court

It is also relevant to note that not very long ago in 2002, the central government dropped the proposal for setting up of a bench of the Supreme Court at Chennai following stiff opposition from the Apex Court on the matter. The Centre then apparently rejected the suggestion from the Parliamentary Committee on Home Affairs for setting up of regional benches of the Supreme Court in Chennai, Kolkata and Mumbai. That decision was primarily in line with the unanimous decision of the full bench of the Supreme Court in 1999 against the creation of such courts on the ground that it would affect the Courts' unitary character, would destabilise it and would affect its integrity.

The question of division of the Supreme Court was addressed even before 1999. More than three decades ago, a comprehensive study by a senior advocate under the auspices of the Delhi-based Indian Law Institute, examined the aspect of creating parallel courts and divisions in the Supreme Court. It was pointed out that there could be two clear divisions in the Apex Court, one concerned with constitutional and administrative law matters and the other with civil and criminal appellate matters. However, this study, the 1999 Supreme Court decision and the government's decision in 2002 were primarily influenced by the reasoning that more judges and benches of the Supreme Court would make it a fragmented institution, with smaller benches deciding similar questions of law in different ways and leading to 'unsettled jurisprudence'.

From the viewpoint of a lawyer, this argument seems better in theory than in practice.

The argument presumes that the court has a unitary character, which presumably has evolved over the years. However, as has been pointed out before,

> In India the organisation of the courts has just not evolved as it has in some other countries. The judicial hierarchy has been deliberately created by the statute, and the whole organisation and the courts are based on a rational plan ... the 'machinery' should be subjected to periodical review ... the judicial system should therefore, be re-examined from time to time in order to ensure that it adapts itself to perform the functions entrusted to it by the constitution and the laws in an efferent manner.[21]

The Supreme Court is a rational structure and a federal judicial institution comprising of individual justices. To say that the entire Court with all its judges has a unitary character, making it a coherent institution having a consistent policy would be a utopian argument.[22]

Report 2: 'Poverty as a Denial of Human Rights': Human Suffering and a Call for Implementation of Pro-Poor Judgements of the Supreme Court

The Law Commission report of April 2009 titled 'Need for Ameliorating the lot of the Have-nots' makes for a stimulating read.[23] In the forwarding letter (attached to the Report) to the Union Minister for Law and Justice, Ministry of Law and Justice, Government of India, the then Chairperson of the 18th Law Commission of India, Dr Justice A.R. Lakshmanan, pointed to the clear link that exists between law and poverty as follows:

> The poor are not poor simply because they are less human or because they are physiologically or mentally inferior to others whose conditions are better off. On the contrary, their poverty is often a direct or indirect consequence of society's failure to establish equity and fairness as the basis of its social and economic relations. Extreme poverty is denial of human rights.

Dr Justice A.R. Lakshmanan also hinted at how human suffering and human rights are to be seen together and as jurist Upendra Baxi had said, 'Those who take rights seriously need to take suffering seriously.'[24] These philosophical insights are the basis for Dr Justice A.R. Lakshmanan's suggestion as to what he calls an 'effective operational mechanism based on the human rights based approach to development'. In his words, an effective operational mechanism, the human rights-based approach to development demands:

- *Participation and transparency in decision-making*: This implies making participation throughout the development process a right, and the obligation of the State and other actors to create an enabling environment for participation of all stakeholders.
- *Non-discrimination*: This implies that equity and equality cut across all rights and are the key ingredients for development and poverty reduction.
- *Empowerment*: This implies empowering people to exercise their human rights through the use of tools such as legal and political action, to make progress in more conventional development areas.
- *Accountability of actors*: This implies accountability of institutions and actors, both public and private, to promote, protect and fulfil human rights and to be held accountable if these are not enforced.[25]

The above approaches and concepts are discussed at some length and the report and the discussion on this becomes the basis for Dr Justice A.R. Lakshmanan to recommend the following, on behalf of the Law Commission of India to the Union Law Minister:

> We are of the view that the Union and the State Governments should accord top priority to implementation of the judgements rendered by our Supreme Court in their letter and spirit in order that the lot of the have-nots is ameliorated.

One can understand the call from the Law Commission of India for the 'implementation of the judgements rendered by our Supreme Court in their letter and spirit in order that the lot of the have-nots is ameliorated'. Indeed, over the last three decades, the progressive provisions of the Indian Constitution have received the widest possible interpretation by the Judiciary. The Courts have always adopted an active approach while interpreting these provisions to ensure that the fundamental needs of a human being can be read into them and can be protected. For example, the right to live with human dignity,[26] the right to livelihood,[27] health,[28] shelter,[29] and so on, have been established as Fundamental Rights of citizens. Any call for implementation of such rights is always welcome at any given time.

A 'Right without Remedies' Legal Regime and 'Justifiable Human Suffering'

In the above context one feels that the Law Commission could have delved a little deeper into why lack of implementation of the Supreme Court judgements can be alarming and a threat to the Rule of Law in the country. Clearly, the pronouncement of rights and their implementation are two different things. The lack of enforcement of these rights can convert a rights regime into a 'right without remedies' regime. Recent judicial data points to the fact that this 'right without remedies' phenomenon may increasingly become the order of the day. Consider the findings of a recent research study: in 2008, writ petitions, where people approach the Supreme Court directly to enforce their fundamental rights, accounted for only about 2 per cent of all admission matters before the Apex Court and none of these were admitted! The data and information that suggests and reveals how accessible the Supreme Court is for public interest litigants, and further adds that in 2008, the court received 24,666 letters, postcards, or petitions asking for its intervention in cases that might be considered public interest litigation. Of these, only 226 were placed before judges on admission days and only a small fraction of these were heard as regular hearing matters. The rest were rejected.[30]

A closer look at the report would reveal that though a clear linkage between the conceptualisation of poverty as 'denial of human rights' and the call to implement the verdicts of the Supreme Court obviously exists, it has not been expressly drawn. For example, Dr Justice Lakshmanan, in his report, touches upon the need to feel the suffering of others but could have gone further to link human suffering with the state of human rights implementation. Possibly, the legal system's exposure to direct experience of pain and suffering has not been enough and perhaps that is a major reason behind the existence of a huge body of 'justifiable' human suffering. Thus, maybe the prevalence of human suffering because of the lack of implementation of rights needs to hurt the executive and judicial psyche harder than what it does presently. The call for enforcement of right and implementation of progressive judgements needs to be sharply put and understood in this context of widespread human suffering.

Having said all of the above, the recommendation that the 'Union and the State Governments should accord top priority to implementation of the judgements rendered by our Supreme Court' is well meaning given that in many contexts and cases, a favourable judgement from the Court is not the end, but the beginning of a struggle to ensure that the implementation of the judgement ensues on the ground.

Report 3: Reforming Practices in Courts and the Habits of Lawyers: Some Suggestions

If the idea of splitting the Supreme Court was a 'structural' response aimed towards a better higher judiciary, the Law Commission of India also came out with another Report, the 230th Report of the Law Commission, which sought to address the inadequacies in management that affect the Courts. The Report titled *Reforms in the Judiciary—Some Suggestions* had some recommendations which in fact were based on the suggestions made by the Hon'ble Justice Mr Ashok Kumar Ganguly, of the Supreme Court. These recommendations included:

1. There must be full utilisation of the court working hours. The judges must be punctual and lawyers must not be asking for adjournments, unless it is absolutely necessary. Grant of adjournment must be guided strictly by the provisions of Order 17 of the Civil Procedure Code.
2. Many cases are filed on similar points and one judgement can decide a large number of cases. Such cases should be clubbed with the help of technology and used to dispose other such cases on a priority basis; this will substantially reduce the arrears. Similarly, old cases, many of which have become infructuous, can be separated and listed for hearing and their disposal normally will not take much time. Same is true for many interlocutory applications filed even after the main cases are disposed of. Such cases can be traced with the help of technology and disposed of very quickly.
3. Judges must deliver judgements within a reasonable time and in that matter, the guidelines given by the Apex Court in the case of *Anil Rai v. State of Bihar*, (2001) 7 SCC 318 must be scrupulously observed, both in civil and criminal cases.
4. Considering the staggering arrears, vacations in the higher judiciary must be curtailed by at least 10–15 days and the court working hours should be extended by at least half-an-hour.
5. Lawyers must curtail prolix and repetitive arguments and should supplement it by written notes. The length of the oral argument in any case should not exceed one hour and thirty minutes, unless the case involves complicated questions of law or interpretation of Constitution.
6. Judgements must be clear and decisive and free from ambiguity, and should not generate further litigation.
7. Lawyers must not resort to strike under any circumstances and must follow the decision of the Constitution Bench of the Supreme Court in the case of *Harish Uppal (Ex-Capt.) v. Union of India* reported in (2003) 2 SCC 45.

The report needs to be taken as a call, especially for lawyers. Habits die hard but if the above suggestions are to take root, existing habits would need to die fast for most lawyers. Almost every practicing lawyer understands the need for it. For example, any lawyer practising in the Delhi High Court, one of the most important High Courts of the country, can testify that on an average, 60–70 cases are listed before a Delhi High Court Judge per day. The sheer quantum of cases forces a judge to adjourn most of the matters, leading to further backlog. The inevitable outcome is that normal adjournments go on for about 4–6 months, the trial dates are not available before two years, and the settlement of suit takes place over 15 years. One feels that all of this amounts to a daily mockery of the fundamental right to speedy trial. The Supreme Court made it clear more than two decades ago that 'a speedy trial is of essence to criminal justice and there can be no doubt that the delay in trial by itself constitutes denial of justice'.[31] Rights are founded on duty bearers that respect and honour them. Lawyers are one of the duty bearers of the right to speedy trial. There is no other way the suggestions of Justice Ganguly need to be understood and internalised by the lawyers.

Proposals in 2009 of the Ministry of Law on Law Reforms

In a recently released vision statement, the Ministry of Law and Justice, Government of India, has also rolled out some significant steps in legal reform some of which are explained in the following sections.

National Mission for Delivery of Justice and Legal Reform

The Ministry of Law and Justice proposes to create a Special Purpose Vehicle (SPV) for the National Mission for Delivery of Justice and Legal Reform, that will manage and implement the Vision prepared by the National Mission for Delivery of Justice and Legal Reform and also service the Bar Council of India. According to the Ministry, the major objectives of the National Mission for Delivery of Justice and Legal Reform are twofold. They are:

1. Increasing access by reducing delay and arrears in the system; and
2. Enhancing accountability through structural changes and by setting performance standards and capacities.

The SPV will define and implement an action plan to provide 'timely justice' to all. It aims to reduce the pendency of cases (arrears) from 15 years to 3 years by means of various innovative strategies, initiatives and definitive action plans. The SPV has a target to eliminate all arrears from the Indian Judicial System by 31 December 2012. All cases pending as on 1 January 2009 will be treated as arrears. The SPV intends to achieve its objective of reducing pendency through a multi-pronged approach which includes Process Re-engineering, Human Resource and Institutional Framework Reforms, Infrastructure Development and Information Technology Enablement.

National Litigation Policy

The government needs to be transformed from a compulsive litigant into a responsible and cautious litigant and the central government is proposing the introduction of a National Litigation Policy to this effect. Perhaps for the first time, the Ministry of Law and Justice has sought to articulate the constituents of a National Litigation Policy that it wishes to work under. According to the Ministry these constituents include:

1. A detailed action plan that shall be launched separately, which shall focus on identification and removal of frivolous and vexatious cases preferred by the central government.
2. This due diligence process shall involve drawing upon statistics of all pending matters which shall be provided for by all government departments (including PSUs). The Office of the Attorney General and the Solicitor General shall also be responsible for reviewing all pending cases and filtering frivolous and vexatious matters from the meritorious ones. An Office for the Attorney General and the Solicitor General is slated to be established as a full-fledged office with a total of 52 lawyers and 26 law researchers.
3. Norms will be formulated for defending cases filed against the government. The approach that 'the Petitioner is always wrong and must be resisted in every which way' must be abandoned. Proper norms will be laid down for appeal and further challenge. The present system viz., 'let the Courts decide every case' must be done away with. This would apply both to the central and the state governments.

4. Setting up of Empowered Committees to eliminate unnecessary litigation needs to be considered.

5. Decisions relating to government and governmental policy must also be put on an identifiable course. This would require collection of data, classification and planning of Court/Bench positions.

National Arrears Grid

Admittedly inspired by the 'Woolf Report of 1996' that had emphasised that the judiciary must generate accurate judicial statistics on a daily basis, the Ministry has proposed the constitution of a National Arrears Grid. The purpose of the National Arrears Grid is to ascertain and analyse the exact number of arrears in every court in the country.

According to the Union Law Ministry the 'deliverables' of the National Arrears Grid shall be as follows:

1. The Grid will have a map which will show the location and manning of every Court in the country including the name of the Presiding Officer, the arrears before him, as well as the facilities available. The Grid, by a process of mutual and quick consultation, will offer mobility so that, wherever required, strengthening is afforded to the Courts.

2. The Grid will efficiently monitor the systemic bottlenecks. Four key bottlenecks causing delays in civil and criminal process (service of process, adjournments, interlocutory orders, appearance of witnesses and accused) will be monitored through the Grid and attention will be provided through a special cell at the High Court and District Court level to resolve issues in coordination with Executive Agencies.

3. The Grid, with the help of sociologists, members of the civil society and the voluntary sector, will also specifically identify action areas/geographical areas concerning the poor and the underprivileged vis-à-vis access to justice. It will pay particular attention to ensure that confidence building takes place in the dispensation of justice in these areas.

Pendency of Cases, Judicial Vacancies and an Open Question

Given the context and the goals to which the National Arrears Grid shall respond to, a close look at the pendency position in all High Courts of the country at the end of the last year is given in Table 3.1.

It may be seen from the above that some of the 'bigger' High Courts have huge problems of pendency with them. Take for example the High Court of Allahabad. Out of the total pendency of over 40 lakh cases in all the 21 High Courts, almost one-fourth is from one single court, i.e.,

Table 3.1 Pendency Position in All the High Courts (as on 31 December 2009)

Sl. no.	Name of the High Court	Civil cases	Criminal cases	Total
1.	Allahabad	668,029	282,835	950,864
2.	Andhra Pradesh	162,470	24,580	187,050
3.	Bombay	295,714	42,469	338,183
4.	Calcutta	273,291	46,555	319,846
5.	Chhattisgarh	42,701	17,717	60,418
6.	Delhi	49,669	11,608	61,277
7.	Gujarat	74,907	25,023	99,930
8.	Gauhati	50,617	8,719	59,336
9.	Himachal Pradesh	45,144	6,499	51,643
10.	Jammu & Kashmir	53,356	2,232	55,588
11.	Jharkhand	30,470	24,736	55,206
12.	Karnataka	154,570	17,732	172,302
13.	Kerala	85,182	28,244	113,426
14.	Madras	394,508	36,882	431,390
15.	Madhya Pradesh	134,881	62,040	196,921
16.	Orissa	231,269	28,649	259,918
17.	Patna	82,646	46,261	128,907
18.	Punjab and Haryana	195,976	47,806	243,782
19.	Rajasthan	200,780	58,407	259,187
20.	Sikkim	64	21	85
21.	Uttarakhand	24,047	7,531	31,578
	Total	32,50,291	8,26,546	4,076,837

Source: Ministry of Law and Justice, Government of India.

Table 3.2 Year-wise Pendency of Cases

Year	Pendency
2007	28,799,567
2008	29,853,043
2009	31,334,354

Source: Ministry of Law and Justice, Government of India.

the High Court of Allahabad. It is interesting to note that the same High Court that has the largest pendency also has the largest vacancy of judges as on 15 February 2009. (See Table 3.3 for present position on judicial vacancies.)

It is also worth nothing that Allahabad High Court—the court with highest pendency and highest judicial vacancies—also caters to the largest percentage of population in India. Some of the other higher pendency at the end of last year is also from populous states. This opens up a straight question as to whether there is a need to raise the number of judges simply on the basis of population size. This argument deserves to be seen more closely. First, of all there should be a good explanation as to why should population not be a criteria for the number of judges. The point is best put in the words of the 120th Law Commission Report which said:

If legislative representation can be worked out, as pointed out earlier, on the basis of population and if other services of the State bureaucracy, police, etc. can also be similarly planned, there is no reason at all for the non-extension of this principle to the judicial services. It must also be frankly stated that while population may be a demographic unit, it is also a democratic unit. In other words, we are talking of citizens with democratic rights including the right to access to justice which is the duty of the State to provide.

Table 3.3 Approved Strength and Vacancy of Judges (as on 15 February 2009)

Name of the court	Approved strength	Judges in position	Vacancies as on 15 February 2009	Judges in position		Fresh appointment made during the year			
				Male judges	Female judges	2006	2007	2008	2009 (up to 15.2.09)
A. Supreme Court of India	31*	24	7*	24	–	3	7	5	–
B. High Courts									
Allahabad	160	73	87	70	3	10	13	–	
Andhra Pradesh	49	31	18	29	2	6	–	3	1
Bombay	75	64	11	57	7	8	1	12	6
Calcutta	58	38	20	36	2	16	–	–	–
Chhattisgarh	18	6	12	6	–	–	–	1	
Delhi	48	39	9	33	6	12	3	10	–
Gauhati	24	22	2	21	1	6	3	2	–
Gujarat	42	29	13	26	3	–	4	–	–
Himachal Pradesh	11	10	1	10	–	3	3	–	–
Jammu and Kashmir	14	12	2	12	–	–	1	3	–
Jharkhand	20	13	7	11	2	4	–	2	2
Karnataka	41	39	2	37	2	4	5	5	–
Kerala	38	33	5	31	2	–	6	6	4
Madhya Pradesh	43	38	5	34	4	3	2	3	–
Madras	60	43	17	39	4	7	7	3	–
Orissa	22	17	5	16	1	1	4	2	–
Patna	43	22	21	20	2	13	2	1	1
Punjab and Haryana	68	48	20	44	4	13	11	7	–
Rajasthan	40	31	9	31	–	3	7	3	–
Sikkim	3	1	2	1	–	–	–	–	–
Uttarakhand	9	8	1	8	–	1	–	2	–
Total	886	617	269	572	45	110	59	78	14

Source: Ministry of Law and Justice, Government of India.

The 120th Law Commission while recommending the five fold increase in judicial strength at all levels of the Indian judiciary (from 10.5 to 50 judges per million of population), also pointed out how India's judge-population ratio stands in poor contrast when compared with several other countries.

National Minimum Court Performance Standards

The vision statement of the Ministry of Law and Justice laid out in October 2009 also says that as suggested by the Hon'ble Chief Justice of India, the following may be set as the National Minimum Court Performance Standards for us:

1. Disposal level of the national system should be raised from 60 per cent of total case load (as at present) to 95–100 per cent of total case load in three years. This target must be established at the district and State levels; and
2. Each court to ensure that no more than 5 per cent of the cases in that court should be more than five years old *(5x5 rule)* within the next three years; and in five years, to ensure that no more than 1 per cent of the cases should be more than one year old *(1x1 rule)*.

The standards that are set by the Ministry are well meaning and well placed, but undoubtedly ambitious. They shall merit a close follow up especially in the coming three years.

Regulation of Public Interest Litigation by Supreme Court

In a Public Interest Litigation (PIL) filed challenging the appointment of Advocate General of Uttarakhand at the age of 62 years, the Supreme Court, on reading of the applicable provisions under the Constitution of India, held that appointment was not bad just because the person is past 62 years, as long as he has the prescribed qualifications.[32] However, the Court noted that the same question has been decided in an earlier case by the Supreme Court and thus repeatedly raising the same controversy

not only wastes the potential time of court but also demeans a very important constitutional office and person who has been appointed to that office. This was thus a clear abuse of process of court in the name of PIL. In this context, the Court went on to discuss in detail, the origin, evolution, nature and scope of PIL in India.

Interestingly, while dealing with the origin and development of PIL, the Court broadly divided it as falling in three phases.

Phase I: It deals with the cases of this Court where directions and orders were passed primarily to protect Fundamental Rights under Article 21 of the marginalised groups and sections of the society who because of extreme poverty, illiteracy and ignorance cannot approach this Court or the High Courts.

Phase II: It deals with the cases relating to protection and preservation of ecology, environment, forests, marine life, wildlife, mountains, rivers, historical monuments, and so on.

Phase III: It deals with the directions issued by the Courts in maintaining the probity, transparency and integrity in governance.[33]

The Court however went on to add:

Unfortunately, of late, it has been noticed that such an important jurisdiction which has been carefully carved out, created, and nurtured with great care and caution by the courts, is being blatantly abused by filing some petitions with oblique motives. We think time has come when genuine and bona fide public interest litigation must be encouraged whereas frivolous public interest litigation should be discouraged... In our considered view, now it has become imperative to streamline the PIL.

This set the premise for the Court to issue a range of directions for regulating public interest litigation (see Box 3.2).

The previous quote adds on to the vast number of cases where the Court had made efforts to regulate PIL. In doing so, it has developed 'some categorical norms that can help it regulate

Box 3.2 Directions to Preserve the Purity and Sanctity of the PIL: Supreme Court

In order to preserve the purity and sanctity of the PIL, it has become imperative to issue the following directions:

1. The courts must encourage genuine and bona fide PIL and effectively discourage and curb the PIL filed for extraneous considerations.
2. Instead of every individual judge devising his own procedure for dealing with the public interest litigation, it would be appropriate for each High Court to properly formulate rules for encouraging the genuine PIL and discouraging the PIL filed with oblique motives. Consequently, we request that the High Courts who have not yet framed the rules, should frame the rules within three months. The Registrar General of each High Court is directed to ensure that a copy of the Rules prepared by the High Court is sent to the Secretary General of this Court immediately thereafter.
3. The courts should prima facie verify the credentials of the petitioner before entertaining a PIL.
4. The court should be prima facie satisfied regarding the correctness of the contents of the petition before entertaining a PIL.
5. The court should be fully satisfied that substantial public interest is involved before entertaining the petition.
6. The court should ensure that the petition which involves larger public interest, gravity and urgency must be given priority over other petitions.
7. The courts before entertaining the PIL should ensure that the PIL is aimed at redressal of genuine public harm or public injury. The court should also ensure that there is no personal gain, private motive or oblique motive behind filing the public interest litigation.
8. The court should also ensure that the petitions filed by busybodies for extraneous and ulterior motives must be discouraged by imposing exemplary costs or by adopting similar novel methods to curb frivolous petitions and the petitions filed for extraneous considerations.

Source: Supreme Court judgement in *State of Uttaranchal v. Balwant Singh Chaufal and Ors*, 2010(1) SCALE 492.

PIL' and help the Court avoid some pitfalls that it may inadvertently slip into while dealing with various PILs.[34] One can only add that such regulation by the Court has increasingly become stricter and tougher. In 2008, the court received 24,666 letters, postcards or petitions asking for its intervention in cases that might be considered public interest litigation. Of these, only 226 were placed before judges on admission days, and only a small fraction of these were heard as regular hearing matters. The rest were rejected.[35] The trend is likely to continue even as the new CJI, Justice Sarosh Homi Kapadia said on his first day in office, while hearing a PIL as part of a three-judge Bench: 'Huge cost will be imposed for filing frivolous PILs.'

The last verdict of the Supreme Court on the need to regulate and streamline PIL discussed above also falls in a pattern. The Court first records the glorious contribution PILs have made before discussing the cases of its abuse and then emphasising on the need for their regulation. However, one good departure from other cases was that the Court made an attempt to see different categories of PIL in three different phases. One feels though, that the Court could have said more, so as to bring in more nuances into the question of regulating PILs. There is a need to understand the various distinct traditions within the PIL jurisprudence resulting from the different categories of public interest issues brought in the higher courts. Such a view can help depart from the conventional understanding that there is a single 'monolithic' lineage of PIL in India. For example, arguably, the PIL cases on large infrastructure projects are shaping a very distinct path for the use of judicial power when compared to PILs on pollution issues. Likewise, separate patterns can be seen in the other categories of public interest cases like cases dealing with 'civil liberties' and say, cases on 'political accountability'. The nature and extent of judicial intervention in each of these categories of cases cannot be explained in terms of a common lineage of PIL jurisprudence. These various categories of cases have evoked different judicial responses as they have provided different contexts for judicial review. Once these distinct areas of judicial intervention through PIL cases are identified and appreciated, the task of understanding specific verdicts within their separate traditions becomes relatively easy.[36] That in turn should help in evolving a more nuanced and effective approach, on the issues and concerns around PIL, for the future.

II

MAPPING KEY COURT CASES FROM THE LAST YEAR

A brief journey through some important judgements of the Supreme Court and various High Courts of India along the last year is useful to understand the nature and extent of judicial intervention in areas that are fundamental to us. This is presented in the following four sections.

Key Cases on Civil Liberties and Gender Justice

Crimes in Custody: Is the Police Listening?

In an important case, a boy aged 17 years lost his life on account of custodial torture and diabolic acts of the police officials. He was studying in the IXth standard. The factual matrix is that the boy was picked up by police officials. The father of the boy was called up at the house and to his the utter shock and surprise, he was informed by the police officers that the boy had committed suicide in a lock up by himself hanging with his shirt. The dead body was covered with injuries, black marks and abrasions all over, and blood was coming out his head, a clear case of getting badly beaten up. However, the FIR came to be registered against erring police officials only for act of abetting suicide, as the police officials gave it the colour of suicide. Aggrieved, the father of the boy approached the Supreme Court and submitted that it was a clear case of custodial torture and death, and by giving a colour of suicide, an attempt is being made to protect the erring police officials.[37] The Apex Court held that Article 21 mandates that no person shall be deprived of his life and personal liberty except according to the procedure established by law, and added that it is difficult to comprehend how torture and custodial violence can be permitted to defy the rights flowing from the Constitution. It further observed, 'The dehumanising torture, assault, and deaths in custody, which have assumed alarming proportions, raise serious questions about the credibility of rule of law and administration of criminal justice system. The community rightly gets disturbed. The cry for justice becomes louder and warrants immediate remedial measures...'

In a significant observation, the Court expressed its dissatisfaction on even the approach of law courts sometimes, when they insist upon the establishment of proof beyond every reasonable doubt by the prosecution, ignoring the ground reality that rarely in cases of police torture or custodial death, there is any direct ocular evidence of the complicity of the police personnel and the police personnel prefer to remain silent and more often than not even pervert the truth to save their colleagues.

The court's observation is worth extracting in full here:

> The exaggerated adherence to, and insistence upon the establishment of proof beyond every reasonable doubt by the prosecution, at times even when the prosecuting agencies are themselves fixed in the dock, ignoring the ground realities, the fact-situation and the peculiar circumstances of a given case, as in the present case, often results in miscarriage of justice and makes the justice delivery system suspect and vulnerable. In the ultimate analysis, the society suffers and a criminal gets encouraged. Tortures in police custody, which of late are on the increase, receive encouragement by this type of an unrealistic approach at times by the courts as well because it reinforces the belief in the mind of the police that no harm would come to them if one prisoner dies in the lock-up because there would hardly be any evidence available to the prosecution to directly implicate them with the torture. The courts must not lose sight of the fact that death in police custody is perhaps one of the worst kind of crime in a civilised society, governed by the rule of law and poses a serious threat to an orderly civilised society. Torture in custody flouts the basic rights of the citizens recognized by the Indian Constitution and is an affront to human dignity. Police excesses and the maltreatment of detainees/under-trial prisoners or suspects tarnishes the image of any civilised nation and encourages the men in 'Khaki' to consider themselves to be above the law and sometimes even to become a law unto themselves. Unless stern measures are taken to check the malady of the very fence eating the crops, the foundations of the criminal justice delivery system would be shaken and the civilisation itself would risk the consequence of heading towards total decay, resulting in anarchy and authoritarianism reminiscent of barbarism. The courts must therefore, deal with such cases in a realistic manner and with the sensitivity which they deserve, otherwise the common man may tend to gradually lose faith in the efficacy of the system of judiciary itself, which, if it happens, will be a sad day for anyone to reckon with.

In another case, a person who was a patient of asthma, and had serious respiratory problem, was kept in a windowless room which was full of dust and cobwebs-allergens, known to trigger an asthma attack. The person eventually died (in custody) of an asthma attack. The trial court charged the concerned police officials for 'culpable homicide not amounting to murder', whereas the High Court in challenge to the same, watered it down to a case of 'simple injury'. On facts the Supreme Court observed, '... the materials submitted by the Investigating Authority in its Final Report... does establish the fact that the deceased had been kept in a room which was highly unsuitable for a person suffering from respiratory problems.'[38] The Court thus gave a clear message that the erring police officials, who lack any concern for basic human rights, are to be dealt with sternly under the law and should not be laid off from bearing the consequences of their acts.

In yet another case, the Madhya Pradesh High Court got an opportunity to hammer the government and its officials for putting a person under illegal detention in jail. In the case, a person found guilty of an offence was sentenced to 10 years rigorous imprisonment and in the subsequent appeal, the sentence was reduced to three years and five months. However, the convict could not be released even after expiry of modified period of the sentence in as much as the modified warrant as required under the Rules could only be issued as late as one-and-a-half years 'after the expiry of the modified period. Therefore, the convict was finally released after this added period of a year and six months for no fault on his part. In this case, the High Court directed the state government to pay a compensation of ₹300,000 to the petitioner.[39]

In another case, the Delhi High Court was also called upon to decide whether the petitioner (a mother) should be compensated by the State of Gujarat, as a public law remedy, by way of strict liability, for the adventure undertaken by its police officials in taking away her minor son, without reason and without the authority of law, from Delhi to a lock-up in Ahmedabad. What compounded the problem was that the Court had to decide this question in the backdrop of the allegation that the petitioner, as also her husband and children, are not citizens of India but, of Bangladesh. On a detailed investigation of facts the High Court found, '[t]he violation of Article 21 is patent and incontrovertible' and added:

Fortunately in this case, nobody has been deprived of his life, but, unfortunately, the minor son was deprived of his personal liberty and that too without following any procedure established by law. There is a clear violation of this hallowed fundamental right which must be guarded at all times and at all costs. Life and liberty are so fundamental to human society that the Constitution, in recognition of this fact, has made the right available to all humans, citizen or alien.[40]

Citing a well-known Supreme Court judgement, the Court held:

Police Officers, who are the custodians of law and order should have the greatest respect for the personal liberty of citizens and should not flout the laws by stooping to such bizarre acts of lawlessness. Custodians of law and order should not become depredators of civil liberties. Their duty is to protect and not to abduct...

Under the circumstances, the State of Gujarat was directed to make the payment of the sum of ₹270,000 to the petitioner by way of compensation to her and her son.

The selection of cases in this section, from both the Supreme Court and the various High Courts, show that illegal detention, custodial torture and death are just refusing to become a thing of the past. Over the years, the most important judgements of both the Supreme Court and the High Courts in this area include the cases relating to prisoners' rights, cases on custodial torture, the rights of a detenu before preventive arrest and the need to balance social security with individual freedom in this regard, cases depicting police atrocities against women and children. The Courts seem to be giving judgements that are giving the right message and the higher Courts, especially the Supreme Court has been doing that for a long time now. The big question is, 'Is the Police-Dom listening?'

Cases in Gender Justice

In a case where the High Court of Punjab and Haryana had ruled that it was in the best interests of a mentally retarded woman to undergo an abortion, the Supreme Court got an opportunity to forcefully assert the rights of mentally challenged women, while reversing the judgement of the High Court.[41] The aforementioned woman had become pregnant as a result of an alleged rape that had taken place while she was an inmate at a government-run welfare institution located in Chandigarh. After the discovery of her pregnancy, the Chandigarh Administration had approached the High Court seeking approval for the termination of her pregnancy, keeping in mind that in addition to being mentally challenged, she was also an orphan who did not have any parent or guardian to look after her or her prospective child.

The High Court had the opportunity to peruse a preliminary medical opinion and chose to constitute an Expert Body consisting of medical experts and a judicial officer for the purpose of a thorough inquiry into the facts. In such cases, the presumption is that the findings of the Expert Body would be given due weightage in arriving at a decision. However, in its order dated 17 July 2009, the High Court directed the termination of the pregnancy, in spite of the Expert Body's findings which showed that the victim had expressed her willingness to bear a child. The Expert Body's finding showed continuance of pregnancy was not harmful to victim physically or mentally. The Supreme Court therefore held that termination of pregnancy of mentally challenged woman at a later stage cannot be permitted when she has previously expressed her willingness to bear child and the also due to the lack of any physical or mental risk on health of victim as determined by the Expert Body. The Supreme Court issued directions to a Trust to provide the victim, the best medical facilities, with proper care and supervision during the pregnancy, as well as for post-natal care. The Supreme Court further observed that the Court's decision should be guided by the interests of the victim alone and not those of the other stakeholders, such as guardians or the society in general. The Courts need to step into the shoes of a person who is considered to be mentally incapable and attempt to make the decision which that said person would have made if that person was competent to do so. The judgement is a landmark in upholding humanity, as well as the rights of the individual.

The fact that 'the State can treat unequal differently' provided the premise for two separate judgements of the Madras High Court that upheld reservation in excess of 50 per cent in favour of women. Thus, the Madras High Court, in the case of a legal challenge by a male staff nurse against the 90 per cent reservation in favour of women for admission to a nursing course, held the policy decision of the state government as being legal and constitutional. The Court held that the process involves adequate care, nourishment, as well as cleanliness, both in respect of the patients as well as their surroundings. Women dominate in this field and take care of the patient as an affectionate sister, a caring mother. Thus, the reservation policy could not be treated as discrimination on the grounds of sex alone, in as much as the discrimination is coupled with certain objective and consideration. In another case, the Madhya Pradesh High Court made a distinction between the criteria applicable for extending reservation to SCs, STs and OBCs, and to women and drew the distinction purposefully in more beneficial terms to women.[42] It held that the decisions of Supreme Court to the effect that reservations in favour of SC, ST and OBC category cannot exceed 50 per cent or cannot be 100 per cent do not apply to a special provision in favour of women under Article 15(3) of the Constitution of India. The Court added, 'It is precisely a lack of opportunity which has led to social backwardness. Reservation therefore, is one of the recognised constitutional methods of overcoming such backwardness, which is permissible for women under Article 15(3) of the Constitution.'

Rights of Homosexuals

A Public Interest Litigation was filed before the Delhi High Court to challenge the constitutional validity of Section 377 of the Indian Penal Code, 1860 (IPC), which criminally penalises what are described as 'unnatural offences', to the extent that the said provision criminalises consensual sexual acts between adults in private. The High Court found Section 377 IPC to be facially neutral and it seemingly targets not identities, but acts. However, in its operation, it does end up unfairly targeting a particular community. The fact is that these sexual acts which are criminalised are associated more closely with one class of persons, namely, homosexuals as a class. Section 377, IPC has the effect of viewing all gay people as criminals.

Justice A.P. Shah writing the judgement on behalf of the bench noted:

> If there is one constitutional tenet that can be said to be underlying theme of the Indian Constitution, it is that of 'inclusiveness'. This Court believes that Indian Constitution reflects this value, deeply ingrained in Indian society and nurtured over several generations. The inclusiveness that Indian society traditionally displayed, literally in every aspect of life, is manifest in recognising a role in society for everyone. Those perceived by the majority as 'deviants' or 'different' are not, on that score, excluded or ostracised.[43]

The Court held that that sexual orientation is a ground analogous to sex and that discrimination on the basis of sexual orientation is not permitted by Article 15 of the Constitution of India. The Court went on to declare that Section 377, IPC, insofar it criminalises consensual sexual acts of adults in private, is in violation of Articles 14, 15 and 21 of the Constitution.

Cases on Freedom of Speech and Expression

In what was a shot in the arm to the cherished freedom of speech and expression, the Gujarat High Court quashed and set aside a notification issued by the state government in August 2009, forfeiting and prohibiting the display, sale, distribution or any kind of use of the book named, *Jinnah—India, Partition, Independence* by Shri Jashwant Singh in Gujarat.[44] In another similar case, where the Maharashtra state government had taken the decision to suspend exhibition of a motion picture called *Deshdrohi*, the Mumbai High Court observed:

> Free speech is of intrinsic value in a democracy. Speech in all its forms is an expression of human personality. To speak is to give creative expression to ideas, thoughts and perceptions. Anguish and appreciation, criticism and acceptance, speech and silence are all forms of symbolism which nature ordains in the evolution of the human ethos. Speech is the quintessence of human life. Article 19(1)(a) is a constitutional embodiment of a right which inhers in nature a right which is inseparable from human existence. But, apart from its intrinsic importance, free speech is of instrumental importance. The instrumental value of the right in a democratic order is that it recognizes the importance of a free expression of ideas in the attainment of democratic values. The intrinsic and the instrumental elements find recognition in the constitutional ethos…[45]

The Court asked that in a constitutional order where these are the underpinnings, can a film which is critical of perceived discrimination be suppressed on the ground of a likelihood of public disorder? It was held that there was absolutely no material before the state government to support an inference that there was a breach of public order or a likelihood of such a breach consequent upon the exhibition of the film. The suspension of the exhibition of the film was ill conceived and the Court proceeded to quash the order of the Maharashtra government.

Case on Implementation of Disabilities Act

The Sikkim High Court in a lesser known case of last year found out that the state government had not yet implemented the provisions of the Persons with Disabilities (Equal Opportunities, Protection of Rights and Full Participation) Act, 1995 in letter and spirit resulting in the total denial of those benefits and opportunities contemplated in the Act to the persons with disabilities. Through a PIL filed by an orthopaedically disabled person who had sought intervention of the Court on the issue, the High Court held:

> We hope and trust that the Government of Sikkim in its administrative fairness, will deliver good governance to the people of Sikkim in general and the persons with disabilities in particular by implementing all the provisions of the Act so as to avoid any such grievances and complaints as reflected in this instant PIL.[46]

Key Cases on Environment and Development

The Yamuna Flood Plain Case

On 13 September 2003, the Commonwealth Games Federation selected Delhi as the venue for the Commonwealth Games, which are now scheduled to be held from 3 to 14 October 2010.

Complaining that the government agencies and the DDA are effecting various steps including massive construction on the periphery of the Yamuna river and in apprehension that the action being taken would not only destroy the river Yamuna but also pose severe threat to the Delhi city as well, the petitioners in the case moved the Delhi High Court. The main claim of the petitioners before the High Court was to the effect that the ongoing construction would affect the ecological integrity of the 'riverbed', besides causing irreversible damage to the 'floodplain'. The Division Bench of the High Court, by an order dated 3 November 2008, refused to interfere with the project in question, but instead directed a Committee to examine and monitor the construction being carried out. Aggrieved by parts of the order, special leave petitions were filed by both sides before the Supreme Court. The case of the petitioners before the Supreme Court was that in as much as the city of Delhi is wholly depending on Yamuna river, its 'riverbed' and 'floodplains' have to be protected. They further highlighted that the site selected for Commonwealth Games Village falls within the river zone wherein the construction activities cannot be carried out without looking into the matter and evaluation by experts like Dr R.K. Pachauri, as directed by the High Court. The Court considered the relevant materials, the National Environment Engineering Research Institute (NEERI) reports of 1999, 2005 and 2008, remedial measures suggested by Central Water and Power Research Station (CWPRS), Ministry of Environment and Forest (MoEF), and other specialised bodies.

The facts above suggested that bone of the central questions involved in the case was whether the site in question was a 'floodplain' or a 'riverbed'. The Supreme Court relied on an affidavit filed by NEERI which said that the site in question was not even 'floodplain', much less a 'riverbed' and then referred to dictionary meanings of these words to conclude that the site in question is neither a 'floodplain' nor a 'riverbed'. This proved decisive and the Supreme Court held, '[t]he observation and conclusion of the High Court that the site in question is on a "riverbed" cannot be sustained', while adding, '[t]he decision of expert and an autonomous body, NEERI supported by the materials placed by other bodies such as CWPRS and MoEF, cannot be lightly interfered with by the Court without adequate contra materials.' Under these circumstances, the Court ruled that the DDA and other authorities are free to proceed with the work at CGV (Commonwealth Games Village) site.

The case threw up some hard questions. The findings of NEERI weighed heavily with the Court despite the fact that in the reports earlier submitted in 1999 and 2005, NEERI itself had not specifically permitted the government or the DDA to use the land in question for any other activities. However, in January 2008, it changed its view, and, as the Counsel in the case argued, only, 'in order to suit the convenience of the organisers of the CGV'. Apart from the NEERI report, only the dictionary meaning of floodplain and riverbed was decisive. In many countries there are specific floodplain legislations, but not in India. Why? A drought prone state like Rajasthan has a flood plain zoning law, but not Delhi. Why? A specific River Boards Act was enacted in 1956, but has never been used, leading to the result that no state in India has a River Board even today. Why? So long as these questions stare at us, the rivers would have to rely on the case by case, and unpredictable judicial determinations for their survival.

The Ganga Expressway Case

In another case where a high profile project was challenged on environmental grounds, a project of the construction of a 8-lane Express Highway (Ganga Express Highway), proposed to be constructed on left bank of river Ganga—from Noida to Ballia—was challenged on the grounds that the whole process of grant of the Environment Clearance was carried out with undue haste. The Allahabad High Court, while quashing the Environment Clearance, and referring to relevant regulations observed, 'Thus, undue haste and hurry in which every step was completed violating mandatory statutory provision proved the non-consideration of relevant environmental issues and acting with a pre-determined mind to somehow grant Environmental Clearance.'[47] In the ultimate analysis, the Court came to the conclusion that in the entire process of obtaining an Environmental Clearance there had been a flagrant violation of statutory provisions and such details, as were necessary to be given on application seeking clearance, were missing, depriving the Regulatory Authority to assess the magnitude of river pollution and vitiating the entire process of grant of Environmental Clearance. Dealing with the objection (always raised in such cases) of the government, that the Court should not interfere in the case as this was a policy question, the High Court held that when a question of Environmental Clearance of mega project comes before a Court in which issues of environmental degradation and pollution of the natural resources is involved, the Court should not shirk from its responsibility of examining as to whether such project violates any constitutional right guaranteed by the Constitution or any other statutory law. The Court in such cases has a duty to see that in the undertaking of the decision no law is violated and the people's fundamental rights are not transgressed except as permissible under the Constitution.

The Aravalli Mining Case

In another well known case on mining in Aravalli hills and in areas in Haryana like Faridabad, the Supreme Court observed:

> The Aravalli hill range has to be protected at any cost. In case despite stringent conditions, there is an adverse irreversible effect on the ecology in the Aravalli hill range area, at a later date, the total stoppage of mining activity in the area may have to be considered. For similar reasons such step may have to be considered in respect of mining in Faridabad district as well.

The jurisdiction and competence of the Apex Court to ban all mining was vehemently contested in the Supreme Court, but it overruled those while laying down the reasons and principle behind banning mining, if the situation warrants so. The principles are best put in the Courts' own words:

> Time has now come to suspend all mining in the above 'Area on Sustainable Development Principle' which is part of Articles 21, 48A

and 51A (g) of the Constitution of India... Mining within the Principle of Sustainable Development comes within the concept of 'balancing' whereas mining beyond the Principle of Sustainable Development comes within the concept of 'banning'. It is a matter of degree. Balancing of the mining activity with environment protection and banning such activity are two sides of the same principle of sustainable development. They are parts of Precautionary Principle.

The above principles became the basis for the Supreme Court to suspend all mining operations in the Aravalli hill range falling in the State of Haryana within the area of approximately 448 sq. km in the districts of Faridabad and Gurgaon including Mewat, till a Reclamation Plan duly certified by the State of Haryana, MoEF, and CEC is prepared in accordance with the applicable statutory provisions. The Aravalli mining case is increasingly important given that it is inspiring significant law and policy reform in Haryana today.

Key Cases on Social and Economic Rights

Case on Right to Water and Duty to Research on It

On 26 March 2009, the Supreme Court passed a detailed order relating to the problem of water shortage in our country and issued a notice to the Secretary, Ministry of Science and Technology asking him to file an affidavit within four weeks stating what measures have been taken to solve the water problem in the country and for implementing the recommendations given by the Court on the said day.[48] In a later order in the same case, the Court strongly opined, 'It is science alone which can solve this problem (as well as the other gigantic problems facing the country).' Citing earlier Supreme Court judgements the Court said, 'The right to get water is a part of the right to life guaranteed by Article 21 of the Constitution.' On this basis, the Court directed the central government to constitute a committee within two months,

> [w]hich shall do scientific research on a war footing for solving the water shortage in most parts of our country because of which our

people are suffering terribly.[49] In particular the Committee shall do the following:

(a) Scientific research on a war footing to find out inexpensive methods of converting saline water into fresh water. This will be very useful in the coastal states because the sea has almost an infinite amount of water reserves and the only problem is to find out inexpensive methods to convert it into fresh water. The present methods like distillation, reverse osmosis etc. are very expensive methods and cannot be afforded by a poor country like India. Hence we have to find out inexpensive methods and this is only possible by scientific research.

(b) Scientific research to find out methods of harnessing and managing monsoon rain water, manage the flood water, to do research in rain water harvesting, and treatment of waste water so that it may be recycled and be available as potable water.

(c) Any other methods or suggestions including for matters for protection and preservation of wet lands and matters connected thereto.[50]

The Court has clearly expressed its intention to monitor the progress from time to time. The Court's anxiety on the issue is understandable. More scientific research is welcome, but to put it mildly, research is just one end of the water problem in the country today.

Right to Safe Education Case

The Supreme Court in an important verdict laid down that the right to education incorporates the provision of safe schools and added that Articles 21 and 21A of the Constitution of India require that India's schoolchildren receive education in safe schools. The Court thus said that in order to give effect to the provisions of the Constitution, it has to be ensured that India's schools adhere to basic safety standards without further delay. This is because, 'It is the fundamental right of each and every child to receive education free from fear of security and safety.'[51] The observation of the Supreme Court on the nature and content of the word 'education' under the Constitution of India is worth reproducing here. The Court said:

The Constitution provides meaning to the word 'education' beyond its dictionary meaning. Parents should not be compelled to send their children to dangerous schools, nor should children suffer compulsory education in unsound buildings. Likewise, the State's reciprocal duty to parents begins with the provision of a free education, and it extends to the State's regulatory power. No matter where a family seeks to educate its children, the State must ensure that children suffer no harm in exercising their fundamental right and civic duty. States thus bear the additional burden of regulation, ensuring that schools provide safe facilities as part of a compulsory education.[52]

Based on the principles, the Court directed that before granting recognition or affiliation, the concerned state governments and union territories must ensure that the school buildings are safe and secured from every angle and they are constructed according to the safety norms incorporated in the National Building Code of India, amongst other such directions.

Right to Health and the Duty of Hospitals

A PIL was filed by All India Lawyers' Union seeking directions for ensuring free medical treatment in terms of the lease agreement entered into between the Government of National Capital Territory of Delhi and Indraprastha Apollo Hospital to establish a multi-disciplinary super specialty hospital. The petition was directed against the inaction of both the government and the hospital towards providing free treatment and medicines to poor and needy citizens at the hospital. Justice A.P. Shah, on behalf of the High Court said that the case presented a situation where 'right to health' of the public at large, recognised the world over (sufficiently delineated in India through Constitutional provisions, as interpreted by the superior courts), was at stake. By agreeing to be a partner with the state in the matter of health care, with stipulations about free health care to the specified extent, IMCL (Indraprastha Medical Corp Ltd) had taken onto itself the mantle of state instrumentality and further held, 'Health is a fundamental human right indispensable for the exercise of other human rights. Every human being is entitled to the enjoyment of the highest attainable standard of health conducive to living a life in dignity.'[53]

The Court surveyed international law in this context and found that the International Convention on Economic, Social and Cultural Rights (ICESCR) provides the most comprehensive article on the right to health in international human rights law. ICESCR calls upon State parties to 'Respect, protect and fulfil' their citizens' right to health. 'Respecting' the right to health means that the government must refrain from taking actions that inhibit or interfere with people's ability to enjoy their right. 'Protecting' the right to health means that the State must seek to protect the people from having their rights infringed by third parties, such as health care providers, private industry, pharmaceutical companies, researchers or vendors. 'Fulfilling' the right to health means that the government is required to take positive action to implement the right to health by adopting policies which allocate public resources to correct the deficiencies in health facilities, goods and services.[54]

In light of the above statements, the Court found that despite the fact that more than 15 years have elapsed since, there has been hardly any implementation of the conditions of the agreement providing for free treatment to indoor and outdoor patients and thus directed the hospital to provide one-third of the free beds, i.e., 200 beds, with adequate space and necessary facilities to the indoor patients, and also to make necessary arrangement for free facilities to 40 per cent of the outdoor patients, among other directions.

Right to Shelter of *Jhuggi* Dwellers

In another case before the Delhi High Court, the intervention of the Court was sought to rehabilitate and relocate the petitioners who were residing at various slum clusters in the Capital city, to a suitable place and providing them alternative land with ownership rights pursuant to demolition of their *jhuggi*s (hutments). It was submitted before the Court that the decision of the authorities for the demolition of their *jhuggi* cluster was in violation of the government policy/Master Plan Delhi 2021. Without making any provision for rehabilitation/relocation for the *jhuggi* dwellers, the demolition order was clearly arbitrary and discriminatory and had rendered the residents of those *jhuggi*es homeless, seriously affecting their Human Rights, as well as the Fundamental Rights as guaranteed under the Constitution. Justice A.P. Shah on behalf of the High Court wrote the judgement on the case and showed remarkable sensitivity towards the needs and the plight of the *jhuggi* dwellers in Delhi. He noted:

> In the last four decades, on account of pressure on agricultural land and lack of employment opportunities in the rural areas, a large number of people were forced to migrate to large cities like Delhi. However, in cities, their slender means as well as lack of access to legitimate housing, compelled them to live in existing jhuggi clusters or even to create a new one. They turned to big cities like Delhi only because of the huge employment opportunities here but then they are forced to live in jhuggies because there is no place other than that within their means. These jhuggi clusters constitute a major chunk of the total population of the city. Most of these persons living in the slums earn their livelihood as daily wage labourers, selling vegetables and other household items, some of them are rickshaw pullers and only few of them are employed as regular workers in industrial units in the vicinity while women work as domestic maid-servants in nearby houses. Their children also are either employed as child labour in the city; a few fortunate among them go to the municipal schools in the vicinity. The support service provided by these persons (whom the Master Plan describes as 'city service personnel') are indispensable to any affluent or even middle class household. The city would simply come to halt without the labour provided by these people. Considerations of fairness require special concern where these settled slum dwellers face threat of being uprooted. Even though their jhuggi clusters may be required to be legally removed for public projects, the consequences can be just as devastating when they are uprooted from their decades long settled position. What is very often overlooked is that when a family living in a jhuggi is forcibly evicted, each member loses a 'bundle' of rights—the right to livelihood, to shelter, to health, to education, to access to civic amenities and public transport and above all, the right to live with dignity.[55] In this regard, comments of Professor Bundy on the large number of forced evictions in South Africa, may be noted:

> 'There is a sense in which these appalling figures have been cited so often that we are

used to them: that we cease to realize their import, their horror—what they mean in terms of degradation, misery, and psychological and physical suffering.'

Bundy makes the point that 'trauma, frustration, grief, dull dragging apathy and [the] surrender of the will to live' are indeed some of the effects of forcible evictions on the human condition. And, the consequences span over multiple areas of social life: frequently it is the case that families are left homeless, their social support structures severed and their welfare services, jobs and educational institutions, rendered inaccessible.[56]

On consideration of applicable facts and law, the Court held that the decision of the government which held that the petitioners were on the 'right of way' and were therefore not entitled to relocation, was illegal and unconstitutional.

Right to Livelihood and Rehabilitation of Tribals

While examining the legal validity of the Kerala Scheduled Tribes (Restriction on Transfer of Lands and Restoration of Alienated Lands) Act, 1975, the Supreme Court had the opportunity to impress upon the Right to livelihood and of rehabilitation of the displaced tribal oustees. Thus the Court observed:

> We must also make it clear that while allotting land to the members of the Scheduled Tribe, the State cannot and must not allot them hilly or other types of lands which are not at all fit for agricultural purposes. The lands, which are to be allotted, must be similar in nature to the land possessed by the members of Scheduled Tribe. If in the past, such allotments have been made, as has been contended before us by the learned Counsel for the respondent, the State must allot them other lands which are fit for agricultural purposes. Such a process should be undertaken and completed as expeditiously as possible and preferably within a period of six months from date.[57]

Key Cases on Rural and Urban Local Governance

Case on Reservation in Panchayats in Tribal Areas

In a significant judgement, the Supreme Court held that in Panchayats located in Scheduled Areas (predominantly tribal areas), the exclusive representation of Scheduled Tribes in the Chairperson positions of the same bodies is constitutionally permissible. This is so because Article 243M(4)(b) expressly empowers the Parliament to provide for 'exceptions and modifications' in the application of Part IX to Scheduled Areas. Upholding the constitutionality of the Jharkhand Panchayat Raj Act (JPRA), the Court made clear:

> The provisos to Section 4(g) of PESA contemplate certain exceptions to the norm of 'proportionate representation' and the same exceptional treatment was incorporated in the impugned provisions of the JPRA.

The Supreme Court also laid down that it is constitutionally permissible to provide reservations in favour of Scheduled Castes (SCs), Scheduled Tribes (STs) and Other Backward Classes (OBCs) that together amount to 80 per cent of the seats in the Panchayati Raj Institutions located in Scheduled Areas of the State of Jharkhand.[58]

It is pertinent to note here that the law in this regard was settled by the Supreme Court in the landmark *Indira Sawhney case* where the Supreme Court had held that the reservations contemplated in Clause (4) of Article 16 of the Constitution of India should not exceed 50 per cent. However, most significantly, the Supreme Court also added in that case as follows:

> While 50 per cent shall be the rule, it is necessary not to put out of consideration, certain extraordinary situations inherent in the great diversity of this country and the people. It might happen that in far-flung and remote areas the population inhabiting those areas might, on account of their being put of the mainstream of national life and in view of conditions peculiar to and characteristic to them, need to be treated in a different way, some relaxation in this strict rule may become imperative. In doing so, extreme caution is to be exercised and a special case made out.[59]

The Supreme Court applied that exception carved out in the *Indira Sawhney case* above to the case of Panchayats in Scheduled Areas while upholding the constitutionality of JPRA, and held, quite significantly, as follows:

We believe that the case of Panchayats in Scheduled Areas is a fit case that warrants exceptional treatment with regard to reservations. The rationale behind imposing an upper ceiling of 50 per cent in reservations for higher education and public employment cannot be readily extended to the domain of political representation at the Panchayat level in Scheduled Areas. With respect to education and employment, parity is maintained between the total number of reserved and unreserved seats in order to maintain a pragmatic balance between the affirmative action measures and considerations of merit... However, the same approach of providing proportionate representation is likely to be less effective in the context of reservations for Panchayats in Scheduled Areas. One reason for this is the inherent difference between the nature of benefits that accrue from access to education and employment on one hand and political participation on the other. While access to higher education and public employment increases the likelihood of gradual socio-economic empowerment of the individual beneficiaries, involvement in local self-government is intended as a more immediate measure of protection for the individual as well as the community that he/she belongs to. Especially in the context of Scheduled Areas, there is a compelling need to safeguard the interests of tribal communities with immediate effect by giving them an effective voice in local self-government...[60]

In laying down the principles of reservation for Panchayats in Schedule V areas the Supreme Court was resonating the words of the Madhya Pradesh High Court from over a decade ago when the High Court had held:

... to safeguard interests of Scheduled Tribes living in remote or hilly areas or forests with primitive culture of their own, the Constitution envisages formation of Scheduled Areas for them, and application of laws to them with 'exceptions and modifications', so that they are able to preserve their culture and occupation and are not exposed to exploitation by forward classes of Urban Population. The protective discrimination in favour of such deprived section of the society can go to the extent of complete exclusion, if the circumstances so justify, of advanced classes in Local Self Governance of Scheduled Areas.[61]

In addition to the above principles, the Supreme Court, while upholding the constitutionality of the JPRA, was following the constitutional value and principle of equality. On the ideas of 'substantive equality' and 'distributive justice' which are at the heart of our understanding of the guarantee of 'equal protection before the law' the Supreme Court said, 'The State can treat unequals differently with the objective of creating a level playing field in the social, economic, and political spheres.'[62]

Formation of Municipal Corporation a Constitutional Requirement

In an important case in the Gujarat High Court, the petitioner sought an order from the court so as to direct the state government to constitute a Municipal Corporation for Gandhinagar City, as required under Part IX-A (i.e., 'The Municipalities') of the Constitution of India. It was argued that it is a constitutional obligation of the state government to constitute a Municipal Corporation for a large urban area like Gandhinagar and the non-fulfilment of such constitutional requirements is a serious erosion of citizens' rights and it would undermine the object and purpose of the 74th Constitutional Amendment Act, 1992. The High Court's exposition of the circumstances under which the 74th Constitutional Amendment Act came into being was instructive. It said:

The manner in which the urban and local bodies were functioning in India was subjected to serious criticism at various levels. It was noticed that in many States the Urban and Local bodies were not able to perform effectively as vibrant democratic units of self-governance. They had become weak and ineffective on account of a number of reasons such as failure to hold regular elections, prolonged suppression and inadequate devolution of powers and functions. Taking into consideration these inadequacies it was felt that the provisions relating to Urban Local Bodies should be incorporated in the Constitution particularly for putting the relationship between the Urban Local Bodies and the State Government on a firmer footing with respect to the functions and taxation powers and the arrangements for revenue sharing, ensuring regular conduct of elections, ensuring timely elections in case of super-session, and providing adequate representation for the weaker sections and Scheduled Castes, Scheduled Tribes and women. Accordingly, by the Constitution (Seventy Fourth Amendment)

Act, 1992, a new part viz. Part IX-A was added in the Constitution to make provisions with respect to Urban Local Bodies. These provisions have been inserted with a view to provide for the setting up of democratic institutions at the grass root level.[63]

The Court then proceeded to observe, '[b]y non-formation of the Municipal Corporation at Gandhinagar, the constitutional require-ment providing above mentioned provisions (of Part IX-A) has been given a complete go-bye'. The Court amplified the observation by further adding, 'Requirement of formation of a Municipal Corporation, in our view, is a constitutional requirement. If statutory re-quirements and constitutional requirements are not complied with, it is the bounden duty of a Constitutional Court to direct the State Gov-ernment to implement those constitutional requirements. Failure to do so by Constitutional Court will be failure to uphold the Constitution and the laws.' 'The High Court thus directed the State Government to form a Municipal Corporation at Gandhinagar in accordance with the constitutional requirement of Article 243Q (under Part IX-A) within a period of six months.'[64]

Slum Development for Minorities: A Constitutional Ideal

In another case before the Gujarat High Court, it had an opportunity to survey various schemes for slum development. The Court noted that through the Integrated Housing and Slum Development Programme and the Jawaharlal Nehru National Urban Renewal Mission, the central government provides assistance to states/union territories for development of urban slums through provision of physical amenities and basic services. However, facts reveal that sizable members of minority com-munities inhabit in slums and the necessity of improving their living conditions need not be over-emphasised. The Court noticed that various urban development programmes envisage that their benefits flow equitably to members of the minority communities and to the cities/slums, predominantly inhabited by minority com-munities. In this backdrop, a PIL was filed which raised the contention that national resources

are being utilised for betterment of a particular religion which is impermissible in law. The High Court noted:

> Welfare of the people is ultimate goal of the State actions. State, if finds, that a minority community is not equally placed with the majority community, socially or economically, can take steps to minimise inequalities and bring that community at par with those com-munities which are otherwise well placed in the social fabrics of the society.[65]

On this premise, the Court categorically held that the funds used to minimise inequalities among minority communities by adopting various social and welfare activities like public safety, health, slum development, improving the deficiencies in civic amenities, economic op-portunities, improving standard of education, skill and entrepreneurship development, em-ployment opportunities, eradication of poverty, and so on, would in no way violate the consti-tutional principles of equality or affect any of the fundamental rights guaranteed to the members of the other communities.

CONCLUSION

A review of some of the key cases of the year gone by shows that there has been a range of positive pronouncements by the Supreme Court and the High Courts in areas of civil liberties, social and economic rights, environment and development, and on issues in rural and urban self governance. Together they tell a story that the Judiciary continues to play its vital role as a guardian of rights and of order in society. Indeed some of the Judges, and in particular, Justice A.P. Shah from the High Court of Delhi, wrote some landmark judgements throughout the last year but the story the cases discussed earlier hide is that some of these cases are occasioned primarily due to judicial pronouncements of the past remaining unimplemented. This trend had motivated the Chairperson of the Law Commission of India to write to the Union Law minister while forwarding the 223rd Report of the Commission to the Ministry in April 2009. He said:

Various laws have been enacted to eradicate poverty: some of them directly deal with them and some of them indirectly. Nevertheless, their tardy implementation makes us lag behind in effectively dealing with the problem... We are of the view that the Union and the State Governments should accord top priority to implementation of the judgements rendered by our Supreme Court in their letter and spirit in order that the lot of the have-nots is ameliorated.

A mapping of key verdicts of the Supreme Court and the High Court, and especially, put together, it gives an impression that the Courts have been accessible to a range of public issues. However, this also is not the whole truth. It has been pointed out in first part of the review that research has established that in 2008, the Supreme Court received 24,666 letters, postcards, or petitions asking for its intervention in cases that might be considered public interest litigation. Of these, only 226 were placed before judges on admission days, and only a small fraction of these were heard as regular hearing matters. The rest were rejected. Numbers may not reveal all but they do suggest that the jury is out on the accessibility of the Supreme Court on public interest issues today. The trends also point to the imperative of understanding the instrument of PIL better. There is a need to understand the various distinct traditions within the PIL jurisprudence resulting from the different categories of public interest issues brought in the higher courts. Such an understanding is central to evolving a more nuanced and effective approaches on the issues and concerns around public interest litigation in future.

As the issues in Judicial corruption and transparency discussed in the first part show, throughout the last year the Judiciary was in the news almost every day, and on many occasions for wrong reasons. Justice Saumitra Sen, Justice Dinakaran and cash at the door of judge scam made repeated appearances in the newspapers. The conduct of the Supreme Court itself on the judges' assets declaration and on the Justice Dinakaran controversy was questionable. However, a range of verdicts and decisions discussed at length in the first half of the chapter, has seen us through some of these controversies.

The role of some of the judges of the Delhi High Court along with the bodies like the CIC, in this regard, needs acknowledgement and appreciation by the civil society. The positive role of Committee on Judicial Accountability, and some senior and respected lawyers should also not be lost sight of as they infused hope and optimism. Some of the new proposals of the Ministry of Law and Justice are also potentially far reaching, though a touch ambitious. Articulation of a National Litigation Policy and proposal to create of a National Arrears Grid deserve a close follow up as we move ahead. Clearly, those who say 'all is lost' are as much as off the mark, as those who say, 'all is well' with the judiciary and the legal system.

NOTES

1   Secretary General, *Supreme Court of India v. Subhash Chandra Aggarwal*, LPA No. 501/2009, Judgement pronounced on 12 January 2010.

2   He referred to Section 2(e)(i) and held that the CJI is a 'competent authority' empowered to frame rules under Section 28 to carry out the provisions of the Act and thus concluded that the CJI and the Supreme Court cannot disclaim being public authorities.

3   The CIC noted that neither the CPIO nor the first appellate authority had claimed that the information asked for is exempted on account of 'fiduciary relationship' or it being 'personal information'. He further noted that the applicant was apparently not seeking a copy (or inspection) of the declaration or the contents thereof or even the names, and so on, of the Judges giving the same. He concluded that the exemptions under Sections 8(1)(e) or 8(1)(j) were not attracted to the case.

4   Secretary General, *Supreme Court of India v. Subhash Chandra Aggarwal*, op. cit.

5   Ibid., para 102.

6   Ibid., para 121.

7   In this case, RTI activist Subhash Chandra Aggarwal had sought the complete correspondence between authorities concerned relating to appointment of Justices H.L. Dattu, A.K. Ganguly and R.M. Lodha, superseding seniority of Justices A.P. Shah, A.K. Patnaik and V.K. Gupta as allegedly objected by Prime Minister's Office. For more information visit the website of the Campaign for Judicial Accountability and Judicial Reforms (CJAR) at www.judicialreforms.org.

8 As a small piece from *Hindustan Times* quipped:

> So is this a tremendously brave move? Well, considering that no one can do anything about the information posted on www. supremecourtofindia.nic.in/assets.htm (ask questions about the posted assets, for instance), it's a touching gesture that's not quite revolutionary. Also, considering that the judges are tax-payers like the rest of us, the matter of their assets being in the 'public domain' should have been a given anyway.

See 'It's Greek to Us', *Hindustan Times*, 3 November 2009.

9 See Iyer, V.R. Krishna. 2009. 'Limits of Judicial Conduct', *The Hindu*, 7 August.

10 It was further alleged that he had acquired a lot of other expensive immovable property, including a commercial complex in the name of his wife in 2001–02 (where he is alleged to have recently spent over 2.5 crore for construction), and a residential house in Anna Nagar, Chennai in the name of his wife in 2004–05 for over 90 lakh. See, Bhushan, Prashant. Undated. 'The Dinakaran Imbroglio: Appointment and Complaints against Judges'. Available online at www.judicialreforms.org

11 For more details on these cases see, 'The Dinakaran Imbroglio: Appointment and Complaints against Judges', supra.

12 See for example, 'Loathing and Fearing in T.N. Village', *Mail Today*, 23 September 2009.

13 *K. Veeraswamy v. Union of India & Others*, 1991 (3) SCC 655 (para 79–80).

14 *R.K. Anand v. Registrar, Delhi High Court*, 2009 (8) SCC 106.

15 The Government of India established the First Law Commission of Independent India in 1955 with the then Attorney-General of India, Mr M.C. Setalvad, as its Chairman.

16 They are cited in courts, in academic and public discourses, and are acted upon by concerned government departments depending on the government's recommendations. The Law Commission of India has so far forwarded 234 reports on different subjects. For more details on the composition and mandate of the Law Commission of India, online at www.lawmin.nic.in.

17 The Report titled, 'Need for division of the Supreme Court into a Constitution Bench at Delhi and Cassation Benches in four regions at Delhi, Chennai/Hyderabad, Kolkata and Mumbai', Law Commission of India, 2009.

18 CJI K.G. Balakrishnan in a recent interview to *The Hindu* said that the Supreme Court must, 'think… seriously' about setting up a constitutional court.

19 Robinson, Nick. 'Hard to Reach', *Frontline*. Available online at: http://www.flonnet.com/fl2703/stories/20100212270304600.htm.

20 Justice Krishna Iyer explained further:

> If democracy is for the people, the Supreme Court should function where the litigants need it most, not where the British for their imperial reasons chose to locate it. It was for historical and geographic-strategic grounds that Delhi was chosen as the national capital. Delhi has no other claim to be the capital seat of the judiciary as well.

See Iyer, V.R. Krishna. 2010. 'Questions of Judicial Access', *The Hindu*, 3 February.

21 See the Report, 'Structure and Jurisdiction of the Higher Judiciary', Law Commission of India, New Delhi, 1978.

22 These arguments have been developed and extracted from Videh Upadhyay (2002) in the article 'More Cases, More Judges, More Courts'. Available online at: http://www.indiatogether.org/opinions/vupadh/videh1102.htm.

23 See Report No. 223 of the Law Commission of India, forwarded to the Law Minister on 30 April 2009.

24 In Dr Justice Lakshmanan's words:

> Increasingly, we are becoming aware that we are all members of a single human family. In a family, the suffering of any member is felt by all, and until that suffering is alleviated, no member of the family can be fully happy or at ease. Few are able to look at starvation and extreme poverty without feeling a sense of failure.

25 Report No. 223 of the Law Commission of India, op. cit., para 1.10.

26 *Francis Coralie Mullin v. Administrator, Union Territory of India*, AIR 1981 SC 746.

27 *Narendra Kumar v. The State of Haryana*, JT (1994) 2 SC 94.

28 *State of Punjab v. Mohinder Singh Chawla*, AIR 1997 SC 1225.

29 *UP Avas Vikas Parishad v. Friends Cooperative Housing Society Ltd.*, AIR 1996 SC 114.

30 Nick Robinson, op. cit.

31 See *Hussainara Khatoon v. State of Bihar*, AIR 1979 SC 1364. It added in another case at the same time, 'There can be no doubt that speedy trial—and by speedy trial we mean a reasonably expeditious trial—is an integral and essential part of fundamental right to life and liberty enshrined in Art 21'. See *Maneka Gandhi v. Union of India*, AIR 1978 SC 597.

32 Thus, Advocate General for the State can be appointed after he/she attains the age of 62 years and similarly the Attorney General for India can be appointed after he/she attains the age of 65 years. See *State of Uttaranchal v. Balwant Singh Chaufal and Ors*, 2010(1) SCALE492.

33 The Court later opined:

> The Public Interest Litigation, which has been in existence in our country for more than four decades, has a glorious record. This Court and the High Courts, by their judicial creativity and craftsmanship, have passed a number of directions in the larger public interest in consonance with the inherent spirits of the Constitution. The conditions of marginalised and vulnerable section of society have significantly improved on account of courts directions in the PIL.

34 *S.P. Gupta v. Union of India*, 1981 Supp SCC 87: AIR 1982 SC 149: (1982) 2 SCR 365; *Bandhua Mukti Morcha v. Union of India*, (1984) 3 SCC 161: AIR 1984 SC 802: (1984) 2 SCR 67; *State of H.P. v. 4 Parent of a Student of Medical College*, (1985) 3 SCC 169: AIR 1985 SC 910; *Forward Construction Co. v. Prabhat Mandal*, (1986) 1 SCC 100: AIR 1986 SC 391; *MC. Mehta v. Union of India*, (1987) 1 SCC 395: AIR 1987 SC 1086.

35 Nick Robinson, op. cit.

36 For further points and more arguments on 'sub-traditions' of Public Interest Litigation, see: Upadhyay, Videh and Lexis Nexis Butterworths. 2007. *Public Interest Litigation in India: Concepts, Cases Concerns*.

37 See AIR 2009 SC 1674.

38 *Indu Jain v. State of M.P. & Ors*, AIR 2009 SC 976.

39 *Pooran Singh v. State of M.P. & Ors*, AIR 2009 Madhya Pradesh 153.

40 *Tasleema v. State (NCT of Delhi) & Ors*, MANU/DE/0870/2009.

41 *Suchita Srivastava v. Chandigarh Administration*, (2009) 9 SCC 1.

42 *Dr Satish Menan v. State of M.P.*, AIR 2009 Madhya Pradesh 185.

43 *Naz Foundation v. Government of NCT and Ors*, 160 (2009) DLT277 at Para 130.

44 *Manishi Jani s/o Thakorlal Jethalal Jani & Anr. v. State of Gujarat thro Chief Secretary and 2 Ors*, AIR 2010 Guj 30.

45 *Kamal R. Khan v. State of Maharashtra*, 2009(4) Bom CR496 at para 12-A.

46 *Paljor Bhutia v. State of Sikkim and Ors*, AIR 2010 Sik 1 at para 8.

47 *Ganga Mahasabha & Anr. v. Union of India & Ors*, 2009 (5) ALJ 588 (DB).

48 *State of Orissa v. Government of India and Anr*, 2009(2) SCALE 271.

49 The Court added:

> This Committee shall have the Secretary, Union Ministry of Science & Technology as its Chairman. Amongst the members of the Committee will be the Secretary, Union Ministry of Water Management. The other members of the Committee will be scientists specialized in the field of solving water shortage problems nominated by the Chairman of the Committee and they are requested to take help from foreign scientists specialised in this field. The members of the Committee should regard this work as a patriotic duty, and the entire people of India including NRIs settled abroad should help this Committee.

See *State of Orissa v. Government of India and Anr*, op. cit.

50 *State of Orissa v. Government of India and Anr*, op. cit., at Para 10.

51 *Avinash Mehrotra v. Union of India (UOI) and Ors*, (2009) 6 SCC 398.

52 Ibid., at para 31.

53 *All India Lawyers Union (Delhi Unit) v. Govt. of NCT of Delhi and Ors*, 172(2009) DLT 319, at para 30 and 31.

54 Kuszzler, Patricia C. 2007. 'Global health and the Human Rights Imperative', *Asian Journal of WTO and International Health Law and Policy*, 2(1) March, and quoted in *All India Lawyers Union (Delhi Unit) v. Govt. of NCT of Delhi and Ors*, op. cit., at para 34.

55 *Sudama Singh and Ors. v. Government of Delhi and Anr*, MANU/DE/0353/2010, at para 44.

56 *Occupiers of 51, Olivia Road, Berea Township, and 197 Main Street, Johannesburg v. City of Johannesburg and Ors.*, (2008) ZACC 1: 2008 (3) SA 208 (CC): 2008(5) BCLR 475 (CC) at para 17 and quoted in *Sudama Singh and Ors. v. Government of Delhi and Anr*, op. cit.

57 *State of Kerala and Anr. v. Peoples Union for Civil Liberties, Kerala State Unit and Ors*, (2009) 8 SCC 46, at para 172.

58 See *Union of India v. Rakesh Kumar*, 2010(1) SCALE 281. The High Court had struck down the relevant provisions of the JPRA as unconstitutional by virtue of reasoning that reservations to the extent of 80 per cent of the seats in Panchayats were excessive, arbitrary and disproportionate, thereby violating Article 14 of the Constitution. The Counsels relied on earlier judgement of the Supreme Court and the Patna High Court which had prescribed an upper ceiling of 50 per cent for reservation of posts in public employment.

59 *Indra Sawhney v. Union of India*, (1992) Supp 3 SCC 217, at para 810.

60 *Union of India v. Rakesh Kumar*, op. cit., at para 34.

61 *Ashok Kumar Tripathi v. Union of India*, 2000 (2) MPHT 193, at para 36 and 37.

62 *Union of India v. Rakesh Kumar*, op. cit., at para 28.

63 *Gandhinagar Saher Jagrut Nagrik Parishard v. State of Gujarat and 2 Ors*, MANU/GJ/0438/2009, at para 7.

64 Ibid., at para 11 and 12.

65 *Vijay Harishchandra Patel v. Union of India (UOI) and Anr*, (2009) 3 GLR 2153, at para 10.

The State of Decentralisation and Local Governance in India: Interrogating Institutions, Programmes and Service Delivery

chapter 4

INTRODUCTION

Decentralised local governance is frequently promoted as a solution to the failure of centralised development not only in India, but also globally. It is assumed that decentralised local governance would facilitate effective people's participation, an enhanced degree of transparency, and ensure greater accountability, which in turn will lead to effective and competitive delivery of services at the local level. The underlying argument is that centralised planning has been relatively unsuccessful in the delivery of developmental goals as it failed to consider local issues and contexts. Grassroots institutions and local people have a better understanding of local issues and context; so they can manage local development better and make development inclusive. Moreover, decentralisation is frequently promoted as a tool for inclusive development, fostering citizenship and democratic practice through effective participation at the grassroots. In this section, we aim to analyse how far these objectives are met. After two decades of decentralisation, has India achieved inclusive development? Does mere existence of local institutions result in effective participation?

The concept of local governance is often used as a synonym for grassroots governance, i.e., at the level of Panchayats and municipalities. However, the concept has a much wider meaning and implications. In recent years however, decentralised local governance has become a fluid and flexible discourse that can be utilised by different ideological interests. Interpretation of the concept is wide enough to include informal community-based participatory initiatives, micro-privatisation, public-private initiatives and formal grassroots institutions of governance. For the purpose of analysis in this report, we focus on the formal aspect of the concept, i.e., the local government. The previous five editions of the *Citizen's Report on Governance and Development* had focused on different aspects of formal local governments in India. The reports analysed the institutional structure, performance, accountability, level of decentralisation and governance process.

In this report, we focus on three key institutions, the State Election Commission (SEC), the State Finance Commission (SFC) and the District Planning Committee (the 3Cs), responsible for ensuring effectively functioning local governments and three Centrally Sponsored Schemes (CSSs), the Mahatma Gandhi Rural Employment Guarantee Act, the National Rural Health Mission and the Jawaharlal Nehru National Urban Renewal Mission, implemented at the local level by local government institutions. The report also interrogates the quality of delivery of basic services at grassroots levels. In this chapter, we aim to assess the effectiveness of local governments in India, make some policy recommendations for improvement of the same and improve the quality of service delivery at the grassroots level. This chapter is organised as follows. The following section provides a brief overview of decentralisation and local governance in India. This chapter examines the importance and performance of three key institutions (3Cs) responsible of ensuring effectiveness of local governments in India. In addition, it also analyses implementation of the three Centrally Sponsored Schemes targeted at the poor and designed to engage local government institutions and the role and effectiveness of local government institutions and quality of service delivery. In the final section, we convey some concluding thoughts, some recommendations for improving formal local governance in India and improving the quality of service delivery for the poor.

DECENTRALISATION AND LOCAL GOVERNANCE IN INDIA: AN OVERVIEW

Decentralisation is not a new concept; it took place all across the globe over the 20th century. Since the 1980s however, the decentralisation of governmental functions for development objectives has become a truly global movement, especially in the developing countries, induced by several pressures like poor governmental performance, rapid urbanisation, democratic transition, societal demands and shifts in lending portfolio of international donors.[1] During this period, the concept of decentralisation has become so popular, particularly among bilateral aid donors and academics that it is referred to as 'the latest fashion'[2] and 'a fashion of our time'.[3]

Decentralisation has conventionally been defined as transfer of power, authority and responsibility from higher to lower levels of government, i.e., from national to sub-national to local levels. In this conventional sense, 'Decentralisation might be seen as a simple structural consequence of a re-allocation of functions within government.'[4] Decentralisation is not so simple, as it can take on numerous forms and degrees with various reasons. Rather, it is a process of redefining structures, governance procedures and practices. Decentralisation as a concept has evolved and transformed over time, undergoing social, economic and political changes and taken diverse and varied meanings, forms and objectives.[5] However, intermittently, we can see the evolution and transformation of decentralisation in India, which culminated in

the formalisation of the concept and formation of local government institutions through Constitutional provisions. Formalisation of decentralisation in India had several objectives:

1. Achieve greater responsiveness and responsibility from the government towards its citizens;
2. Promote effective bottom-up planning;
3. Ensure functional division between policy-making and execution; and
4. Ensure democratic participatory governance.

Before we assess how far these objectives have been met, we shall briefly analyse the structure of local governments, the constitutional provisions and implementation in this section.

The 73rd and 74th Constitutional Amendments followed the precept of the failed Rajiv Gandhi's 64th and 65th Constitutional Amendment Bills' strategy of avoiding changes in the 7th Schedule to strengthen local government. The twin constitutional amendments attempted to accomplish this through a few mandatory provisions and a number of optional provisions on devolution of powers, functions and finances to local governments that the states have ignored but which the Centre has been pursuing though without any success. While the mandatory provisions have been complied with by the states, the most important fallout of these amendments has been the changed constitutional right of existence of local bodies from their earlier discretionary creation and abolition by the states. This follows from the elected nature of local bodies along with their claim on peoples' sovereignty that they now share with the states and the Centre. This fundamentally changes the nature of state–local relations that need to be reflected in law and practice in the future. The earlier concept of the state 'as the mother of local bodies' has now been replaced by the state 'as the nurse of local bodies'. The mandatory provisions under the 73rd and 74th Constitutional Amendments are presented in Table 4.1, which indicates the relative success of the tenure and election of local bodies compared to limited achievement in the other areas, viz., typology, working of the SFCs, and of the planning committees, as noted

Table 4.1 Mandatory Provisions under the 73rd and 74th Constitutional Amendments for the Panchayats and Municipalities

Areas	Mandatory provisions	Implementation
1. Typology: tiers and levels	• Three tiers of Panchayats—at the district, intermediate and village levels and three levels of municipalities—municipal corporation, municipal council and town council (*Nagar* Panchayat) for large, small and transitional areas; • large municipalities with >300,000 population to have ward committees.	• This meant business as usual, except adding *Nagar* Panchayats as the smallest level of municipalities; • for Panchayats, allocation of functions and taxes among tiers is made arbitrarily; • for municipalities, municipal councils and *Nagar* Panchayats have same functions, taxes, elected executive, staffing and control; as in the past; • municipal corporations have larger functions, taxes and an appointed executive, as in the past; the ward committees do not act as decentralised units of large municipalities.
2. Tenure and duration	• Five years; if dissolved, election is to be held after expiry of the original tenure.	This turned out to be the most important provision; dissolution of local bodies is permitted if there is political deadlock in the council; judicial review.
3. Election and council composition	• To be conducted by State Election Commission (SEC); • reservation of seats for scheduled castes/tribes in reserved constituencies, one-third of seats reserved for women.	• This has engaged most attention from the states for (a) constituency delimitation, (b) preparation of electoral rolls, (c) widening the reservation quota to include other backward classes, (d) seat reservation for office bearers of the councils and (e) dual council membership with state legislature/Parliament.
4. State Finance Commissions	• To be recommended by the State Finance Commissions (SFCs); • the Central Finance Commission (CFC) to assist the states for grants to the Panchayats and municipalities on the basis of SFCs' recommendations.	• This had limited success due to the states' reluctance to: (a) devolve exclusive and additional functions to the local bodies; (b) increase grants to the local bodies and (c) inability of the SFCs to suggest grants on 'normative' gap filling method, as adopted by the CFCs.
5. District and metropolitan planning committees	• District and metropolitan planning committees in each district and metropolitan area to prepare 'draft development plans'.	• This has been a non-starter due to (a) the failure of DPC to take off and (b) except West Bengal, no other state has constituted MPC.

by the 2nd Administrative Reforms Commission (SARC).[6]

The 'discretionary provisions' of the amendments included:

1. Devolution of powers and functions;
2. Local domain of functions and taxes;
3. Extent of local autonomy;
4. Introducing political executive and separate staffing in local bodies;
5. Voter-accountability;
6. Local fiscal responsibility and budget management; and
7. Declaring local bodies as units of '*local* self-government'.

In other words, the entire issue of institutional empowerment of local bodies was left to the discretion of the states. The SARC recommended following the South African model of enacting a 'framework law' within which these issues could be resolved but this required its adoption by a few states to start with for other states to follow. This meant that a Constitutional Amendment is needed to override the 7th Schedule power of the states.

The other two options considered and rejected by the Commission were, (*a*) inserting a local list of functions and taxes in the 7th Schedule, and (*b*) transferring the subject 'local government' from the state list to the concurrent list.

Both these options were considered by the Commission as infeasible. The Centre, since passing the twin amendments, has lost interest in local government reforms and continues with its policy to treat the 7th Schedule arrangement as sacrosanct, until it musters enough political strength to initiate a second constitutional reform to strengthen local government. Meanwhile, the states would be incentivised through a 'Devolution Index' (DI)[7] attached to the CFC grants.

The two strategies advocated by the Ministry of Panchayati Raj (MoPR) for the states are:

1. Undertaking activity mapping, and to delineating functional activities between the state and the Panchayats; and
2. Application of the subsidiary principle for allocating functions among the three tiers of Panchayats.

A look at the completed activity mapping undertaken by a state shows the hollowness of such claim, as shown in Box 4.1.

We now turn to a closer look at the strategy of the twin amendments on decentralisation to local governments covering functions, finances and functionaries, or the 3-Fs. The inclusion of functionaries is a purely Indian innovation. The underlying idea is that as a result of decentralisation, the states find it difficult to deal with their surplus staff and send them to the local bodies without assessing their need, their ability to pay, or allowing them the option of outsourcing some of their activities. In other words, any increase in financial devolution would be tied to pay the salary of the transferred state staff and cannot be more economically spent on the transferred functions.

The MoPR is operating an incentive scheme called, 'Panchayat Empowerment and Accountability Incentive Scheme' (PEAIS) to (*a*) empower the Panchayats for 3-Fs devolution in terms of a Devolution Index prepared by the National Council of Applied Economic Research (NCAER), and (*b*) to establish accountability systems for the Panchayats. Box 4.2 presents the details of the scheme.

A study by Alok and Chaubey (2010) assesses the enabling environment that the states have created for the Panchayats to function as institutions of self-governance. In terms of devolution, states have moved with differential pace vis-à-vis one another and have not observed changes in different dimensions in a concomitant manner. The study provides a comprehensive ranking of states based on four devolution indices: mandatory frames, functions, finances and functionaries. It finds that no state has secured the same rank in all dimensions, but it also shows that high ranking states have shown a remarkable congruity in most of the indicators of devolution. The top five states are Kerala, Karnataka, Tamil Nadu, West Bengal and Maharashtra respectively. While 10 states are above the national average, 13 states are below national average. All of the southern states have performed better than the national average (see Annexure 4.4). Notwithstanding the fact that Panchayats are evolving, the states have to go a long way in devolving powers to Panchayats to enable them function as institutions of self-governance.

Both the NCAER and the IIPA Devolution Indices suffer from similar disabilities for mixing up the issues of devolution and accountability in the same index, and also for not raising relevant questions on the degree of devolution by the states. Both the studies seek to measure the extent of devolution by the states to the Panchayats in terms of 3-Fs, i.e., functions, finances and functionaries, by transferring powers and finances, but not by empowering them to take decisions in their sphere of activities. Even within the limited scope of empowering the Panchayats, the studies do not seek the relevant issues in the 3-Fs. For instance, no attempt is made to find out the extent of exclusive functions/activities that the Panchayats are supposed to do on their own. Similarly, on the financial front, the focus of the studies should have been on the extent of fiscal autonomy the Panchayats enjoy and the proportion of central and state grants in Panchayats' revenue. The functionaries aspect is introduced on the assumption that the Panchayats would depend on the transferred state employees to carry out their activities instead of enabling them to have staff of their

---

Box 4.1   Activity Mapping in a State

- Executive order by the state's Panchayat department issued in November 2005 remains inoperative as matching orders have not been issued by the functional departments.
- The order was not based on the principles of devolution.
- Functional devolution was not accompanied by transfer of related staff.
- Fund placement was left at the discretion of the line departments.
- No arrangement was made to transfer the activities of the parallel state agencies to the Panchayats.
- Most of the activities related to identification of beneficiaries of plan schemes, monitoring the activities of agencies without any control, the Panchayats have some control over only two subjects—drinking water, and health sub-centres.
- The order seeks to control the internal management of the Panchayats in respect of transferred schemes.
- GPs have no role in managing primary education and *anganwadi* centres.

Source: Ghosh, Buddhadeb: 'Activity Mapping- search for a methodology', ISS, New Delhi, n.d.

Box 4.2   Panchayat Empowerment and Accountability Incentive Scheme (PEAIS)

The Panchayat Empowerment and Accountability Incentive Scheme (PEAIS) is a Central Sector Scheme funded by Government of India to the State Governments/UTs.

Objectives of PEAIS: The Scheme was formulated with an objective to empower Panchayats as institutions of local self-government as per Article 243G of the Constitution and provide incentives to the States to undertake reforms concerning Panchayati Raj. The aims of the scheme are to (a) incentivise states to empower Panchayats, and (b) incentivise Panchayats to put in place accountability systems that go a long way towards making them transparent and efficient.

Basis of Incentives: The performance index of State Governments/UTs to devolve the 3-Fs (functions finance and functionaries) to Panchayati Raj Institutions (PRIs) is based on Working Devolution Index (DI) formulated by the NCAER and by the IIPA.

Source: Government of India (MoPR).

own, which is a highly centralist approach of promoting decentralisation. On all these fronts, the studies fail to focus their queries to relate to issues of devolution and instead fall prey to the current agenda of the MoPR that has little to do with devolution *per se.*

The scheme of devolution to the local bodies under the 73rd and 74th Constitutional Amendments was optional for the states, who took full advantage of the discretion under Articles 243G (for the Panchayats) and 243W (for the municipalities), along with the two illustrative lists of areas of functions/activities to be devolved. For the Panchayats, the issue is of vital significance as the state legislations do not delegate specific functions/activities to them in exclusive terms and expect them to act as implementation agencies for central and state schemes for rural development. The issue here is whether the Panchayats are to continue as agency institutions or institutions for providing local services. The Planning Commission and the 13th Finance Commission had divergent views in this matter. The implementation of a myriad of rural and urban development schemes may keep the local bodies busy, but this has nothing to do with decentralisation.

Local governments as delegated entities are legally accountable to the states and this is known as 'vertical accountability'. With the constitutional recognition of their right of existence, there is a case for shifting their accountability to the constituency level. This would change the ethos of the local bodies as mere delegates to the position of primacy in the provision of local services. The key to constituency or 'vertical accountability' is availability of relevant information to the citizens. With the enactment of the right to information (RTI) law, popular

interest in the activities of local government is on the increase. The states are also expected to incorporate citizen's charter in the Panchayat and municipal legislations; the problem is an absence of statutory listing of Panchayat functions across the states, except in Kerala.

The 73rd and 74th Amendments provided for institutional arrangements for 'downward accountability' through mandated wards committees in the large municipalities and optional village assemblies (*Gram Sabhas*[8]) at the village level, but these are yet to be effective. The municipal ward committees need to be backed by a decentralised set-up of municipal service delivery, while the *Gram Sabhas* could be involved in the design and implementation of village level schemes and projects. A detailed discussion on the role, functions and performance of *Gram Sabhas* is provided in our previous report (see *Citizen's Report on Governance and Development 2007*).

INSTITUTIONS OF LOCAL GOVERNANCE: STATUS OF 3Cs

State Election Commission

The State Election Commissions (SECs) are key institutional players in ensuring effective local government institutions in India. SECs for all States and Union Territories were constituted under Articles 243K[9] and 243ZA[10] of the Constitution of India, and are vested with the powers to conduct elections for local government institutions. With less than two decades' experience, the SECs have been playing an important role in local governance by conducting elections for more than three million representatives to local government institutions with a combined electorate of 714 million voters (larger than the electorate of European Union and United States combined).

While the SECs perform functions similar to that of the Election Commission of India, they are independent of the latter. However, the powers, functions and performance of the SECs, to some extent, varies across states and are in some cases constrained by authority vested with the respective State Legislatures to define the role of SECs and to make provisions in connection with election to local government (see Article 243K, Clause 4 and Article 243ZA, Clause 2). For instance, in most states, the delimitation of constituencies is neither under the control of the SEC, nor under its influence. In fact, SECs in many states do not have any say in the reservation of constituencies either, rather it is the state governments that finalise reservations of seats. Delimitation and reservation are two important initial activities of the electoral process. Often, finalising delimitation and reservation become reason for irregularity in local elections; but paradoxically SECs are not associated with it.

Despite the limitations in institutional capacities, the SECs have successfully completed local elections in a fairly appreciative manner. In all states (except for Panchayats in Jharkhand), elections to Panchayats and municipalities have been held regularly. States like Rajasthan, Madhya Pradesh and Chhattisgarh conducted the 4th round of local government election from December 2009 to February 2010. However, the situation is different in different states because of differences in state Acts and willingness of state governments to institutionally strengthen local governance in the state. Accordingly, powers and authorities of the SECs vary from state to state.

In Jharkhand, the Panchayat elections have yet not been held so far because of the contested issue of reservation. Similarly, elections to many municipalities could not take place in the past because the state government either did not complete delimitation in a timely fashion, or some political hurdles were created against delimitation. State Election Commissions often find themselves helpless in conducting elections in a smooth and timely manner because of lack of authority on these issues. The Government of India has also—in the Model Panchayat Elections Bill, 2007—proposed that the powers of delimitation, notification of an election, reservation of seats, as well as reservation in the offices of Chairpersons should be given to the State Election Commission. Though SECs have successfully conducted elections to Panchayats and municipalities, very few states associate the SEC with elections to District Planning Committees.

Article 243K however vests in the SECs, the powers to prepare electoral rolls for local elections. The SECs prepare electoral rolls on the basis of a ward as a unit. It may be noted that the Election Commission of India (ECI) prepares electoral rolls for assembly and Parliament elections, which means that most of the states have two voters list, separately prepared by the ECI and the SEC. So, while a citizen could be a voter for the Panchayat election, he/she may not be lucky enough to be able to vote in the Parliament election in the same year if his/her name is not there in electoral rolls prepared by the ECI. Some states have made efforts to build upon the ECI voters list to prepare voters list for local elections. However, there is a need to bring

---

Box 4.3   SEC, Rajasthan

The Rajasthan SEC is a single-member commission headed by the State Election Commissioner. The SEC has come up with many innovations to make local elections free, fair and informed. SEC has been very positive in making voters informed about importance of participation in election. It has provided all possible supports and guidance to voters' awareness campaigns conducted by CSOs in the state.

To make Panchayat/Municipal elections 2009–10 free and fair, the SEC has also appointed election observer for the polling for Zila Parishad member (which has been in practice only in case of MLA/MP election).

To enable daily wage earners vote without tension of losing their one-day wage, the SEC has also recommended that the NREGA worker must get a paid holiday on the day of the polling.

The SEC has also ensured CSOs that appropriate measures would be taken to safeguard SCs, STs and women against their vulnerabilities during voting.

However, the SEC is constrained and so, not able to implement many enabling initiatives because of lack of resources and lack of appropriate authorities. In fact, most of the works, which SEC has been able to achieve, is because of personal efforts and rapport of the current Chairperson and Secretary of the Commission.

in suitable amendments in national and state election rules to provide for a single (updated) voters list for all spheres of governments, from the Panchayat to the Parliament.

The SEC performs functions similar to that of the ECI but the tenure and conditions, qualifications and conditions of service of SECs vary greatly across states and are not as good as that of the ECI. The SECs are usually single-member commissions with a Secretary and a small staff usually assisting the chairperson of SEC. In Madhya Pradesh, the SEC is appointed for six years while in Tamil Nadu, the tenure of the SEC is just two years. Though Karnataka and Kerala do not prescribe any qualification, however, in different states, qualification for SEC ranges from the rank of a High Court Judge to a District Court Judge, from the rank of a Chief Secretary to a Joint Secretary. As per the report of the Working Group of the Planning Commission/MoPR (2006), even salaries and other service conditions for chairpersons of SECs vary greatly from state to state.

SECs have to depend heavily on the state governments for allocation of appropriate resources to discharge their constitutional duties. Often, SECs are appointed on political-bureaucratic considerations rather than competency considerations. Also, financial and functional dependence of the SEC on state government affects the independence of the Commission. SECs are also vulnerable to extraneous pressures. The National Commission to Review the Working of the Constitution (NCRWC) had recommended in 2002 that SECs should be accorded the status of a High Court Judge in the same manner as Election Commissioners in the ECI are accorded the status of a Judge of the Supreme Court. The Second Administrative Reform Commission has recommended for appointment of the SEC on the recommendations of a collegium comprising of the Chief Minister, the Speaker and the Leader of Opposition in the Legislative Assembly. It has also proposed that an effective institutional mechanism should be evolved and strengthened to bring the ECI and the SECs on one platform. This will facilitate regular interaction, logistical coordination, infrastructure sharing and technical support to the SECs. It will also help SECs to draw upon the institutional strength and credibility the ECI has established over the decades. In addition, the Commission is of the view that the impressive infrastructure of Electronics Voting Machines (EVMs) available with ECI should be deployed for local elections, given their success in the Parliament and Legislative Assembly elections. For this purpose, the State laws should specifically provide for use of EVMs.

State Finance Commission

State Finance Commissions are constituted under Article 243I of the Constitution of India, which mandates the Governor of every state to set up a finance commission, 'within one year from the commencement of the Constitution (73rd Amendment) Act, 1992, and thereafter at the expiration of every fifth year.' Since this Act came into force on 24 April 1993, all the states, which were in existence at that time, should have had, by now, reports by three finance commissions with the fourth one in the process of finalising its report. However, the states have not strictly complied with this mandatory provision. In fact, the first finance commission was set up within the mandated period only by ten states, as a result of which, the cycle originally envisaged has been substantially disturbed.

As per Articles 243I and 243Y of the Constitution of India, the SFCs are required to review the financial position of the Panchayats and municipalities and make recommendation regarding the principles which should govern:

Box 4.4 SFC, Odisha

The five-member Third State Finance Commission of Odisha appointed in September 2008 with initial tenure up to 31 October 2009 later extended up to 31 January 2010, is on the verge of submitting their final report to the State Government after having submitted an interim.

To ensure that the report is based on an understanding of the real state of Panchayati Raj Institutions (PRIs) and to get a direct feel of the ground realities, the commission visited several PRIs in different parts of the state. The chairperson of the commission who is active in establishing liaison with CSOs revealed that the commission had visited many states like Karnataka, Kerala, Andhra Pradesh and West Bengal to gain experience and learning.

The commission is sceptical about the acceptance of their recommendations by the State Government and mentioned that a major hindrance in actualising the recommendations by the SFCs for financial betterment of the PRIs/ULBs is the lack of systematic data on local governance and local development. With very limited resources at the disposal of SFC, it is very difficult to generate quality data because of the lack of sincerity on the part of the ERs in providing timely and authentic data.

1. (a) The distribution between the state on the one hand and the Panchayats and municipalities on the other, of the net proceeds of the taxes, duties, tolls and fees levied by the state, and the allocation between the Panchayats and the municipalities at all levels of their respective share of such proceeds.

    (b) The determination of the taxes, duties, tolls and fees, which may be assigned to, or appropriated by the Panchayats and the municipalities.

    (c) The grants-in-aid to the Panchayats and the municipalities from the consolidated fund of the state.

2. The measures needed to improve the financial position of the Panchayats and the municipalities.

3. Any other matter referred to by the Governor in the interest of sound finance of the Panchayats and the municipalities.

The functional domain of SFCs and CFC is similar. Clause (3) of Article 243I of the Constitution of India authorises the SFCs to determine their procedure. Almost all the SFCs follow a procedure similar to the CFC in respect to their functioning. On account of over five decades of existence, the CFC has become well known across the country, however, the same is not true of SFCs, which have been in existence for barely over a decade and a half. Also, while input data required by CFC is more or less available in systematic forms, data at local government levels are either non-existent or are very poor in quality. This makes the task of the SFCs more complex as they have to first generate data and then analyse it to make suitable recommendations. This could be unrealistic for the financially and functionally constrained SFCs.

As per the Constitution, the CFC is required to make recommendations as to the measures needed to augment the consolidated fund of a state to supplement the resources of the local bodies, on the basis of the recommendations made by the SFC. It would, therefore be desirable that the SFC reports should contain estimation and analysis of the finances of the state government, as well as of the local bodies. The SFCs must also clearly identify the issues which require action on the part of the central government to augment the consolidated fund of the state and list them out in a separate chapter for the consideration of the central finance commission. However, all central commissions so far, have not been able to use all SFC reports in the desired manner. Even the 13th Finance Commission had to get its own data, generated on the financial aspects of local governments to make recommendations about local government finance. It has interacted with Panchayats, municipalities and some of the SFCs to generate ideas and information, but institutional linkages between Central and State Finance Commissions, as stipulated in Article 280 of the Constitution, are still missing.

The 12th Finance Commission examined the functioning of the SFCs in great detail and made some very important recommendations. It recommended that the SFCs should be constituted at least two years before the required date of submission of their recommendations, and the deadline should be decided, so as to allow the State Government at least three months' time for tabling the ATR, preferably along with the budget for the ensuing financial year. Synchronisation of the award periods of the SFC with the Central Finance Commission does not mean that they should be co-terminus. What is necessary is that the SFC reports should be readily available to the CFC when the latter is constituted, so that the CFC, on the basis of uniform principles, could make an assessment of the state's need. This requires that these reports should not be too dated. As the periodicity of constitution of the CFC is predictable, the states should time the constitution of their SFCs suitably. In order to fulfil the overall objective, the procedure and the time limits would need to be built into the relevant legislation.

District Planning Committee

As per Article 243ZD of the Constitution, District Planning Committees (DPCs) shall be constituted at the district level in every state to consolidate the plans prepared by the Panchayats and the municipalities in the district, and to prepare a draft development plan for the district as a whole. The legislature of a state may, by law, make provision with respect to, (*a*) the composition of the District Planning Committees, (*b*) the manner in which the seats in such Committees shall be filled, provided that not less than four-fifths of the total number of members of such Committee shall be elected by, and from amongst, the elected members of the Panchayat at the district level and of the municipalities in the district in proportion to the ratio between the population of the rural areas and of the urban areas in the district, (*c*) the functions relating to district planning which may be assigned to such Committees and (*d*) the manner in which the Chairpersons of such Committees shall be chosen.

Every District Planning Committee shall, in preparing the draft development plan, have regard to (*a*) matters of common interest between the Panchayats and the municipalities including spatial planning, sharing of water as well as other physical and natural resources, the integrated development of infrastructure and environmental conservation, (*b*) the extent and type of available resources, whether financial or otherwise. It shall consult such institutions and organisations as the Governor may, by order, specify. The Chairperson of every District Planning Committee shall forward the development plan, as recommended by such Committee, to the state government.

The provision for district planning under Article 243ZD seeks to strengthen the local bodies' planning capabilities first, and then enjoins the DPC to consolidate these plans for the district. This presumes functional and fiscal devolution to the Panchayats, in particular, to undertake planning of their own activities from their own resources. In the absence of such devolution, planning has no meaning. Second, the district planning exercise now being carried out is a state responsibility that has no formal linkage with that of the DPC's local sector planning. The plan funds are earmarked for the states' district planning exercise, and not that of the DPC. The SARC thought that the DPC experiment was a non-starter and recommended its abolition, a suggestion on which the Centre has to take a considered stand.

A study conducted by PRIA found that while in most states, the DPCs are constituted on paper, they are however not done so in the constitutionally desired ways. In Madhya Pradesh, Andhra Pradesh, Gujarat, Karnataka, Haryana, Himachal Pradesh and Odisha, the supervising agency for the DPC elections is the state government or the Deputy Commissioner rather than the SEC. Besides this, the DPCs are not functional in their truest sense in most states. Several states such as Chhattisgarh, Himachal Pradesh, Gujarat, Madhya Pradesh, Maharashtra, Punjab and Orissa have ministers as Chairpersons of DPCs. This severely vitiates the participative grassroots nature of the planning process, which is expected to be employed. Among the states considered in the study, the DPCs are functioning regularly only in a few states (Kerala, Karnataka, Rajasthan and Haryana to some extent) and there too the quality of functioning needs to improve significantly. Quite often, they meet to discuss bottlenecks in planning without being able to sort them out. The study did not come across a single DPC constituted as per

---

Box 4.5 DPC, Madhubani, Bihar

In all the districts of Bihar, election for the DPC was held in 2007. However, even after the constitution of the DPCs, many of them remain almost non-functional. Madhubani is somehow an exception in the sense that the members and the chairperson of DPC are relatively more proactive. However, DPC lacks appropriate functions, finance and functionaries to anchor district-planning processes. The Bihar State Government has yet not provided powers to the DPC despite many formal and informal requests from the chairperson and the members of the DPC in this regard.

Even without a formal orientation on planning, the DPC actively participated in participatory district planning during 2008–09 when the BRGF pushed Integrated District Planning was initiated in the state. The DPC, rather than sticking to just the Backward Region Grant Fund (BRGF) plan, approved a comprehensive district plan and submitted it to the state government through the district administration. The state government in turn, culled out the BRGF plan from it to send it to the Ministry of Panchayati Raj to get the conditional BRGF funds sanctioned to it. Once the BRGF formalities were over, peoples' plan of Madhubani lost its relevance after getting informally stamped as 'not of appropriate quality'. The usual district plan, prepared by the bureaucracy, was implemented later.

Normally people get disenchanted after getting such neglecting treatment towards their efforts but Madhubani's DPC has once again started district planning process this year. There are many pressures, constraints and political divisions on DPC. All these collectively indicate a similar fate of the process but it would be worthwhile to watch if the actual grassroot planning gets precedence over incremental bureaucratic budgeting based district plan for 2010–11.

the Constitution. The DPCs have also not been able to effectively enable rural–urban linkages, there is an absence of coordinated planning and any joint project planning has not necessarily resulted in integrated project implementation. Block level integration of rural and urban plans was not being achieved which was important, especially in the case of small towns that have strong links with the rural hinterland. Inter-sectoral coordination was not realised and was often resisted on account of being inconvenient, as well as being against the status quo.

In a letter to the Secretary, Department Panchayati Raj of the Bihar State Government, the Chairperson of Madhubani DPC has delineated problems faced by the DPC (see Annexure 4.5). The letter bears evidence on the current plights of not only the Madhubani DPC, but also of the other DPCs in the state. It would be interesting to note here that DPCs are being 'used' or 'forced' to approve the Back-ward Region Grant Fund (BRGF) plan, so that the district/state could access the funds from Ministry of Panchayati Raj. Once BRGF plan is approved, no one bothers about district plan. Even if a participatory district development plan is prepared and approved, it remains on paper. It is not implemented and no one is accountable to implement it. It is striking that this pathetic progress in establishing and energising DPCs has occurred, in spite of the Planning Com-mission's decision that from 2006 to 2007, consideration of Annual Plans of the states will be contingent upon the state which includes setting up of DPCs in all their districts and enable them to be functional.

Studies find that though the Planning Com-mission along with the Ministry of Panchayati Raj initiated the push for energising DPCs, the momentum was lost from the very beginning. Now it seems as if it was a mere formality. The Planning Commission and the Ministry know it very well that functional District Planning Committees mean a shift in the planning para-digm and so, institutional and attitudinal changes are required in this regard. This means that the whole processes of planning needs to be closely monitored, and supported continuously and appropriately. Leaving DPCs and planning processes at the mercy of red tape and vested

interests is injustice to the aspirations of the people. The Planning Commission does not appear to have gone beyond its circular letter to the states' Chief Ministers in 2006–07, which for all practical purposes, remains on paper.

IMPLEMENTING CENTRALLY SPONSORED SCHEMES: ROLE OF LOCAL INSTITUTIONS

Mahatma Gandhi National Rural Employment Guarantee Act (MGREGA)[11]

Though local government institutions were established almost two decades ago, most of the central schemes/programmes in the functional domain of local governments, since then, have largely ignored them or given them only a per-functory role. However, MGREGA (formerly NREGA) has broken ground in this regard by, legally declaring Panchayati Raj Institutions (PRIs) as, 'the principal authorities for planning and implementation' of the scheme. Incidentally, MGREGA is the first developmental legislation which assigns a definite and important role to PRIs. At the same time, avoiding institutional displacement, MGREGA does not entail creation of parallel bodies for implementation. The Act has created the legal framework to enable the political executive to structure effective de-centralisation. The Guidelines reaffirm this by declaring the PRIs as the 'key stakeholders'.

Mahatma Gandhi Rural Employment Guarantee Scheme (MGREGS), in synergy with other schemes like the Backward Region Grant Fund (BRGF), the National Rural Health Mission (NRHM), Rashtriya Swasthya Bheema Yojana (RSBY), has provided a launching pad for empowerment of PRIs and their transformation into 'institutions of self-governance' though the jury is still out on whether this potential has been fully realised and given concrete shape in practice. MGREGS combines the economic development and social justice functions, in the context of local planning and implementation. While the local government institutions only have the potential to perform these functions, the outcome regarding the further realisation of entitlements, broadening of the capabilities of the disadvantaged and ensuring democratic participation (the Constitution itself assigns these roles to them), will depend on the institutional health of local governments. If the potential for empowering local governments using MGREGA as the entry point is not emphasised enough and not given operational features, then there is every danger of them being converted into mere agencies.

PRIs are assigned with the most critical role in the implementation of MGREGA. Some of the salient provisions of the Act, as evidence, are provided as follows:

- Section 12(1) mandates the inclusion of representatives of the PRIs in the State Employment Guarantee Council, which is the vital institution for the implementation of the Act at the state level, with wide ranging powers and functions.
- Section 13 declares PRIs as the 'principal authorities' for planning and implementation, and outlines the functions of intermediate and district level Panchayats in planning and supervision of implementation. The District Programme Coordinator (DPC), who is often the District Collector, is obliged to assist the District Panchayat.
- Section 15 speaks of the Programme Officer at the intermediate Panchayat level. It further states that all or any of the functions of the Programme Officer can be discharged by the *Gram* Panchayat or any other local authority.
- Section 16 expands the role of the *Gram* Panchayat and mandates that at least 50 per cent of the work in terms of cost has to be implemented through the *Gram* Panchayat. Further, it has given the responsibility of allocating employment opportunities among the applicants to the *Gram* Panchayat.
- Section 17 endows the *Gram Sabha* with the authority to conduct social audits and monitor the execution of works (see Box 4.6).
- Schedule II explains the duties of the *Gram* Panchayat in registering the households, issue of job cards, assigning of work, maintenance of records, and so on.

It is evident that MGREGA assigns a wide ranging role to the PRIs right from registering

of workers up to monitoring and social auditing. It vests powers of planning and implementation (at least 50 per cent) with them and casts an obligation on them for transparency and accountability, especially on the Panchayats. Probably the only deficiency with reference to local governments is the non-mention of the DPC in the Act. Ideally, the DPCs should have been assigned the task of coordinating the planning and preparation of the Perspective Plan, Labour Budget and the Annual Plan.[12]

Since MGREGS is a demand driven programme, the role of PRIs has become vital in tracking the demands from the grassroots. Another reason for putting PRIs as nodal agencies for successful implementation is that these institutions are to a great extent responsible for maintaining the transparency and accountability in its functioning. For instance, under the provisions of MGREGA, it is mandatory for a job seeker to obtain a job card by applying to the Panchayat. The *Gram* Panchayat, in turn, is responsible for providing the applicant with job cards within 15 days of the application. This mandate of reciprocal relation between the Panchayat and the applicant aims to maintain the transparency of the programme. However, data suggests that many of the states have been unable to keep pace with the demand for job cards and making them available to the applicant within the mandated time. According to the MGREGA website, as of March 2009, there were total 99 million households that demanded employment, while only 14 million of households were working under MGREGA. Similar is the case with providing timely work and payment of wage within the stipulated time of 15 days after the completion of the work, where the mandates are often violated by the Panchayats.

One of the serious constraints the Panchayats are facing in implementing the programme is shortage of functionaries. According to a study, out of 214 Centrally Sponsored Schemes targeted at the rural communities, Panchayats are supposed to be implementing 151 and play partial role in the implementation of 23 schemes. On an average, they are supposed to maintain accounts for as many as 76 schemes. Responsibilities of Panchayats have increased

---

Box 4.6   Social Audit of MGREGS

MGREGS is a special programme that is not just a scheme but also a law which has a social audit built into the legislation. Social audit is a dynamic tool by which people are able to make officials accountable for their performance in the delivery of legally enshrined rights. It is a process where people (beneficiaries) work jointly with government to monitor and evaluate the planning and implementation of a scheme/programme. Social audit is conducted jointly by the government and the people, especially those people who are being affected or the intended beneficiaries of the scheme being audited. The objective of having the provision for social audit is to bring in transparency in the process, empower the beneficiaries, and ensure good governance. Social audit is not only a tool of monitoring or evaluation but also a key tool for strengthening democracy at the grassroots. It is a tool to strengthen village democracy by empowering the *Gram Sabha*, the lowest level of local government institutions. However, the outcome in terms of effectiveness of social audit is contestable. The process of social audit has a long way to go before it can achieve its real and intended objective.

MGREGS was planned as a 'bottom-up' programme where work would be 'demand driven' and decided by the needs of the local community. However, lack of awareness and shortage of technical support has meant that the scheme has fallen into the old pattern of directions flowing from the top. The scheme is faltering in one of its key provisions and instruments, that is, the social audit. Social audit is the differentia specifica of the scheme. Yet, there are very few instances of a social audit in reality. Though a standard format for a social audit has been devised, it is hardly utilised. Rather than being an instrument of strengthening the *Gram Sabha*, monitoring employment scheme, and providing input from the bottom, social audit has been reduced to a process of information sharing from the top, bringing in some (though restricted) transparency. On the other hand, any recommendation or complaint emerging from institutions is hardly taken up by the higher authorities or institutions.

A study on social audits in Andhra Pradesh finds that it has emerged as a source of receiving information for the stakeholders regarding the utilisation of allotted money. It has been able to unearth several financial frauds and misdeeds at the small levels but what is yet to be known is the status of several recorded scams involving large sums of money. At the same time, there is delay and inaction, in most cases, in taking action in response to any detected fraud.

If MGREGS has to be effective, produce real benefits for the poor, and promote bottom-up development practice, we recommend that social audit has to be strengthened not only as a tool of information sharing, monitoring, and evaluation, but also as a tool of strengthening the *Gram Sabha* and democracy at grassroots. That would require establishment of proper accountability mechanism between the *Gram Sabha* and higher institutions of governance, and training and technical support to the *Gram Sabha*s so that they can ensure accountability.

Source: Gopal, K.S. 2009. *Delivering NRGES: Challenges and Opportunities, A Practitioners Guide*, Centre for Environment Concerns (CEC).

---

many folds, without a proportionate increase in capacity, which makes them vulnerable to the blame game of the bureaucracy and others. In such a situation, sometimes Panchayats take refuge in the excuse that they lack support from line departments.

Central Operational Guidelines of MGREGA provide for one Employment Guarantee Assistant (EGA) or Rozgar Sahayak, for each *Gram* Panchayat. Considering the volume of work that the Panchayats have to do, ranging from planning to executing to monitoring, one EGA falls short of fulfilling the requirement. Maintenance of muster rolls, release and distribution of payments, measurement of the work, procurement of materials, are all under the purview of the Panchayats' functioning. To add to this, not all *Gram* Panchayats across the country have an exclusive secretary for this work. As a result, the absence of these functionaries severely constraints timely payment, acceptance of applications and allotment of work, which means Panchayats are quite vulnerable to gain a bad rapport.

However, the Ministry of Rural Development has come up with a scheme to appoint a Lok Karmi and Lok Sevak, adding them to the functionaries as advocates of citizens' rights and their facilitator. Due to the widespread illiteracy

among rural poor which is a major stumbling block for the effective implementation of MGREGS, the Central Government is considering the appointment of an educated person from Schedule Caste, Schedule Tribe, or a minority group as Lok Karmi in each Panchayat to help the job seekers. In the draft proposal,[13] the Ministry of Rural Development is proposing to engage NGOs in the programme by designating them as Lok Sevaks, who would in turn appoint and guide Lok Karmis in their territorial jurisdiction, which would not be more than four blocks in a district. The proposal, however, has received some criticism on the ground that it lacks discussion and consultation with state governments.

Another issue is that the Panchayat is not responsible for maintaining the quality of the work, as the focus of this programme is simply on securing 100 days of employment in a year. Thus, it often happens that the road built under the scheme gets washed away the following year. This puts a serious question mark on the role of the Panchayat as the institution for grassroots bottom-up participatory planning, if considered from the perspective of envisioning the overall development of the area. Similar is the case with no provision for the upgradation of the unskilled workers, where the Panchayat is only bound to provide employment to the job seekers.

Though formation of a Vigilance and Monitoring Committee (VMC) for each *Gram* Panchayat is mandatory for monitoring of the work provided under MGREGA, the *Gram* Panchayat officials often handpick these committees and even when the *Gram Sabha* selects them, often they lack orientation regarding their roles and responsibilities. Representation of the marginalised section in the VMC still remains a concern. Many *Gram* Panchayats have volunteered proactive disclosure mentioning the fund received, spent and work done, but at the same time a large number of *Gram* Panchayats have refrained from doing this. Social audit as a tool for accountability and transparency is also limited to certain cases. Though much has been said in praise of social audits conducted under MGREGA, these audits have achieved much less on the ground. The social audit process still has a long way to go before it can substantially contribute to transparency, empowerment and good governance (see Box 4.7). Reports of corruption by government officials and the *Sarpanch* are ever increasing and poses a threat, not only to MGREGA, but also to the whole concept of local self-governance.

To conclude, it could be mentioned that the MGREGA has acted significantly in reducing the rural poverty, placing Panchayat at the core and rendering decentralisation its due respect. Yet, these local government bodies are hugely constrained in planning, executing and monitoring such a huge national programme due to lack of resources in terms of functionaries, experiences and at times, due to the lack of positive will.

National Rural Health Mission (NRHM)

The NRHM, 2005–12, was launched by the Central Government with the stated objective to provide, 'integrated comprehensive primary healthcare services, especially to the poor and vulnerable sections of the society'. At the heart of the mission lies the concept of enabling community ownership and mobilising demand for services for strengthening the public health systems for efficient service delivery alongside enhancing equity, accountability and promoting decentralisation. The NRHM intends to ensure better delivery of services by undertaking, 'architectural correction of the health system to enable it to effectively handle the increased allocation for public health through increased community ownership, decentralisation of the programmes to the district level, inter-sectoral convergence, and improved primary health care'.

Local governments perform an important function of establishing a link between the vote and public good, citizens and service providers, authority and accountability, taxes paid and services received. They can establish such linkages, more so in the case of health sector, as people value health service more than any other basic service. Therefore, it is assumed that local political control (for planning and monitoring) can significantly improve the quality of service and accountability in health service delivery. With this assumption, the NRHM intends to empower PRIs to manage and control various public health services (see Box 4.7). The *Zila Parishad* is given a lead role in the District Health Mission (DHM) to conceptualise and implement health programmes based on local needs. DHM have complete control over the District Health Fund and public health institutions such as

---

Box 4.7   Role of PRIs in NHRM

The mission envisages following roles for the Panchayati Raj Institutions:

- Commitment by states for devolution of funds, functionaries and programmes for health service delivery to PRIs.
- The DHM to be led by the *Zila Parishad*. DHM will guide and manage all public health institutions in the district, sub-centres, PHCs and CHCs.
- ASHAs would be selected by and be accountable to the *Gram* Panchayat.
- The Village Health Committee of the Panchayat would prepare the village health plan, and promote inter-sectoral integration.
- Each sub-centre will have an Untied Fund for local action at ₹10,000 per annum. The fund will be deposited in a joint bank account of the Auxiliary Nurse Midwife (ANM) and sarpanch, and operated by the ANM, in consultation with the Village Health Committee.
- PRIs involved in *Rogi Kalyan Samiti*s for good hospital management.
- Provision of relevant training to the members of PRIs.
- Making available health related database to all stakeholders, including Panchayats at all levels.

Primary Health Centres and Community Health Centres. At the village level, the *Gram Sarpanch*, along with ANM (Auxiliary Nurse Midwife), will jointly operate the untied funds of the sub-centres. PRIs will implement the sanitation programmes and they will also lead the hospital management committees. The village Panchayat selects the village level health facilitator ASHA (Accredited Social Health Activist) and payments to ASHA are subject to approval of the village Panchayat. The guidelines of NRHM also states that it is 'preferable that line functionaries at each level be managed by the corresponding Panchayati Raj Institutions'.

NRHM is the combination of national programmes like the Reproductive and Child Health II project (RCH-II), the National Disease Control Programmes (NDCP) and the Integrated Disease Surveillance Project (IDSP). The core strategy of NRHM includes decentralisation of village and district level rural planning and management. Appointment of ASHA within the mission is to create awareness on health related issues, to counsel women and to mobilise the community towards demanding and accessing health related services. ASHA is also supposed to assist and facilitate pregnant women to have institutional delivery to First Stage Referral Units or to Primary Health Centres.

Under NRHM, the *Gram* Panchayat has the role of developing the Village Health Plan with the support of the ANM, ASHA, AWW (Anganwadi Worker) and other self-help groups. Another major role of the Panchayat is to select ASHA, preferably from the village to facilitate trust building between the ASHA and the community. As NRHM facilitate integration of other programmes, the village plan should encompass the immediate health related concerns through building awareness of the community towards developing a broader vision. However, the Panchayat faces several constraints in realising the goal envisaged by NRHM. There is a clear lack of coordination among various departments and institutions involved in the mission like Health and Family Welfare, PRIs, Rural Development, and so on. Though there are proper guidelines for training of the ASHA, in most of the cases she has not been able to deliver the envisioned role due to

lack of capacity and clear cut instructions of her role (in comparison to the ANM). The Village Health Committee (VHC) of the Panchayat has remained non-functional to a great extent. Preparation of a Village Health Plan should have ideally been the role of the DPC originating through the *Gram Sabha*, who is supposed to prepare a comprehensive development plan for the *Gram* Panchayat. Existence of a separate health department and transaction of funds for health related activity to them again violates the mandate of devolution of functions, functionaries and funds to the Panchayats as per the 73rd Constitutional Amendment. This also hampers the accountability and transparency mechanism of the mission, which lies at the heart of PRIs.

Jawaharlal Nehru National Urban Renewal Mission (JNNURM)

The JNNURM is a mission of macro economic growth wherein ground conditions would be created through reform measures and select infrastructural investment in 65 select (special mission) cities. Importantly, the scope of JNNURM has now been extended to cover another 780 urban centres of the country although the share of total funds allocated to other than the special mission cities is less than 20 per cent.

The JNNURM, besides attempting infrastructural development and reform in governance in the 65 select cities through its Infrastructural Development (ID) component[14] (accounting for over 60 per cent of the total stipulated funds of ₹500,000,000), it is also expected to provide the poor in these cities access to basic services and land with tenurial security under its other component, Basic Services for Urban Poor (BSUP).[15] The latter accounts for about 40 per cent of the total funds. Interestingly, the ID component is being looked after by the Ministry of Urban Development, while BSUP is being administered by the Ministry of Housing and Urban Poverty Alleviation. An analysis of the information regarding the projects and schemes launched under ID component in different cities reveal that most of these have been designed to increase the total capacity of the services, basically water supply, sanitation and sewer treatment, at the city level. There is no explicit provision to improve the delivery of the facilities in the deficient areas within the cities or to improve the access of the poor to these. Given the emphasis on reform, financial efficiency and cost recovery for each of the facilities, and promotion of public private partnership, it is understandable that much of the benefits from this augmented system will be cornered by those who have affordability.

JNNURM is the first holistic programme aimed at urban renewal, taking the concerns of the urban poor as one of its agenda. The BSUP and Integrated Housing and Slum Development Programme (IHSDP) are directed towards the urban poor in the mission and non-mission cities respectively. Besides these, there are other reforms like internal earmarking of funds for the poor, provision of basic services to the urban poor and household level services, where a comprehensive policy on providing basic services to all urban poor has to be formulated by the concerned state government or the Urban Local Body (ULB). Among various services to be provided to the poor, security of tenure figures in the reform agenda. An analysis of the programme reveals that while one component of BSUP may be achievable, it is quite ambiguous how the other component of security of tenure would be addressed, since this issue has not been clearly discussed. The proposed scheme for 'affordable housing through partnership', and the scheme for 'interest subsidy for urban housing' which would be dovetailed into the Rajiv Awas Yojana would extend support under the JNNURM to states that are willing to assign property rights to people living in slum areas. It would be important to ensure that property rights are assigned to people occupying slums in prime locations within the metropolitan cities. One positive step taken to bring about inclusive development is the repeal of Urban Land Ceiling and Regulation Act (ULCRA). It is nonetheless difficult to believe that the market, through the repeal of the ULCRA, is expected to do as is envisaged under the mission. In fact, the repeal of the ULCRA raises an immediate area of concern, as it would result in further accumulation of land with the private developers, wherein market forces would

determine access to housing. In such a situation, there would be no other instrument which would help the poor to access land at affordable prices. In fact, there has been demand by the People's Movement for Housing Rights for strengthening of the ULCRA, rather than its repeal. If some mechanism is not devised to deal with the land tenure issue then the urban poor is unlikely to benefit from the mission. The BSUP would also be cosmetic in nature because land tenure remains the key issue, which at the moment seems unaddressed.

An immediate concern regarding the implementation of the JNNURM is that it would lead to massive dislocation of the poor and the informal activities in the cities. The cleansing drive taken up in most cities, in a bid to beautify them, has already led to dislocation and removal of slums and petty hawkers. The construction of Rapid Mass Transport System and flyovers has started having a similar impact. In fact, the policy-makers have made it explicit that these sanitising drives would not harm the poor since they would be given alternate accommodation under JNNURM. However, even under such a conducive policy environment, economic dislocation of the poor would need serious attention because it will require examination that whether those evicted under such development projects satisfy the minimum eligibility criteria for relocation or not. It may be noted that no standardised criteria have been worked out for identifying the beneficiaries under the BSUP programme. This may come in the way of housing the urban poor in the Indian cities, which are already fragmented and highly corrupt.

Introduction of a user charge policy is another reform which seeks policy attention. Various state governments and ULBs are introducing user charge policies spelling out the coverage, rate, and periodicity of revision, and so on. The main objective of the policy is to recover the full cost of operation and maintenance by levying proper user charges from the services; ensure that each service, sale or use of municipal goods or resources provided to the general public is self-sustaining; and also allow the private sector to compete with the ULBs without disadvantage in supplying comparable or better services, resources, or goods wherever applicable. Under the above policy, ULBs are to charge for water supply, sewerage, solid waste management, public transport and 'others'. For many of the ULBs, 'others' include street lighting, toll roads, municipal library, primary health/dispensary services provided by the ULB, education, parks, crematoriums and hiring of municipal assets like community halls, water tankers, cesspool cleaners, and so on. Lack of affordability to pay for water tankers or streetlights would result in pricing out of the urban poor from these services. Further, under the user charge policy, ULBs are encouraged to reduce non-revenue water. This policy, if implemented, would again have adverse effects on the poor. Also, adding the tag of user charge to health and education would negate the social concerns of the government.

An attempt has been made to work out the per capita spending by the central government on the MGREGA in rural areas and the JNNURM in both mission and non-mission cities in urban areas during 2005–09. The big city bias of JNNURM is reflected in this exercise where the mission cities receive ₹219 per capita per annum compared to ₹91 and ₹73 for the non-mission cities and rural areas under MGREGA respectively.

Under the provision of 'household level basic services' reforms under JNNURM, housing is to be provided among other basic amenities. Under this scheme, private agencies are being encouraged to take up slum redevelopment where existing slums are being rebuilt with multi-storied structures. However, substantial land thus acquired in the name of housing for the poor is being earmarked for commercial and residential uses of the non-poor. The subsidies directed to the poor are thus cornered by the private agencies, either for themselves or for the section of the population who can afford to pay market prices at prime locations in cities.

Earmarking 20–25 per cent of developed land for the Economically Weaker Section (EWS) and Low Income Group (LIG) category is another promising area under the central reform consideration. Here too, ULBs are in a state of ambiguity in implementing this reform. Many private builders are seeking ways of waiving this clause by paying lump-sum penalty of contribution to the shelter fund of the concerned state.

The increased participation sought from the private sector in providing municipal services by making it mandatory to frame state level regulatory and policy initiatives for the purpose is another reform which calls for attention. If municipal services are managed by the private sector and determined by the market, there would be chances of the poor being priced out.

The past few years have witnessed attempts being made to involve the communities to manage services within the cities. This was essentially the fall out of the limited success of decentralised governance through WDCs institutionalised by the enactment of the 74th Constitutional Amendment Act in 1992. Citizen Groups or Resident Welfare Associations (RWAs) are being encouraged by the local governments to take up maintenance of services and capital investment. The municipal

Table 4.2 Comparison of Per Capita Spending by the Central Government on MGREGA and JNNURM, 2005–09

Per capita MGREGA spending by the Central Government during 2005–09	
Total central release till September 2009 (₹ lakh)	2,414,750.53
Annual per capita MGREGA spending by the Central Goverment (₹)	73.38
Per capita JNNURM spending (inclusive of BSUP) by the Central Government in Mission Cities during 2005–09	
Total amount of funds released till September 2009 (₹ lakh)	1,389,916.95
Annual per capita JNNURM spending by the Central Government (₹)	219.41
Per capita UIDSSMT spending (inclusive of IHSDP) by the Central Government for non-mission during 2005–09	
Total amount of funds released till September 2009 (₹ lakh)	691,655.00
Annual per capita UIDSSMT spending by the Central Government (₹)	91.39

Source: Calculated from information obtained from Ministry of Urban Development, 2010, http://nrega.nic.in & http://jnnurm.nic.in

responsibility of provision of services is being increasingly passed on to the RWAs. Civil society activism has opened up new opportunities for representation, as they are able to exercise significant influence on the governments. However, such opportunities hardly extend to the 'urban poor'.

The participatory framework of governance functioning through RWAs has for the first time led to the active involvement of citizens in the provision and maintenance of services. Micro-level research shows that it is only the more powerful RWAs who are able to voice their concern to the exclusion of the poor. Unfortunately, even under the much acclaimed Bhagidari system in Delhi, there is no involvement of slums and unauthorised colonies. The observation of Union Minister of State for Urban Development on the concept of the 'Bhagidari' scheme of the Delhi Government may be cited to corroborate the above argument. He remarked that although its intentions were noble, the Bhagidari programme had not been able to penetrate deep across different sections of population in the Capital and had ended up becoming elitist in nature. A large chunk of the population does not have any representation in this scheme, as the RWAs representing the colonies that account for over 69 per cent of Delhi's population that resides in slums and unauthorised colonies, have been largely left untouched by the Bhagidari scheme. Unfortunately, however, this holds true for the other cities like Mumbai, Chennai and Bangalore and others, as well. The RWAs function only in the elite and middle income colonies to the exclusion of the marginal areas inhabited by the 'urban poor'.[16]

Those RWAs, which are not partners with the Bhagidari scheme, also have a role in urban governance independent of government support. These RWAs take up activities like cleaning of the colony streets, solid waste management, water supply, payment of electricity bills, maintenance of security through installation of colony gates, and so on. A few RWAs have in fact taken up maintenance activities even without the support of the local bodies or other agencies. An RWA in the capital restored the greenery of a small park in their block. Each member contributed

₹2,500 to ₹3,000 and collected ₹60,000 with which they bought plants, made a boundary wall and appointed a gardener for maintenance. The RWAs functioning as *Bhagidar*s had a much greater role in local governance. In addition to provision of civic services and maintenance of security in their neighbourhoods, these RWAs took up capital investment projects through participatory budgeting, raised protests in the city against hike in power tariffs, helped the distribution companies in collection of electricity bills, involved the Municipal Corporation of Delhi and the Delhi Development Authority to evict squatters, as well as formed political parties to stake their claim. The only difference found between RWAs functioning as *Bhagidar*s, in comparison to the other RWAs, was in terms of financial and institutional support. Further, RWAs were found to be more organised and vocal in South Delhi, which has a higher concentration of elite colonies.

An analysis of RWAs in Delhi shows that the very mechanism of the functioning of RWAs is likely to accentuate and institutionalise disparity within the cities. Involvement of RWAs in contributing to partial cost of the capital projects is contributing to accentuation of disparity within cities. It is not because of corruption but the simple logic of easier access to community funds, which is helping in attracting investment from the local bodies and other agencies. Those RWAs, which are in a position to generate funds from among themselves, are eligible to access municipal revenues for development work in their locality.

In Mumbai, local NGOs and the corporate sector have become active in some localities in organising ALMs (Area Locality Management), which is a variant of RWAs. The success of the ALMs led the municipal commissioner to delegate more functions to them. These include beautification of the localities, and maintenance of gardens, parks and roads.

Attempts are being made to increase the number of RWAs in the capital and other cities, but there are serious bottlenecks coming in the way of success. Understandably, the unauthorised colonies, and the slums and squatter settlements located on public land, with the residents having no legal ownership or tenancy rights, have shown little initiative in forming the associations or registering them with the registrar of societies. Although tenurial rights are not formal requirements for registration, the absence of that creates informal barriers. In Delhi, the government would not support RWAs as *Bhagidar*s, which is located on land it wants to clear for its development projects. Understandably, rarely have the slum colonies been able to form RWAs or get the municipal officials to their areas to discuss their problems or seek redressal.

Importantly, several of the RWAs are being drawn into city or state politics due to the existing government structure not addressing the local problems. A few have issued circulars for casting their vote-favouring candidates who could represent specific local needs in the Assembly or the Municipal Council. Some may consider this as a desirable trend as it would force the authorities at higher levels to take greater interest in local issues and provisioning of basic services. There is, however a risk that higher level decisions would be influenced by local infighting, incapacitating the system to take a broader inclusive view of the issues.

DECENTRALISED SERVICE DELIVERY IN INDIA

The future of public service delivery, particularly to the poor, has been an issue of contention in the developing countries, at the level of national and sub-national governments, international financial institutions, development organisations and social movements. The contention is so intense that, in recent years, we have seen major shifts in global policy paradigm for public service delivery, from state provision of the services, to market oriented reforms in 1990s, to introduction of 'democratised governance' in service delivery systems during the current decade. In all these paradigms however, the quest has been towards improving efficiency and effectiveness in service delivery. The current paradigm of democratic governance in service delivery emphasises on 'decentralisation' and 'participation' of service users. While the intrinsic values of decentralisation and participation makes them desirable goals in

their own right, as the proponents claim, it has mostly been promoted to improve efficiency and effectiveness of public services through equitable, responsive and efficient management. However, the jury is still out on it.

Provision of basic services such as health, education, water and electricity, all of which have largely been provided by the state, have systematically failed, and especially failed for the poor.[17] Centralised state provisioning of basic services has ended up in non-uniform and inefficient delivery patterns,[18] and a weak relationship between the service providers and the users[19] undermining its objective of uniform provision. The result is a very limited access to modern infrastructure and services among the poor, particularly in low-income countries. Where there is physical access to these services, the quality, reliability and effectiveness remains poor. Public spending on these services seems to have a weak relationship with effective outcomes[20] due to systemic problems like under-management, weak accountability mechanism, corruption and rent-seeking.[21] This has led to questioning of the state's capability and centralised approaches to deliver local public services.

In response to the perceived failure of the 'statist' model and market reforms in public service delivery, drawing on analytical critiques provided an alternative perspective emerged that emphasised 'public control over governance' or 'democratisation of governance' as a solution to the crises in public services.[22] This alternative perspective traces the roots of the crisis to the strong control wielded by vested interests in public, as well as in private service delivery mechanisms. It emphasises 'management of affairs in the public (non-private) domain of society, in order to serve the public interests at large' and thus bring in transparency, accountability and participation in governance of service delivery.[23] In the wake of these changes and with the objective to bring in transparency, accountability and participation, governance of many public services has been decentralised to local governments and newly established micro-institutions of users.

Decentralisation is believed to address the existing problems and bring in economic and administrative (or managerial) efficiency through accounting for costs in decision-making, increasing accountability, reducing transaction costs, matching service to needs, mobilising local knowledge, improving coordination and providing resources. At the same time, decentralisation is also expected to improve equity through greater retention and fair distribution of the benefits accrued.[24] However, the other objectives are not ignored, even if not given equal importance in public service reforms. In case of public service decentralisation, efficiency and effectiveness gain, and local empowerment are often projected as explicit objectives to gain public support for reforms. Though the objectives of public expenditure reduction and retaining central control are given significant importance in design of decentralisation initiative, they are rarely spelt out.

Decentralisation, in essence, is a process of institution building; its success depends on 'strengthening the managerial and technical capabilities' of local governance institutions.[25] It not only strengthens the existing local institutions, but also creates new institutions to take on specific functions. In recent years, many community-based functional institutions have been created to share responsibilities of public service delivery at micro level. The proliferation—pluralising the institutional network at grassroots—has littered the development landscape 'with committees... mandated as "user groups" to take on some of the functions of provisioning, regulation, and management that previously resided with the state'.[26] Success and sustainability of these institutions will largely depend on public participation in these institutions.

India has taken bold steps to strengthen the voice of poor through decentralising many of the public service delivery mechanisms to the local governments established through 73rd and 74th Constitutional Amendments. The amendment specifies a list of 29 subjects that states can choose to devolve to local governments. The objective was to bring the government closer to the citizens, reduce the accountability gap between service providers and users, and improve the match between diverse local preferences (varying according to local context and realities) and public services.

Decentralisation in service delivery is expected to strengthen the voice of the poor, improve accountability of public sector decision-making towards them through democratic process and improve transparency in the process, as local activities are more visible to local people. All these potentials and expectations have made decentralisation the critical core of India's strategy to improve public service delivery. However, outcome of decentralisation in service delivery varies to a great deal across states. Since decentralisation is defined by the Constitution as a state subject, states have pursued varying strategies to empower local governments.

In the previous section, we have analysed role of PRIs in the decentralised delivery of some public services (employment and health) and their effectiveness. In this section, we consider few more services like education, sanitation and drinking water and present an overall picture of the status of decentralised service delivery in India. The evidence suggests that the current state of decentralised public service delivery in India is far from effective. It has a long way to go before it can claim to produce real benefits for the poor in terms and access and quality.

Though decentralisation has been able to improve physical access to basic services, the quality of service is still to be improved. Illiteracy is still high in rural areas and teacher absenteeism is rampant. Local public dispensaries and other public curative services do not match the demand from local people due to doctor absenteeism and poor infrastructure. As a result, much of these services are now being provided by the private providers, which imposes additional costs on the rural poor. The situation is not better in the case of drinking water and sanitation either.

Why has decentralisation not helped much in improving the quality of service? First, in most cases across sectors, the state line departments continue to hold control and play a predominant role in service delivery, even though it has been devolved to the local governments. Due to unclear allocation of responsibilities, practices that do not follow the spirit of the law, inadequate access to discretionary funds, lack of powers over state-level functionaries and inadequate local capacity, the ability of PRIs to influence outcomes in service delivery is limited.

Box 4.8   Sarva Shiksha Abhiyan and PRIs

Sarva Shiksha Abhiyan (SSA), 'education for all' was launched by the Government of India with the intention to universalise elementary education through community ownership of the school system. It emerged as a response to the demand for quality elementary level education for all the children of the country. SSA has two aspects: (a) It provides a wide convergent framework for implementation of Elementary Education schemes; (b) It is also a programme with budgetary provision for strengthening crucial areas to achieve universalisation of elementary education. The framework, rather than a guideline aspect for the programme, actually renders a lot of scope to the state and the local level governments to plan according to the specific context and local realities. This also leaves the scope for bottom-up participatory planning that could address the needs of the community. The emphasis is on mainstreaming out-of-school children through diverse strategies, bridging the social and the gender gap, and on providing eight years of schooling for all children in the age group of 6–14 years. Though the objectives are expressed nationally, it is expected that various districts and States are likely to achieve universalisation in their own respective contexts and in their own time frame.

Since the programme aims at involving the community, there are provisions for involving the community through various committees and associations at the Panchayat level. Thus there are provisions for School Management Committees, Village Education Committee, Parent Teacher Association, Mother Teacher Association, Tribal Autonomous Councils and other grassroot level structures to be involved in the management of the school. The programme also ensures pro-active disclosure of funds received and spent, number of student and related information on the school wall. SSA, therefore, was envisioned to decentralise delivery of education by rooting its planning and implementation through participation of the grassroot beneficiaries. Considering the fact that education is also one of the 29 functions mentioned in the 11th Schedule, the importance of Panchayats in delivering the programme increases manifold.

However, having mentioned that the programme has provisions for involving every section of the community, it is needed to be highlighted that these provisions are in contradiction to the institution of local governance at the grass root level, i.e., the *Gram* Panchayat. To start with, the VEC is a parallel body existing beside the mandatory standing committee for education at the GP level. There seem to be no reason for creating an alternative mechanism for the same purpose, subduing the roles and responsibility of the GP towards local governance. Second, the fact that all the funds directed towards education are directly transferred to the VEC rather than to the GP once again violates the integrity of the Panchayati Raj System as the mandated body to plan and implement for social justice and economic development of the grassroot. This is enhanced by the fact that SSA committees are not accountable to the GP for the funds received and expenditure incurred. Though recently there has been a circular issued from the Department of School Education and Literacy to plan for SSA through *Gram Sabha*, in reality this is a distant cry. Further, the members of the VEC, who are supposed to be selected by *Gram Sabha*, are often chosen without any consultation with them. In short, though SSA has developed transparency and accountability measures for itself by creating representative committees, by doing so it has not only created parallel bodies undermining the importance of PRIs but also has failed to maintain the same.

Second, there is a contradiction between provisions (law) and practice. While law requires devolution of implementation functions to local government institutions, in practice most of the key functions are implemented by state governments. While the allocation of responsibilities to PRIs is limited, whatever is allocated is not supported by either financial or administrative powers. The outcome is a weaker relationship of accountability and services that do not meet local expectations.

CONCLUSION

To conclude, the state of decentralisation and (formal) local governance is far from effective. There is a long way to go before decentralised local governance can produce real gains for the marginalised sections of the society, produce inclusive development and facilitate democratic practice. Mere establishment of decentralised local institutions, without effective devolution to match the responsibilities, does not mean

---

Box 4.9   Decentralised Public Service Delivery in Karnataka: Key Findings

Drinking water:
- Majority of households (69 per cent) depend on public sources of drinking water.
- Public taps are most accessible (by 85 per cent users) but also experience frequent breakdowns (once in three months as reported by 48 per cent users).
- However, taking all factors together more users are satisfied (65 per cent) than dissatisfied (35 per cent) with the service provided by Village Panchayats.

Sanitation:
- Only one-fifth households have individual toilets and almost none have access to toilets.
- Garbage disposal scheme is almost unheard of.
- Slightly more than one-third of the surveyed households have wastewater connection to drains.
- Marginally more users are satisfied (55 per cent) than dissatisfied (45 per cent) with the quality of drainage services provided by Village Panchayats.

***Gram Sabha* and development schemes: Public awareness**
- Awareness on *Gram Sabha*s is low: only 40 per cent respondents are aware, of them only 47 per cent have attended one.
- Only 18 per cent among those who attended a *Gram Sabha* found it useful, while 54 per cent found it discriminatory.
- Awareness on development schemes is very low, ranging from 14 per cent to 25 per cent.

Cost (including frequent visits, resultant wage loss and travel costs, and bribe) to avail these schemes is high.

Source: Sekhar, S., M. Nair and A.V. Reddy. 2008. *Decentralised Service Delivery in Panchayats: A Pilot Citizens' Audit.* Bangalore: Public Affairs Centre.

achievement of the goals. In its current form, decentralisation in India seems to be a tool for reinforcing central control in local governance. The belated action to activate local government in India after more than half a century of the country's independence, through the 73rd and 74th Constitutional Amendments, had a limited success mainly due to opposition from the states as also because of the limited scope, bureaucratic drafting and faulty method of functional and fiscal devolution. The main shortcoming of these Amendments was the political strategy to empower local government from outside the 7th Schedule. This has not worked and any future attempt to energise local government must, of necessity, start from restructuring the 7th Schedule to conform to the ethos of a multi level governance system through an open system of reform.

There is a dire need to bring in clarity in decentralisation, i.e., clarity in responsibilities delegated and need to be delegated to the local government institutions, matching devolution of finances and administrative autonomy to meet with the responsibilities. Empowerment of, not only local government institutions, but also the other institutions responsible for making local governance effective is required to gain the real benefits of decentralisation for the poor. In its current form, decentralisation and local governance serves to the interest of a small group of well-offs as it promotes rent-seeking. The problem is not only in the implementation, but also in design of local governance in India. The institutions of local governance, like many other public institutions in India, are designed in a way that they serve perverse interests and endorse rent-seeking. States have to release more resources to the local government institutions and endorse their self capability and sustainability rather than mentoring and controlling them. Thus, improving local governance in India would require breaking down the nexus of perverse interests, bringing in radical changes, and probably, institutional shifts.

NOTES

1 Diamond, Larry. 1999. *Developing Democracy: Towards Consolidation*. Baltimore: The Johns Hopkins University Press, pp. 120–21.

2 Conyers, Diana. 1983. 'Decentralization: The Latest Fashion in Development Administration?', *Public Administration and Development, 3*(2): 97.

3 Manor, Manor. 1999. *The Political Economy of Democratic Decentralization*. Washington DC: The World Bank, p. 1.

4 Scott, Ian. 1996. 'Changing Concepts of Decentralisation: Old Public Administration and New Public Management in the Asian Context', *Asian Journal of Public Administration, 18*(1): 3.

5 Also discussed by Rondinelli, Dennis A. 2005. 'Decentralization and Development', in A.S. Huque and H. Zafarullah (eds), *International Development Governance*. New York: Marcel Dekker-CRC Press.

6 Government of India. 1977. *Local Governance: An Inspiring Journey into the Future*. Report of the Second Administrative Reforms Commission, 6th Report, New Delhi.

7 DI was first introduced by the 11th CFC with 20 per cent weightage, but was abolished by the 12th CFC; now the 13th CFC has reintroduced it with 15 per cent weightage.

8 The romantic idea of *Gram Sabha* originates from Gandhian concept of village republic. It has a large following in India with divergent concepts of local government. *Gram Sabhas* function outside the formal structure of three-tier Panchayats.

9 Article 243K: 'The superintendence, direction and control of the preparation of electoral rolls for, and the conduct of, all elections to the Panchayats shall be vested in a State Election Commission.'

10 Article 243ZA: 'The superintendence, direction and control of the preparation of electoral rolls for, and the conduct of, all elections to the Municipalities shall be vested in a State Election Commission.'

11 Vajayanand, S.M. 2008. 'NREGA and Panchayati Raj Institutions: Learnings from Kerala'.

12 National Rural Employment Guarantee Scheme, implemented by the National Rural Employment Guarantee Act, was renamed as Mahatma Gandhi Rural Employment Guarantee Scheme (MGREGS) on 2 October 2009.

13 The proposal to appoint Lok Sevak and Lok Karmi, issued by the Ministry of Rural Development, was in draft form till the report went to press.

14 The JNNURM has two sub-missions: (*a*) Urban Infrastructure and Governance (UIG) and (*b*) Basic Services to the Urban Poor (BSUP). Projects such as road, public transport, trunk network of water supply, sanitation and storm water drains, construction of multi-level parking lots and city beatification have been taken up under the UIG.

15 The BSUP is supposed to take care of the shelter and basic services of the urban poor in the 65 designated cities.

16 Kundu, Debolina. 2009. 'Elite Capture and Marginalization of the Poor in Participatory Urban Governance: A Case of Resident Welfare Associations in Metro Cities', in *India: Urban Poverty Report* (ed.). New Delhi: Oxford University Press.

17 See *World Development Report 2004: Making Services Work for Poor People*. New York: The World Bank and Oxford University Press.

18 Bardhan, Pranab and Dilip Mookherjee. 2006. 'Decentralisation and Accountability in Infrastructure Delivery in Developing Countries', *The Economic Journal, 116*(508-01): 102.

19 See Barnes, Douglas F. (ed.). 2007. *The Challenges of Rural Electrification: Strategies for Developing Countries.* Washington DC: RFF Press & ESMAP.

20 Ahmad, Junai, Shantayanan Devarajan, Stuti Khemani and Shekhar Shah. 2005. 'Decentralization and Service Delivery', *World Bank Policy Research Working Paper 3603*, p. 1. Washington DC: The World Bank.

21 Chand, Vikram K. (ed.). 2006. *Reinventing Public Service Delivery in India: Selected Case Studies,* pp. 18–22. New Delhi: Sage Publications and World Bank; World Bank. 2006. *Reforming Public Services in India: Drawing Lessons from Success.* New Delhi: Sage Publications, pp. 1–4.

22 See Wagle, Subodh and Kalpana Dixit. 2006. 'Revisiting Good Governance: Asserting Citizens Participation and Politics in Public Services', in D. Chavez (ed.), *Beyond the Market: The Future of Public Services,* pp. 21–30. Amsterdam: Trans National Institute & Public Services International Research Unit.

23 Ibid., p. 26.

24 See Ribot, Jesse C. 2002. 'African Decentralization: Local Actors, Powers and Accountability', *Democracy, Governance and Human Rights-Paper No 8*. Geneva: UNRISD.

25 Dennis A. Rondonelli, op. cit., p. 401.

26 Cornwall, Andrea and John Gaventa. 2001. 'From Users and Choosers to Makers and Shapers: Repositioning Participation in Social Policy', *IDS Working Paper 127*, p. 9. Sussex: Institute of Development Studies.

ANNEXURE 4.1

Number of Panchayats in Major States and Last Election Held

State	Number of Panchayats			Last elections held
	Village Panchayat	Intermediate Panchayat	District Panchayat	
Andhra Pradesh	21,807	1,097	22	2006
Arunachal Pradesh	1,779	161	16	2008
Assam	2,202	185	20	2007–08
Bihar	8,463	531	38	2006
Chhattisgarh	9,724	146	18	2010
Gujarat	13,693	224	26	2006
Haryana	6,155	119	21	2005
Himachal Pradesh	3,243	75	12	2005–06
Jharkhand	4,562	212	24	*
Madhya Pradesh	23,012	313	50	2010
Punjab	12,225	141	20	2008
Rajasthan	9,166	248	33	2010
Tripura	511	23	4	2009
Uttar Pradesh	52,001	820	70	2005
West Bengal	3,351	333	18	2008
Total	**171,894**	**4,628**	**392**	

Source: IRMA. 2010. *State of Panchayati Raj Report 2008–09: An Independent Report*. Ministry of Panchayati Raj, Government of India.
Note: * First election is scheduled to be held in 2010.

ANNEXURE 4.2

Strengthening Local Bodies: Recommendation of 13th Finance Commission of India

The 13th Finance Commission recommendations relating to local bodies inter alia aim at strengthening local government finances and governance in India. The 13th Finance Commission, making a departure from the previous Finance Commissions, has divided the grants to be distributed to the states for local bodies into two parts: general basic grant and general performance grant. The performance grant can be accessed, only if the state complies with nine conditions or reforms. They are:

1. The State Government must put in place a supplement to the budget documents for local bodies.
2. The State Government must put in place Audit System.
3. The State Government must put in place a system of independent local body ombudsmen.
4. The State Government put in place a system to electronically transfer local body grants provided by the Commission.
5. The State Government must prescribe through an Act the qualifications of persons eligible for appointment as members of the SFC.
6. All local bodies should be fully enabled to levy Property Tax without hindrance.
7. The State Government must put in place a State Property Tax Board.
8. The State Government must gradually put in place standards for delivery of essential services.
9. All municipal corporations with a population of more than one million (2001 Census) must put in place a Fire-hazard Response and Mitigation plan for their respective jurisdictions.

States are given one year, i.e., 2010–11 to comply with these conditions before they can access the performance grant from 2011–12. Complying with these conditions within the stipulated timeframe, require comprehensive understanding and capacity at the State level.

Summary of Key Recommendations on Local Bodies

- Article 280 (3) (bb) & (c) of the Constitution should be amended such that the words 'on the basis of the recommendations of the Finance Commission of the State' are changed to 'after taking into consideration the recommendations of the Finance Commission of the State'.

This recommendation seems to strengthen state control over SFCs. It poses a danger of recommendation of SFCs being undermined. The state governments, if the recommendation is accepted, will be free to reject recommendation from SFCs regarding augmentation of Consolidated Fund of a state to supplement the resources of the local bodies.

- Article 243(I) of the Constitution should be amended to include the phrase 'or earlier' after the words 'every fifth year'.

This recommendation mandates establishment of new SFCs every five years or earlier to review financial position of local bodies.

- 13th Finance Commission recommends that local bodies be transferred a percentage of the divisible pool of taxes (over and above the share of the states) after converting this share to grant-in-aid under Article 275. The general basic grant, as well as the special areas basic grant should be allocated amongst states as specified. The state-wise eligibility for these grants is provided till 2015.
- State Governments will be eligible for the general performance grant and the special areas performance grant only if they comply with the prescribed stipulations. These grants will be disbursed in the manner specified. The state-wise eligibility for these grants is provided till 2015.
- The states should appropriately allocate a portion of their share of the general basic grant and general performance grant, to the special areas in proportion to the population of these areas. This allocation will be in addition to the special area basic grant and special area performance grant recommended by us.
- State Governments should appropriately strengthen their local fund audit departments through capacity building, as well as personnel augmentation.
- The State Governments should incentivise revenue collection by local bodies through methods such as mandating some or all local taxes as obligatory at non-zero rates of levy, by deducting deemed own revenue collection from transfer entitlements of local bodies, or through a system of matching grants.
- To buttress the accounting system, the finance accounts should include a separate statement indicating head-wise details of actual expenditures under the same heads as used in the budget for both Panchayati Raj Institutions (PRIs) and Urban Local Bodies (ULBs). The Finance Commission recommends that these changes be brought into effect from 31 March 2012.
- The Government of India and the State Governments should issue executive instructions so that their respective departments pay appropriate service charges to local bodies.
- Given the increasing income of State Governments from royalties, they should share a portion of this income with those local bodies in whose jurisdiction such income arises.

- State Governments should ensure that the recommendations of State Finance Commissions (SFCs) are implemented without delay and that the Action Taken Report (ATR) is promptly placed before the legislature.
- The Finance Commission provides a template for SFC reports and recommends that SFCs should consider adopting the template as the basis for their reports.
- Bodies similar to the SFC should be set up in states which are not covered by Part IX of the Constitution.
- Local bodies should consider implementing the identified best practices.
- A portion of the grants provided by us to urban local bodies be used to revamp the fire services within their jurisdiction. Local Bodies should be associated with city planning functions wherever other development authorities are mandated this function. These authorities should also share their revenues with local bodies.
- The development plans for civilian areas within the cantonment areas (excluding areas under the active control of the forces) should be brought before the district planning committees.

State Governments should lay down guidelines for the constitution of *Nagar* Panchayats.

ANNEXURE 4.3

State of Panchayats

State of Panchayats Report 2008–09, analysing different themes that are implicated in the processes of strengthening local self-governance and Panchayats, claims that there has been a visible progress on many counts. However, a few but key efforts could hasten institutionalisation of authentic decentralised governance as mandated by the constitution. Such participatory local self-governance is inevitable and necessary for deepening the processes of development and democracy and for making them more inclusive. In an ideal world the Panchayats could assume their constitutionally mandated role of 'planning for economic development and social justice' and function as institutions of self-government without outside help or support. However, in the real world, a lot more has to be accomplished on the road of devolution, capacity building and animation of Panchayat processes for realising the constitutional ideals. The journey until now has been modest; it must continue with vigour.

Centrally Sponsored Schemes (CSSs) and Panchayats

A substantial portion of resources for local development is provided by the Central Government through its various Schemes. In the last few years, a number of significant schemes have been introduced in the social sectors which channel funds for employment, sectoral development and basic services in rural (and in some cases urban) areas. The design of these programmes, particularly the structure and procedures prescribed for implementation at the district level and below has important implications for the roles and functioning of local governments, particularly as they relate to some of the functions listed for transfer to Panchayats in the 11th Schedule.

The design of these schemes provide a varying degree and nature of space for Panchayat involvement; NREGS was found to have recourse to greatest reliance on Panchayats. The report concluded that Panchayats have largely been involved in 'agency functions' of implementation; their roles and responsibilities in planning for these CSSs could be enlarged. The degree of involvement has varied, based on the specifications available in the scheme guidelines, as also the extent of devolution of functions, functionaries and funds the States have enacted.

Participation and Representation

The Constitutionally mandated structure and composition of Panchayats, in a bold move brought a million women, half a million people from the Scheduled Castes and a third of a million from the Scheduled Tribes—in all, 1.6 million of the systemically marginalised—into political positions in local government. It was a historical action of a kind the world had not seen, that sought to redress centuries of marginalisation with a few strokes of the pen. It also presented a monumental task to those who would craft a more egalitarian and democratic India—of helping the representatives elected by these groups to understand and actively play the public roles they were stepping into, for most of them would not be familiar with the territory, or even public engagement. Over time, more of those elected are stepping into their positions and taking on the entailed responsibilities, and both numbers and quality of participation have improved over the years, and more, some elected women representatives are going on to political careers in unreserved constituencies. But what it also shows is that there is yet a long way to go, for this improvement is still slim—a significant gender gap remains in the participation of women and men, and SC representatives—both men and women—not only still face social and institutional barriers but also, in many places, a violent backlash.

The report finds that institutional and organisational factors—specified rules, procedures, organisational arrangements and cultures have a greater bearing on levels of participation than social factors, which include prevailing customs and norms of behaviour, expected social and domestic roles and social structures in the community. Even when representatives mentioned/discussed social factors, in most cases they were framed as failures of the institutional/organisational arrangements.

Decentralised Planning

Among the more important Constitutional provisions for instituting local self-governance is the specification that Panchayats (and ULBs) be capacitated to plan for 'economic development and social justice' in their jurisdictions, and that local government plans be 'consolidated' by the District Planning Committee. This is critically important to strengthening panchayats, as planning is a core governance function and important to the articulation of panchayat identity as institutions of local self-governance. The report finds that the situation in 10 states is reassuring, for there has definitely been a strengthening of the fledgling processes observed two years ago. DPCs were constituted in all 10 states, and though in most were active only in the BRGF districts, in some states, the processes initiated for BRGF plans had been set in motion in all districts. District Visions and Draft Development Plans had been produced in most of the BRGF districts, and in many more in the latter states. Some processes of visioning, preparation of annual plans (and in some locations, perspective plans also) had been undertaken at *Gram* Panchayat and intermediate Panchayat levels in many districts. However, both process and products need re-orientation and transformation. The process remained top-down in most cases, starting with the District Vision which was expected to frame Panchayat (and ULB) plans. Plans were developed scheme/programme-wise, with little cross-sectoral integration, and none were spatial.

Integration across rural and urban jurisdictions was also absent. Capacities for undertaking the comprehensive, integrated spatial planning, through a participatory, bottom-up process as envisaged in the Constitution are weak at best—in the DPCs, administrative structures, and often with TSIs involved in the process. In fact such competencies are sparse in the country and concerted action to develop a cadre of such planners is sorely necessary.

Panchayats and Natural Resource Management (Water)

The stark pattern that emerges across states is that the transfer of activities to panchayats has centred on drinking water, to a greater or lesser extent, but participatory management of irrigation and watershed development has been mostly through user-groups that have little formal linkage with or accountability to Panchayats. Even in the case of drinking water provision, the predominant pattern is of transfers of O&M activities, but only in some exceptional cases (eg. WB) more of the core *governance* functions—planning, monitoring—have been devolved. But there has not been concomitant transfer of watershed and irrigation activities to Panchayats; this has in fact been noticeable not only by its absence, but also, in that the functions have been transferred to *user* groups. This not only undercuts the identity and authority of Panchayats as local governments, but also brings into play the dangers of localisation significantly.

Source: IRMA. 2010. *State of Panchayati Raj Report 2008–09: An Independent Report.* Ministry of Panchayati Raj, Government of India.

ANNEXURE 4.4

State of Devolution in India: A State-level Analysis

Devolution Index (D) and Sub-indices

Rank	States/UTs	D_1	D_2	D_3	D_4	D
1	Kerala	92.59	80.76	69.62	61.25	**74.73**
2	Karnataka	90.74	77.95	56.11	64.08	**69.45**
3	Tamil Nadu	89.63	77.11	58.76	49.58	**67.06**
4	West Bengal	96.30	70.90	61.56	46.25	**66.51**
5	Maharashtra	73.52	65.52	62.78	44.17	**61.49**
6	Madhya Pradesh	74.44	63.52	53.50	54.17	**59.78**
7	Gujarat	54.44	59.78	51.56	44.58	**53.07**
8	Andhra Pradesh	70.74	45.01	53.77	35.83	**50.10**
9	Sikkim	87.04	59.11	24.59	40.17	**47.43**
10	Himachal Pradesh	88.15	53.89	25.30	43.83	**47.01**
11	Haryana	51.67	44.66	40.15	40.17	**43.23**
12	Orissa	67.04	56.76	27.17	31.67	**42.93**

(Annexure 4.4 continued)

(Annexure 4.4 continued)

Rank	States/UTs	D_1	D_2	D_3	D_4	D
13	Uttar Pradesh	80.00	42.47	35.31	23.17	**41.73**
14	Bihar	73.33	53.98	22.69	30.33	**41.20**
15	Lakshadweep	74.44	28.46	33.33	41.25	**39.62**
16	Rajasthan	70.37	30.72	34.83	28.00	**37.56**
17	Goa	64.81	29.78	25.81	34.17	**34.52**
18	Chhattisgarh	48.70	28.80	37.28	26.25	**34.24**
19	Punjab	62.41	34.25	11.07	40.17	**31.54**
20	Uttarakhand	41.67	28.75	22.52	30.83	**28.92**
21	Assam	63.70	23.08	26.56	12.67	**28.31**
22	Arunachal Pradesh	46.48	19.71	3.17	21.25	**18.25**
23	Chandigarh	33.33	23.44	5.46	16.25	**17.19**
National Average		**69.37**	**47.76**	**36.65**	**37.40**	**45.04**

Source: Alok, V.N. and P.K. Chaubey. 2010. *Panchayats in India: Measuring Devolution by States.* New Delhi: Macmillan.
Notes: The following dimensions construct the sub-indices D_1 = Mandatory Frames; D_2 = Functions; D_3 = Finances; D_4 = Functionaries.

The Figure 4.1A presents comparative ranks of all the states with their respective values for the composite devolution index, with a horizontal line showing national average.

Kerala is ranked at the top in the composite devolution index as well as in two most important sub-indices of functions and finances. Indicator-wise analysis shows that the state has devolved the maximum in terms of functions/activities for which a detailed activity mapping has been carried out. The transparency mechanism of the state is also considered the best. The Panchayats in the state of Kerala have been found to have the good capacity to collect revenue and utilise them. In other words, the Panchayats in Kerala have been made more autonomous than that of other states. Kerala is far ahead in using criteria based objective allocation formulae for Panchayats. The state has also developed the best structure for physical infrastructure and capacity building.

Karnataka follows Kerala in the composite devolution index. Karnataka is at the top in the sub-index for functionaries and occupies second place in that for functions. Panchayats in Karnataka have the maximum role in the vertical schemes. The state has also devolved good number of functions to Panchayats, in that respect the state is second only to Kerala. Panchayats in the state also have an effective role

Figure 4.1A   Devolution Index: Ranking of States

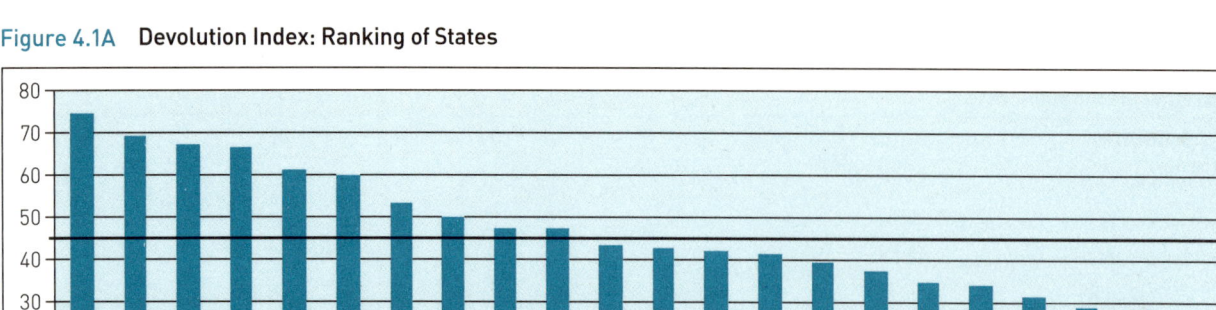

Source: Alok, V.N. and P.K. Chaubey. 2010. *Panchayats in India: Measuring Devolution by States.* New Delhi: Macmillan.

in parallel bodies and control over line department functionaries. Interestingly, Panchayats in the state enjoy the maximum taxing power and has the best system of fiscal management and monitoring among all the states. Kerala follows Karnataka in this respect.

Tamil Nadu is ranked third in the overall devolution index as well as in the sub-index of functions and occupies fourth place in all other sub-indices. The State Finance Commission in Tamil Nadu is found to be effective, only second to Himachal Pradesh. The state government timely constitutes the commission and prepares action taken reports in time. Tamil Nadu substantially involves Panchayats in vertical schemes. It is reported that the *Gram Sabha* conducts its various roles thoroughly.

West Bengal is ranked fourth in the composite devolution index along with the sub-index of functions and is ranked first in the sub-index of mandatory frames, third in that of finances. The state finance commission in West Bengal is found to be as effective as in Tamil Nadu. The state has devolved good number of tax handles to Panchayats. In this connection, the state is second to only Karnataka. The state has the robust fund flow management system and did not default even a single instalment of 12th Finance Commission grant to Panchayats. The state shares this position with Andhra Pradesh, Gujarat and Uttar Pradesh.

Maharashtra occupies the fifth place in the overall devolution index and the sub-index of functions. However, the state is second to only Kerala in the most important sub-index of finances. The Panchayats in the state utilise funds adequately and shares the top slot with their counterpart in Kerala in so far as the indicator related with fund utilisation is concerned. The provisions related to *Gram Sabha* in the state are considered far better than that of many others. The functioning of Panchayats in the state is considered transparent and ranked second only to Kerala.

Madhya Pradesh is ranked in overall index and sub-index of functions. The state scored high and ranked third in the sub-index of functionaries. It seems the state attaches utmost importance to Panchayats having a role in parallel bodies involved in development activities. The state is ranked second only to Karnataka in this indicator. The Panchayats related fiscal management and monitoring mechanism in the state is found good. The state is behind only to Kerala and Karnataka in this indicator. Functionaries at local level are accountable to Panchayats in Madhya Pradesh. The state is second to only Karnataka. Similarly, the state is second to Karnataka in the indicator related to the role of Panchayats in parallel bodies.

Source: Alok, V.N. and P.K. Chaubey. 2010. *Panchayats in India: Measuring Devolution by States*. New Delhi: Macmillan.

ANNEXURE 4.5

District Planning Committee, Madhubani

Memorandum
(Translated)

Dated: 09/12/2009

To
The Secretary
Department of Panchayati Raj
Government of Bihar

Sub: *Regarding problems/difficulties in the preparation of Integrated District Plan*

Sir,

73rd and 74th Constitutional Amendment Act has promoted the process of integrated district planning. According to Article 243ZD of the Constitution, in every district there should be a District Planning Committee, which shall be responsible for the preparation of Draft District Plan based on the proposals prepared by Panchayats and Municipalities for economic development and social justice.

According to the above mentioned Act a District Planning Committee has been set up in Madhubani District also. District Planning Committee, Madhubani is engaged in the preparation of an Integrated District Plan for the year 2010–11. During the process of preparing, the plan there are some problems/difficulties DPC is facing. District Planning Committee, Madhubani wants to draw your attention towards the problems/ difficulties mentioned below:

1. DPC has tried to prepare the database of resources and amenities available at District, Block, Panchayat(s) and Municipality/Municipal Council level to prepare an Integrated Plan. But, departments are not willing to provide this data/ information related to three tiers of Panchayats and Urban Local Body level.

2. For the purpose of preparation of an Annual Plan, District Planning Committee tried to set up a District Planning and Block Planning Units at District and Block level respectively. But, it has not been materialised because of the absence of clear guidelines for the setting up of such units in the Bihar District Planning Committee Byelaws 2006.

3. For the preparation of integrated district plan, it is necessary for the DPC to have detailed information of schemes carried out in the district and assisted by Central and State Governments. In this context, DPC has requested all the departments for the information and financial resources available under different schemes at district, block, Panchayat and ULB level. But no

department had supplied/shared such information till date. In the letter sent to departments, the District Planning Committee sought information regarding last three years' expenditure and physical achievements under different schemes at District, Block, Panchayat and Municipalities level. But, the departments do also not provide this information.

4. DPC, Madhubani issued a Press release carrying an appeal to organise *Gram Sabhas* on 15th of August 2009 to prepare Annual work plan for the preparation of 2010–11 annual plan. But, the *Gram Sabha* could not be organised. Again on 14, 15 and 16 September a direction has been issued by the DPC through the Chief Executive Officer of Zila Parishad (DDC) to all the *Gram Panchayats* to organise *Gram Sabhas*, so that, the annual work plan could be prepared for the year 2010–11 and it could be sent to State Government for incorporation in the 2010–11 State Plan. Madhubani District Planning Committee wants to know that what should be the role of DPC in preparing an Annual Work Plan in a given time frame. Does the DPC has the right to direct Panchayats and Urban local bodies to prepare a plan in advance and to ask for its submission to DPC?

5. In the absence of a standard Planning calendar for the annual planning exercise, the Madhubani District Planning Committee is not able to prepare the annual work plan for the year 2010–11 in time.

6. The Urban local bodies are sending their plans directly to the DPC as per statutory provisions causing problems in integration of rural and urban plans at Panchayat Samiti or Block level.

7. During the process of preparation of Annual Work Plan the need of professionals was felt to integrate rural and urban plans and consolidation of plans at Block/Panchayat Samiti level.

8. DPC, Madhubani require employees and financial resources to prepare an Integrated District Plan.

Because of the shortage of officials, DPCs day to day functioning too seldom suffer and in the absence of financial resources the important works like capacity development and publicity of draft plan are being hampered.

9. The DPC devoid of the right to sort out complaints regarding the execution of plans. Guidelines have been issued in August 2008 by Ministry of Panchayati Raj regarding execution of BRGF Schemes. In these guidelines, the DPC was awarded the right to set up an evaluation committee, but nothing has been done so far in this regard.

10. Because the main objective of funds available under BRGF is for filling the critical gaps identified after using the financial resources available under different schemes and programmes to execute the works undertaken.

Hence, Madhubani District Plan Committee would not endorse the BRGF annual work plan for the year 2010–11, until the Annual work plan vetted by Zila Parishad is not integrated by different departments in their Annual Plans for the year 2010–11.

Therefore, we request you to give a serious thought to the above-mentioned problems of DPC. We expect help and guidance for necessary amendment in the Bihar District Planning Committee Byelaws 2006 for the effective execution of functioning and the empowerment of the district planning committee for the preparation of Integrated District Plan.

Yours faithfully,
Chairperson
Zila Parishad and
District Planning Committee, Madhubani

Copy to:

1. Secretary, Planning Board, Bihar
2. Director, Department of Panchayati Raj, Bihar

ANNEXURE 4.6
State-wise Allocation of Funds under JNNURM

S.N.	States/Union territories	ACA committed 2007–08	ACA released 2007–08	ACA committed 2008–09	ACA released 2008–09	ACA committed 2009–10	ACA released 2009–10
1	Andhra Pradesh	91,532.30	48,916.54	34,993.75	18,898.95	13,935	24,885.07
2	Arunachal Pradesh	0	2,006.94	8,215.65	2,053.91	0	2,006.94
3	Assam	25,284.60	791.26	0	6,321.15	9,000	7,112.41
4	Bihar	0	461.93	37,628.03	1,955.62	0	7,441.39
5	Chandigarh	0	1,544.92	0	405.20	10,738.80	0
6	Chhattisgarh	0	1,272.80	10,000	0	0	12,145.60

(Annexure 4.6 continued)

(Annexure 4.6 continued)

S.N.	States/Union territories	ACA committed 2007–08	ACA released 2007–08	ACA committed 2008–09	ACA released 2008–09	ACA committed 2009–10	ACA released 2009–10
7	Delhi	0	0	17,472.30	2,220.58	186,904.60	15,100
8	Goa	0	0	0	0	0	0
9	Gujarat	70,210.79	24,563.54	54,381.69	47,035.34	20,604.09	47,788.21
10	Haryana	5,359.35	1,339.84	2,4674.50	9,147.46	0	0
11	Himachal Pradesh	0	0	5,788.80	0	3,880	2,619.01
12	Jammu & Kashmir	13,353.30	6,877.36	10,000	2,500	0	0
13	Jharkhand	0	0	48,268.46	6,682.46	0	5,384.66
14	Karnataka	59,596.2	18,766.61	32,222.25	12,992.94	4,332	22,782.60
15	Kerala	1,964.80	6,319.93	18,405.20	3,350.50	1,105	2,439.45
16	Madhya Pradesh	23,129.06	7,914.35	24,275.82	15,931.43	20,115.70	12,343.27
17	Maharashtra	75,275.77	56,827.52	141,678.39	88,349.54	10,336.86	88,649.86
18	Manipur	2,322.64	580.66	2,308.34	0	9,225.12	2,883.37
19	Meghalaya	0	0	19,616.15	4,904.04	0	0
20	Mizoram	1,513.62	378.41	0	0	0	756.82
21	Nagaland	2,273.04	179	0	389.26	4,538.19	1,702.81
22	Orissa	0	9,978.37	18,818.40	3,338	4,500	2,491.60
23	Punjab	21,389	4,145.29	3,624.50	4,939.22	2,289	3,346.62
24	Puducherry	16,272	4,068	3,972.80	993.20	0	0
25	Rajasthan	27,561.44	10,654.03	24,551.97	20,281.38	0	2,826.10
26	Sikkim	2,152.81	538.20	0	538.20	6,535.49	1,663.87
27	Tamil Nadu	60,731.11	16,093.02	101,845.69	28,446.11	9,000	37,723.44
28	Tripura	0	0	7,043.40	1,760.85	9,000	2,250
29	Uttar Pradesh	87,189.91	21,365.55	143,592.93	43,078.75	31,500	47,632.21
30	Uttarakhand	9,867.30	1,523.85	13,205.62	2,678.56	4,628	7,546.69
31	West Bengal	18,275.18	5,687.25	55,685.13	22,857.17	44,822.75	27,717.88
	Total	**615,254.44**	**252,795.17**	**862,269.77**	**352,049.82**	**406,990.60**	**389,239.88**

General Annexures

Key Indicators of Development

Category	Country	Population Millions 2008	Population Average annual % growth 2000–08	Population Density people per sq. km 2008	Population age composition % ages 0–14 2008	Gross national income GNI USD billions 2008	Gross national income GNI USD per capita 2008	PPP gross national income USD billions 2008	PPP gross national income USD per capita 2008	GDP per capita % growth 2007–08	Life expectancy at birth Male years 2007	Life expectancy at birth Female years 2007	Adult literacy rate % ages 15 and older 2007
South Asia	Bangladesh	160	1.6	1,229	32	82.6	520	230.6	1,440	4.7	65	67	53
	India	**1,140**	**1.4**	**383**	**32**	**1,215.5**	**1,070**	**3,374.9**	**2,960**	**5.7**	**63**	**66**	**66**
	Nepal	29	2.0	200	37	11.5	400	32.1	1,120	3.6	63	64	57
	Pakistan	166	2.3	215	37	162.9	980	448.8	2,700	3.7	65	66	54
	Sri Lanka	20	0.9	310	24	35.9	1,790	89.9	4,480	5.8	69	76	91
BRIC	Brazil	192	1.2	23	26	1,411.2	7,350	1,932.9	10,070	4.1	69	76	90
	Russia	142	–0.4	9	15	1,364.5	9,620	2,216.3	15,630	7.5	62	74	100
	India	**1,140**	**1.4**	**383**	**32**	**1,215.5**	**1,070**	**3,374.9**	**2,960**	**5.7**	**63**	**66**	**66**
	China	1,326	0.6	142	21	3,899.3	2,940	7,984.0	6,020	8.4	71	75	93
Others	Australia	21	1.4	3	19	862.5	40,350	727.5	34,040	1.9	79	84	–
	United Kingdom	61	0.5	254	18	2,787.2	45,390	2,218.2	36,130	0.1	77	82	–
	United States	304	0.9	33	20	14,466.1	47,580	14,282.7	46,970	0.2	75	81	–
	Low Income	973	2.1	52	38	509.6	524	1,368.8	1,407	4.1	57	60	64
	Middle Income	4,651	1.1	60	27	15,159.6	3,260	28,619.5	6,154	5.0	67	71	83
	High Income	1,069	0.7	32	18	42,041.4	39,345	39,686.3	37,141	0.0	77	82	99
	World	6,692	1.2	52	27	57,637.5	8,613	69,309.0	10,357	0.8	67	71	84

Source: *World Development Report 2010*, World Bank.

ANNEXURE II
Key Indicators of Poverty

Category	Country	National poverty line				International poverty line							
		Population below national poverty line		Survey year	National %	Survey year	Population below USD 1.25 a day %	Poverty gap at USD 1.25 a day %	Population below USD 2 a day %	Survey year	Population below USD 1.25 a day %	Poverty gap at USD 1.25 a day %	Population below USD 2 a day %
		Survey year	National %										
South Asia	Bangladesh	2000	48.9	2005	40.0	2000	57.8	17.3	85.4	2005	49.6	13.1	81.3
	India	1993–94	36.0	1999–2000	28.6	1993–94	49.4	14.4	81.7	2004–05	41.6	10.8	75.6
	Nepal	1995–96	41.8	2003–04	30.9	1995–96	68.4	26.7	88.1	2003–04	55.1	19.7	77.6
	Pakistan	1993	28.6	1998–99	32.6	2001–02	35.9	7.9	73.9	2004–05	22.6	4.4	60.3
	Sri Lanka	1995–96	25.0	2002	22.7	1995–96	16.3	3.0	46.7	2002	14.0	2.6	39.7
BRIC	Brazil	1998	22.0	2002–03	21.5	2005	7.8	1.6	18.3	2007	5.2	1.3	12.7
	Russia	1998	31.4	2002	19.6	2002	<2.0	<0.5	3.7	2005	<2.0	<0.5	<2.0
	India	1993–94	36.0	1999–2000	28.6	1993–94	49.4	14.4	81.7	2004–05	41.6	10.8	75.6
	China	1998	4.6	2004	2.8	2002	28.4	8.7	51.1	2005	15.9	4.0	36.3

Source: *World Development Report 2010*, World Bank.

ANNEXURE III
Basic Capabilities Index 2009

Category	Country	BCI 2009	BCI level	BCI evolution
South Asia	Afghanistan	46	E	
	Bangladesh	56	E	<<
	India	**68**	**E**	>>
	Nepal	58	E	<<
	Pakistan	71	D	>>>>
	Sri Lanka	96	B	=
BRIC	Brazil	90	B	>>
	Russia	100	A	>>
	India	**68**	**E**	>>
	China	94	B	<<
Others	Australia	100	A	=
	United Kingdom	99	A	=
	United States	98	A	=
	Israel	100	A	=
	Japan	100	A	=
	Singapore	100	A	=
	Denmark	100	A	=

Source: http://www.socialwatch.org
Notes:

BCI level		BCI evolution	
A	Acceptable	>>>>	Significant Progress
B	Medium	>>	Slight Progress
C	Low	=	Stagnant
D	Very Low	<<	Regression
E	Critical	<<<<	Major Regression
			No data on evolution

ANNEXURE IV
Gender Equity Index 2009

Category	Country	GEI 2009	Education	Economic activity	Empowerment
South Asia	**Afghanistan**				
	Bangladesh	53	85.8	53.5	18.9
	India	**41**	**77.5**	**36.6**	**7.9**
	Nepal	51	74.1	57.1	22.5
	Pakistan	43	75.9	34.2	18.0
	Sri Lanka	58	98.0	43.0	32.4
BRIC	Brazil	68	96.5	64.6	43.6
	Russia	71	97.3	74.6	42.0
	India	**41**	**77.5**	**36.6**	**7.9**
	China	68	92.4	73.3	38.6
Others	Australia	75	95.2	75.0	55.0
	United Kingdom	74	97.5	72.8	51.1
	United States	74	97.0	72.3	52.3
	Sweden	88	96.3	83.8	82.9
	Finland	84	98.6	78.5	75.7
	Rwanda	84	88.2	84.6	77.8
	Norway	83	96.2	82.0	69.8

Source: http://www.socialwatch.org

ANNEXURE V
State of Hunger across Indian States

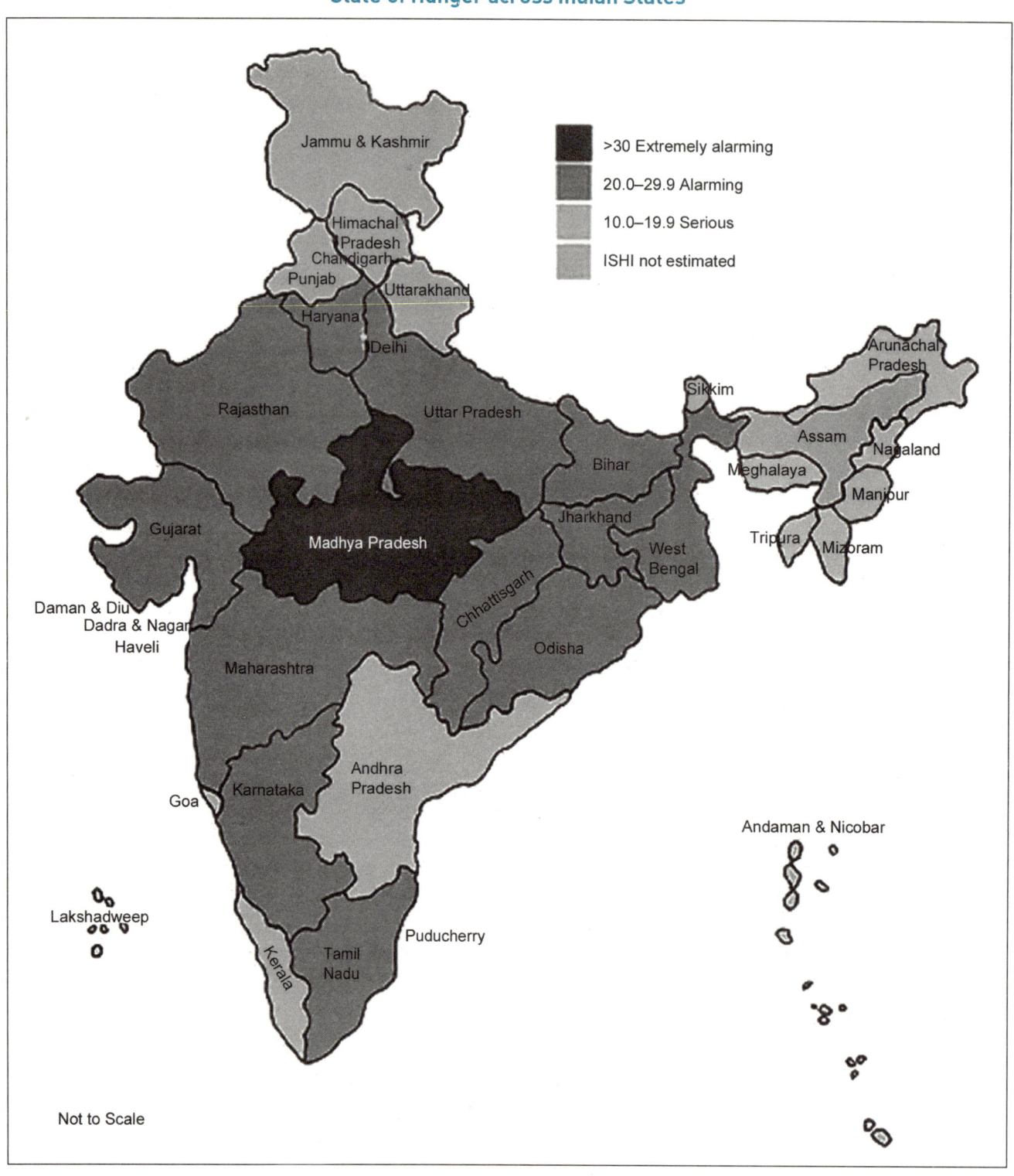

Source: Adapted from Menon, P., A. Deolalikar and A. Bhaskar. 2009. *India State Hunger Index: Comparisons of Hunger Across States*. Washington DC, Bonn and Riverside: IFPRI, Welt Hunger Hilfe & UC, Riverside.

ANNEXURE VI
The India State Hunger Index and Its Underlying Components

State	Prevalence of calorie under-nourishment (%)	Proportion of under-weight among children <5 years (%)	Under-five mortality rate (deaths per hundred)	India state hunger index score	India state hunger index rank
Punjab	11.1	24.6	5.2	13.63	1
Kerala	28.6	22.7	1.6	17.63	2
Andhra Pradesh	19.6	32.7	6.3	19.53	3
Assam	14.6	36.4	8.5	19.83	4
Haryana	15.1	39.7	5.2	20.00	5
Tamil Nadu	29.1	30.0	3.5	20.87	6
Rajasthan	14.0	40.4	8.5	20.97	7
West Bengal	18.5	38.5	5.9	20.97	8
Uttar Pradesh	14.5	42.3	9.6	22.13	9
Maharashtra	27.0	36.7	4.7	22.80	10
Karnataka	28.1	37.6	5.5	23.73	11
Orissa	21.4	40.9	9.1	23.80	12
Gujarat	23.3	44.7	6.1	24.70	13
Chhattisgarh	23.3	47.6	9.0	26.63	14
Bihar	17.3	56.1	8.5	27.30	15
Jharkhand	19.6	57.1	9.3	28.67	16
Madhya Pradesh	23.4	59.8	9.4	30.87	17
India	**20.0**	**42.5**	**7.4**	**23.30**	–

Source: Menon, P., A. Deolalikar and A. Bhaskar. 2009. *India State Hunger Index: Comparisons of Hunger Across States*, Washington DC, Bonn and Riverside: IFPRI, Welt Hunger Hilfe & UC, Riverside.

STATE PARTNERS

Madhya Pradesh

Samarthan, Bhopal and Madhya Pradesh Voluntary Action Network (MPVAN), Bhopal. Samarthan promotes participatory governance and development thus encouraging leadership of Women, Dalit, Tribals and other disadvantaged sections of the society.

Orissa

Centre for Youth and Social Development (CYSD), Bhubaneshwar works towards achieving people-centred development for the deprived and under privileged through direct intervention, as well as building up alliances with agencies of shared intent.

Maharashtra

Youth for Voluntary Action (YUVA), Mumbai, implements its development agenda by engaging with local, community-based organisations strengthening existing organisations to respond effectively to local development issues.

Vikas Sahyog Pratisthan (VSP), Mumbai, is a group of voluntary organisations working for the upliftment of poor and deprived sections of society. Its area of expertise is in nature farming, water conservation, promoting role of youth in village governance and co-operatives.

Karnataka

(Karnataka Social Watch) Rejuvenate India Movement (RIM), Bangalore, which is a conglomerate of 11 Non-government Agencies. It works towards effecting positive changes by generating actions that are practically effective and morally compelling while upholding the principles of participative democracy, genuine volunteerism and self-empowerment.

Community Development Foundation (CDF), Bangalore believes in collective efforts to bring about meaningful change and sustainable development in adult literacy, children and human rights, gender issues, education and health aspects.

Tamil Nadu

Tamil Nadu Social Watch (TNSW), Chennai is a resource-cum-research centre involved in social public policy monitoring and lobbying at the State level. The major contributions have been Dalit budgeting and in budget awareness in civil society, along with the Tamil Nadu Social Development Report 2000.

Centre for Policy Studies (CPS), Gandhigram Rural University, Dindigul Distt., Tamil Nadu People's Forum for Social Development (TNPFSD), Chennai.

Andhra Pradesh

Centre for World Solidarity (CWS), Hyderabad, is a support organisation with partners in nearly five states working with a rights-based development approach towards Panchayati Raj, Minorities, Tribal Rights, Education, Forestry, Alternative Agriculture and Natural Resource Management, Human Rights Issues and women's rights and gender mainstreaming.

Dalit Bahujan Shramik Union (DBSU), Hyderabad, working with Dalit organisations on Dalit issues and rights.

Uttar Pradesh

Uttar Pradesh Voluntary Action Network (UPVAN), Lucknow, is a conglomerate of nearly 225 vibrant civil society organisations of UP. It operates through the advocacy resource centre, networking, alliance-building centre, gender resource and information resource centre and takes up issues for advocacy which affects the voluntary organisations and their struggle to ensure justice and equity for the marginalised.

Bihar

Vidyasagar Samajik Suraksha Seva Evam Shodh Sansthan, Asian Development Research Institute.

Chhattisgarh

Mayaram Surjan Foundation (MSF), Raipur runs a research and documentation centre and conducts programmes to build up grassroot democratic values and practices, promote value-based and development-oriented journalism and prepare youth to take lead in building and safeguarding a pluralistic society.

Gramin Yuva Abhikram (GYA), Raipur, works in the areas of community empowerment, campaign for people's right to water, campaign for accountable governance, media advocacy, women empowerment, apart from networking with like-minded agencies and policy research.

Rajasthan

Centre for Community Economics and Development Consultants Society (CECOEDECON), Institute of Development Studies, Pratham.

West Bengal

Institute for Motivating Self Employment (IMSE) along with Forum of Voluntary Organisations, West Bengal, Kolkata. The Forum is comprised of 98 voluntary organisations representing Christian Missionaries, Leftist Social Action Groups, Human Rights Groups. The Forum apart from supporting the achievement of food sovereignty of the people and their rights over land, water, forest and seed, also opposes imperialist globalisation.

Kerala

Representatives of Kerala Sastra Sahitya Parishad, Centre for Development Studies, Indian Institute of Information Technology and Management, led by C. Gouridasan Nair, Special correspondent, The Hindu, Thiruvananthapuram.

Jharkhand

Currently coordinated by National Social Watch Coalition supported by SPAR, Gene Campaign, Agragati, SPAR, LJK, HOPE, SAFDAR, Adivasi Sanghamam, Swaraj Foundation.

Himachal Pradesh

RTDC—Voluntary Action Group (RTDC–VAG), People's Campaign for Socio-Economic Equity in Himalayas (PcfSEEiH).

SANSAD (South Asian Network for Social and Agricultural Development), aimed at making South Asia free from hunger and poverty and taking global and regional initiative for sustainable agricultural and rural development and human dignity aimed at putting collective pressure on policy-making.

NATIONAL COALITION PARTNERS

ADR

Association for Democratic Reforms aims to work towards improving and strengthening democracy and governance in India. The main objectives of ADR are electoral reforms, right to information and greater transparency of those in power, empowerment of the ordinary citizen and reform of the government and bureaucracy.

Centre for Youth and Social Development

CYSD works with the deprived and the underprivileged towards the goal of people-centred development. Its participatory development action enables people to pursue their need fulfilment through their own institutional means. Its training and capacity building support to development organisations produced a cascade of effective learning at the grass-roots and increasing professional efficiency in development action at all levels. By building up alliances with agencies of shared intent, it attempts to bring on a pro-poor agenda in the mainstream of development policies and practices.

The Centre for Budget and Governance Accountability

CBGA, New Delhi, is an attempt to promote transparent, accountable and participative governance. CBGA has been proactively engaged in tracking public policies and economic issues from the perspective of the poor and the marginalised.

Ekta Parishad

Ekta Parishad is a Gandhian organisation, it works towards community based governance (*Gram Swaraj*), local self-reliance (*Gram Swawlamban*) and responsible government (*Jawabdehi Sarkar*). It is a mass movement based on Gandhian principles of non-violence. It mobilises people (especially the poor and deprived sections) on the issue of proper and just utilisation of livelihood resources (i.e., primarily land, but also forest and water).

Kabir

Kabir is a communications organisation dedicated to the increased awareness and use of the Right to Information (RTI) Act by all individuals and organisations across all segments of Indian society. It envisions a culture of transparency and accountability in government that allows for meaningful participation of citizens in their own governance.

National Centre for Advocacy Studies

NCAS is a membership-based organisation that has been working on various people-centred advocacy initiatives across the country. NCAS has a decade-long history of training people on advocacy and undertaking people-centred advocacy initiatives. NCAS works on various socio-economic rights essentially from the perspective of the marginalised. NCAS is also involved in Media Advocacy initiative, Advocacy Learning and Praxis and Governance and Advocacy. The theme in NCAS work is bridging people and building ideas. NCAS sees the Social Watch Process as an essential component towards this end.

PRS Legislative Research

PRS Legislative Research is an independent research initiative that aims to strengthen the legislative debate by making it better informed, more transparent and participatory. PRS is the first initiative of its kind in India.

Samarthan Centre for Development Support

It promotes participatory governance and development. The organisation is committed to strengthen democratic processes building leadership of Women, Dalit, Tribals and other disadvantaged section. Civil society organisations have a critical role as social change agent, therefore promotion support and strengthening civil society institutions in development is also key endeavour of Samarthan. Samarthan also believes in building examples of participatory development and governance, therefore, is actively involved in field action at the grassroots to build people's institutions.